OKLAHOMA ROCK
A Climber's Guide
by Tony Mayse

Oklahoma Rock: A Climber's Guide by Tony Mayse
©2018 Sharp End Publishing, LLC

Published and distributed by:
Sharp End Publishing LLC
PO Box 1613
Boulder, CO 80306
t. 303-444-2698
www.sharpendbooks.com

ISBN: 978-1-892540-98-0

Cover photo: Tony Mayse on the Quartz classic *Wild Child* 5.11d RX | Photo by Andrew Burr

Cover photo on Limited Edition: Doug Robinson climbing *Amazon Woman* 5.10b R circa 1984. Prolific climber, author, and mountain guide. Embracing the clean climbing ethos which has influenced many generations of climbers and changed the very way climbers interact with the cliffs and mountains we climb. | Photo by Marion Hutchison

Opening page photo: John Tarkington climbing *Bombs Away* 5.11c | Photo by Tony Mayse

Artwork in cover interior by Dray Bullard

READ THIS BEFORE USING THIS BOOK

WARNING:

This book is dedicated to Lori, the kindest, most gentle and happy person that I have ever known—always considering everyone other than herself and always giving without ever expecting anything in return.
~I love you, Lolo.

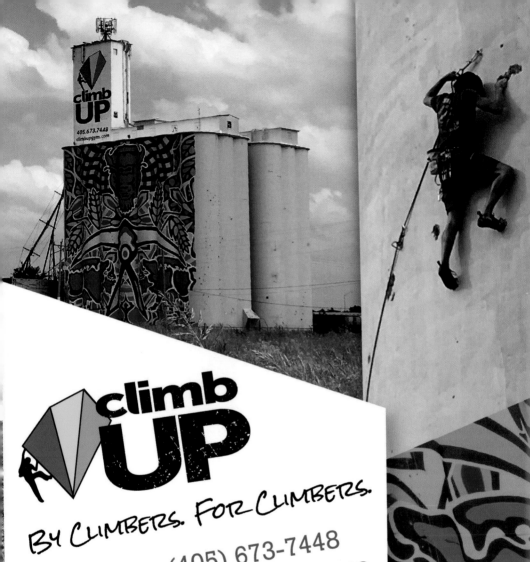

These areas can also be approached from the Sunset parking area.

I'D LIKE TO THANK...

When I decided to write an updated full-color guidebook the task seemed overwhelming at times.

This is your guidebook. It truly is an Oklahoma climber's guide. Friends, climbing partners, and climbers from across the country have come together to contribute, making this one of the best new guidebooks in the country.

THANK YOU...

Contributions of articles on geology and conservation, artwork, historical images, modern climbing images, route information, help making icons and correcting photos...the list goes on and on of the support I have received while developing this endeavor.

I was able to reconnect with old friends and make new ones. It was grueling at times, it was unbelievably hard work, but in the end it was worth every moment. After all, it's not about the destination, it's all about the journey.

A special thanks to Doug Robinson, the climbing legend, for taking a gamble and agreeing to write the foreword in my first guidebook *Oklahoma Select*. Your words cannot be replaced so I retained your foreword in this guide. Wonderful writing combined with your knowledge of our rock climbing history made your foreword irreplaceable. I also appreciate the cool photos! Thank you, Doug.

Thank you, Duane Raleigh for all the stories and route information, I really enjoyed the chats, and of course I enjoy hearing about the "lines of strength and power!"

Thank you, Jimmy Ratzlaff for trusting me with your personal collection of guidebooks, photos, and slides. That plastic "tub" blew me away. Getting to know you and reliving those early days of Oklahoma climbing have provided a priceless experience for Lori and me. I especially enjoyed our phone conversations! I am forever grateful, thank you, Jimmy.

To Jon Frank: I took a chance at giving you a call and you answered in a big way! The stories you shared with us are treasures. Your books *Oklahoma on the Rocks* and *Oklahoma on the Rocks II* were my first guidebooks, and I still appreciate them to this day. Looking forward to roping up with you, Jon!

To Marion Hutchison: Thank you for the articles, photos, and for always being the voice of reason. Without you and all your efforts, Marion, the landscape of accessible climbing in Oklahoma and this book would look very different. I always enjoy our conversations, they are timeless and funny! You are the best.

Thanks to Mark Herndon for your contribution on geology. I have enjoyed the conversations and stories. Lori and I appreciate all your hard work and value your friendship.

To Terry Andrews: I remember it like it was yesterday...I was jonzin' to climb with anyone and you show up to Quartz, with your partner Russell Dutnell, and I asked if I could follow you up a climb and you said yes. Now here we are almost 30 years later and you are still the same guy. I always enjoy seeing you out on the rock.

Thank you, Keith Egan for the historical information, much appreciated Keith.

To Tony Wilson for taking the time to write about the days climbing with Russell Hooper A.K.A. "Corndog." I know Russell is smiling on us! Your photo of *Yellow Beard* says it all. Don't suck!

To my good friend Joe Romero, thank you for everything, bro! You are my true brother and selfless friend. You have seen me at my best and seen me at my worst and you continue to be a constant support. I love ya, man!

Thank you to my good friend the "Czech Machine" Stanley Vrba. I am so happy to have met you at Lost Dome several years ago. Shortly after we met we took off like a flash to the Verdon Gorge in southern France with our wives on the coolest trip! I'm also excited that you love Oklahoma climbing, especially Quartz! Let's make some plans!

Thank you Chris Corbett for making the journey out to the refuge on this current endeavor and taking the time to take photos and edit some of the pages in this book. Our trip to Yosemite was a memorable one. I appreciate our lifelong friendship. Always a pleasure hanging out with you, Chris!

Thank you, Andrew Burr for your amazing photos. Its was a cool happenstance meeting you in Vail, Colorado while you were shooting some ice climbing and then taking me up on my offer to come to Oklahoma to check out our stone! Glad it all worked out! Thanks, bro.

John and Sierra Tarkington: It's always a pleasure being around you both! The two of you are some of our favorite people! Sierra, thank you for the historical information and photo, I appreciate the help.

Thank you Molly Hennesy for all of your help and enthusiasm with this guide. Your dog icons are great, we love them. The photos you selflessly took are outstanding and make all of us look much better than we actually are! You are always quick to help us get the job done and that is a fine and rare attribute for such a young person. You are high on our list, besides Lori thinks you're a superstar!

Thank you, Preston Pettigrew for taking the initiative and writing Quartz Mountain's first bouldering guide, *Small Rocks in a Wheatfield*.

Thank you, Elisha Gallegos for providing the wonderful artwork that graces the pages of this new book and the awesome photos for all to enjoy!

Thank you, Colby and Sally from Rock n' Resole. Love you guys.

Thank you, Freddy Harth, you are a lifelong friend, our ascents on El Cap span two decades. You are still as hardcore as you were when I first met you. I love ya, man!

Thank you, Aaron Gibson for your photo and route information.

Thank you, Steve Cate for your information on cycling, looking forward to some ride time!

Thank you, Ryan and Trish Ray for your photo contributions.

I would like to thank Logan and Kali Jo Boren for being the best grandkids and enjoying the hike to Crab Eyes then roping up with me! Quartz was fun too! I love you both!

When I first started rock climbing I bought Clay Frisbee's guidebook *The Natural: A Climbers Guide to Sam's Throne*. This book had it all! First ascent information, easy to read topo's, gear descriptions and route lengths. Shortly after, I met Clay and we became life long friends with many El Cap adventures. Clay, you are a climber that sets the standard in life and climbing. Thank you, my dear friend Clay.

Thank you, Todd Johnson for being the consummate cool guy that I always aspired to be as a young man. The off-the-couch athlete that can do it all! From sub 7 hour ascents on the Captain in such a laissez-faire way then walking off the top without shoes! Climbing with you on the Captain and pushing me past my comfort limit opened my eyes as to what is possible up there! You are my inspiration in so many ways! I'm glad we are friends. Love ya bro!

Scott Deputy: I thank you for your friendship and words of wisdom. A lawyer turned full-time climber and "King" of YOSAR! Your friendship to me means more than I can put down on these pages. Thanks, bro!

Thank you to Fred and Heidi Knapp for taking a chance several years ago on a brief phone conversation and now here we are 15 years later on our 3rd book *Oklahoma Rock*! It was great to finally climb with you Fred! So cool to watch you climb! Can't wait to hook-up for some long days on the stone!

Thank you Sarah Nicholson for all of your hard work on this book! Great climbing with you here in Oklahoma! Your visit was so fun for us, especially Lucy!

Finally, I would like to thank all my pups for being patient while I wrote this guide. I'm ready to get out and play with you guys.

Happy climbing.

Photo by Andrew Burr

WICHITA MOUNTAINS A BRIEF TIMELINE

The Wichita Mountains cover a large area of about 1500 miles and extend into several counties of southwest Oklahoma, including those of the Quartz Mountain area and the Wichita Mountains Wildlife Refuge, which has the largest and tallest rock formations.

The name "Wichita" means "Man of the North," and the area is named after its first known inhabitants, the Native Americans. The people of the Wichita Tribe were related to the Pawnee, a peaceful people. Ancestral Wichita tradition and belief was that the tribesmen were born from the rugged rocks in these sacred lands. More than 100 years ago, this very land was home to several tribes of Native Americans who lived along the creeks and streams here. They hunted buffalo which not only provided food, but clothing and shelter for their families. The Wichitas enjoyed all the seasons in this wilderness domain. One should reflect on this very aspect while visiting the Wichita Mountains. We are just passing through.

Below is a brief time line of the Wichita Mountains Wildlife Refuge:

1834—Colonel Henry Dodge was the first American to contact the Native American tribes.

1869—Major General Phillip Sheridan established Fort Sill, an Army Post.

1874—Commanches, Kiowas, and Southern Cheyennes went on a warpath. Quanah Parker, a Comanche Chief, remained on a warpath as he didn't trust the white man's word. The following year he and his tribesman surrendered to Fort Sill. It also needs to be noted that Quanah Parker was not only a brave warrior and Chief to his people, he was a smart man that would later self-educate and learn Spanish and English, as well as how to integrate into and be successful in the white man's world, becoming a leader once again of his people as a judge in the Indian Court of Affairs. Quanah Parker was born in Elk Valley of the Wichita Mountians.

1876—Geronimo fled to Mexico to avoid being moved to a reservation out west.

1894—Geronimo and 341 of his tribe surrendered and were brought to Fort Sill's military outpost. The white man had succeeded in running the Native Indian off their lands.

Quanah Parker posing with two of his wives.

1901—President William McKinley set aside a portion of the Wichitas as a Forest Reserve.

By this time over hunting had reduced the bison herd from 60 million across America to an astounding and unthinkable herd count of 550 buffalo.

1905—A proclamation was announced renaming the area as the Wichita National Forest and Game Preserve. This was also the nation's first big game and animal wildlife preserve encompassing 59,020 acres of land with 22,400 acres set aside as Public Use Area, for activities such as picnicing, camping, hiking, and hunting by lottery.

1905—The American Bison Society demanded protection be given to the buffalo.

1907—New York Zoological Society offered 15 American bison to the new Wichita National Forest and Game Preserve. Two years after demanding protection for the buffalo, the bison arrived in Cache, just next door to the Wichita National Forest and Game Preserve by railway on a 1500-mile journey from New York.

1909—Geronimo dies of pneumonia. Prior to his death, he was allowed to travel with Pawnee in Wild Bill's Wild West Show.

1911—Not only did the buffalo suffer under the reckless overhunting after the white man first set foot in this region, but elk also faced extinction from overhunting. In 1911, elk were introduced to the Wichitas. Five

WICHITA NATIONAL FOREST
—v— & GAME PRESERVE —v—

U.S.
1920

"Entrance to the Wichita National Game Preserve. Woman posing beside car under stone gate."

The photo was taken by Dr. J. Allen Perisho, circa 1920. The first entrance was on two wooden poles, back around 1908.

Photograph provided through the Oklahoma Historical Society.

Rocky Mountain elk were transported from the National Elk Refuge in Jackson, Wyoming and then an additional 15 elk were transported from the same herd the following year. The entire elk herd in the refuge today is directly descended from those 20 animals.

1913—Apache Indians remained prisoners of war until this year.

1933—The Civilian Conservation Corps (CCC) was begun through President Roosevelt's New Deal Program, providing jobs during the Great Depression for young men, and also serving the much-needed purpose of conservation work on the nation's public lands. More than 3 million jobs were provided by this program, one of the most popular of Roosevelt's presidency.

Some of the CCC's jobs were to build dams, buildings, and fencing to keep the wildlife in. The program was set up for unmarried, unemployed, abled bodied and sound young men ages 18-26. They were paid $30 per month, of which $25 was automatically sent home to their families.

1935—The area was transferred to the Bureau of Biological Survey, a predecessor of the now Fish and Wildlife Service and is now known as the Wichita Mountains Wildlife Refuge.

1938—The Works Progress Administration and a private firm Public Work Administration completed blasting a 3-mile-long road up Mount Scott using dynamite and nitroglycerin, often having to break through 60-foot-plus tall walls. This road, which winds its way up the side of Mount Scott, serves no purpose other than that of convenience for modern visitors to enjoy driving their vehicles to the top thus taking in the scenic vistas from its 2462 foot elevation (though, fortunately, it also enables ready access to two excellent climbing crags). The CCC Program ended in 1942.

Mount Scott was named after General Winfield Scott "The Grand Old Man of the Army," who served active duty longer than any other person in Army history.

"Resting here until day breaks and shadows fall and darkness disappears."

~Quanah Parker

Reference material:

• Oklahoma Historical Society.

• Outdoor Trail Guide to the Wichita Mountains.

• Images of America Medicine Park Oklahoma's First Resort.

• Photo Credits: Oklahoma Historical Society

THE OTHER GRANITE STATE BY DOUG ROBINSON

Granite, the finest stone for climbing ever to erupt from the flanks of Mother Nature. It can be so smooth, you have to get your eyeball down this close to see the wrinkles in it, and bite your fingernails to get a tip's worth of purchase. Or maybe there's no wrinkle but just a ripple, like the least hollow on flowing water, and you smear with your best conviction as if scrubbing gum off your shoe on the burnished side of the courthouse, in hopes of hanging on. Despite of this asperity you've been gyrating upward anyway, insinuating your presence with a high-pressure delicacy, when suddenly there's a big hold. I mean one you don't have to squint down the millimeter scale to find. It's fully as thick as a thumb under your big toe and a couple of inches wide, so you get a rest. Maybe you find a bolt to clip your rope to here. Or maybe not. The locals are stingy with their hardware. They call it style. Some of us step up to it with a respect bordering on fear, and secretly admire their guts.

Of course there is far more granite on both coasts. Out east they chiseled a state from it. And clear across the other side, in the la-la-land that your politicians—when they're having a polite day—would call the Left Coast, we've got so much of it we can get a touch blasé. Still, it inspired enough awe to give birth to the very idea of a National Park, and then lock up Yosemite and the heart of it into the largest stretch of wilderness this side of Alaska. Coming from California, I must admit that we can sometimes take granite as a given.

Not here. Here only the wind is forgiven. Here, in the great aching-prairie middle of North America where the granite crops out sparingly, folks appreciate it. Here, sprouting up out of the grassland, is the core of the oldest granite range in the country. Modest pieces of rock, but finely wrought. And here, not in spite of this scarcity but because of it, has arisen a stout tradition of hard rock climbing in a bold style. This fine granite has drawn together an exceptional group of climbers, made them feel at home in patches of verticality, and evoked from them a creative renaissance.

Here Tony Mayse has risen to become one of the leading climbers of the latest generation, and is inspiring the next as a teacher and guide. Now Tony has become its spokesman as well, gathered into this volume the best efforts on Oklahoma's granite. It says a lot that working with a scarce commodity, these local climbers have created so prolifically that Tony's book can, for the first time, select among their achievements. He has done it well, adding the latest to a fine tradition of guidebooks. But if you find Tony's description of your favorite climb feels restrained, just remember that he's carrying on an understated tradition marked by a terse pride and gentle humor. Just check out the quotes Tony has generously included from those earlier guides. Then when you bump into him at Quartz, watch Tony's eyes light up.

If you ever start taking all this good climbing for granted, pause to recall that in the last fifteen years every boulder of it has been threatened. First the Wildlife Refuge looked like they would throw climbers out, then Quartz nearly got turned into ranchettes. Climbers rallied, creating the Wichita Mountains Climbers Coalition, and finessed their relationship with the wildlife managers who now view us as allies. Then we bought Quartz, raising nearly $20,000 in small bills to match a grant from the Access Fund, and turned it all over to the adjoining State Park. With access guaranteed forever. All of this was so well done that the Access Fund offered our local leader, Marion Hutchison, the job of National Director.

Two more reminiscences: The first happened next door to this granite state, in Kansas. We piled into the car before dawn, clutching mugs of coffee, to make the long pilgrimage out to local sandstone. Chris Nickel, who had invited me to climb there, was driving. As we backed out into the darkness, I glanced at her dashboard. There was a handmade sign: "Drive ah so careful." I smiled. It's a good idea to climb that way too. Climbing is a fine mistress. She can also be a bitch. The only way to stay by her side is with the respect of a good juggler, constantly adjusting that volatile blend of pride and humility.

Then there's Ted Johnson. Ted was a farmer, and Quartz Mountain, the jewel of Oklahoma climbing, stood in his wheat field. The local climbers I was coming to know and respect had, by the early 1980s become his friends. I stood with Ted at the foot of his rock, watching them up there. There was Duane Raleigh, their leader by virtue of his hard climbing and his bold style. Duane's style still sets the tone here; although he has moved on to work the larger climbing world as the publisher of Rock & Ice. There was Marion Hutchison, who after Ted died, would pull us all together into the WMCC to save the granite resource itself. There was Mark Herndon, who would not only climb El Capitan, but then leap off the top, floating out to the meadow under his BASE-jumpers canopy. Mark went on to walk the wild side more than even Edward Abbey, alone all summer across the Arctic National Wildlife Refuge, where he cast his petroleum geologist's eye on its imminent desecration and called its bluff.

The future was all still ahead for this band of brothers; they weren't yet anything beyond gleeful locals, playing out their pure love of climbing on the rocks at hand. Ted stood there in his baggy blue overalls, watching these boys at their serious play on his rock. "It's a great sport," he said. And then he reconsidered, casting another eye on a luminous brotherhood, "No, it's a grand sport."

Doug Robinson climbing Amazon Woman 5.10b R circa 1984. | Photo by Marion Hutchison

ABOUT THE GUIDEBOOK

Duane Raleigh and Bill Thomas produced the first Oklahoma rock climbing guidebook, in the 1970s, with *Southern Exposure*. This guidebook got the ball rolling for all subsequent Oklahoma guidebooks. First ascent information was passed down to the second and third guidebooks for Oklahoma, namely *Oklahoma on the Rocks* and *Oklahoma on the Rocks II* by Jon Frank, Jack Wurster, and Duane Raleigh in the 1980s. The next book was the *Oklahoma Climber's Guide* by Chuck Lohn, produced in 1999; this book had climbing areas outside of the Wichita Mountains Wildlife Refuge and Quartz Mountain.

The next two guidebooks were the *Oklahoma Select* guides, published by Sharpend Books in 2004 and 2010. These books were a selection of some of the more popular climbs for the wildlife refuge and Quartz Mountain.

This guidebook *Oklahoma Rock* is the first full color guide for the Wichita and Quartz Mountain climbing areas. This book includes full color topos, a section of Oklahoma climbing history and early first ascent photos, stories from the first ascentionists, more than 400 routes, a bouldering section for Quartz Mountain, and the historic Steak Dinner Bouldering Area, as well as GPS information for the climbing areas.

Guidebooks are constantly evolving as new routes are being climbed and new areas discovered.

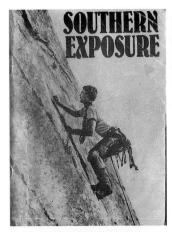
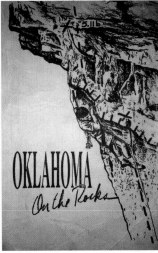

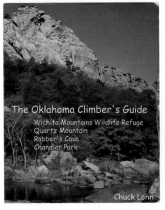
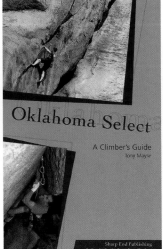
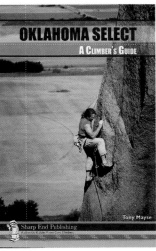

THERE WILL BE ERRORS...

This book will have mistakes, and for that I apologize. These inaccuracies were not intentional, they were not done to keep someone's favorite route out of the book, nor to not include someone on the first ascent, or credit someone else for an ascent they did not climb. This book was a lot of work and at times frustrating. Besides spending months behind the computer, I have also spent countless hours away from home and my family while working on this guide, as have other climbers who have produced guidebooks. Nowadays it's easy to bash someone on the internet with the flick of a keyboard quip...

Please keep this in mind before you start bashing this or any guidebook for inaccuracies, it's a lot of work.

CLIMBERS AND DOGS...

Most climbers have dogs, including me. I enjoy having my furry companions hanging out with me while I'm at the crag. I know my dogs enjoy being out there with me, they have told me this on many occasions. There are hazards in these areas for dogs. Snakes are a biggy. A healthy rattlesnake can kill your pet before you make it back to the parking area, so be aware! In warmer months when the snakes are active my pups stay home. For this guide I have added an icon to let the climbers know which area is dog friendly or not. This is from my personal experience in the refuge. If you feel different I'd like to hear about it. The icon has a photo of a dog with a green border, meaning the area is pet friendly and with the red border and slash, it is not a good place for your pet. Some considerations for non-friendly areas were places with big drop-offs, technical approaches, and no shade. If you want to feel how hot it is for your pet on a summer day, put on your jacket and take off your shoes, then stand on the baking granite slab in full sun! Remember the granite warms up in the hotter months making it hard on their paws. Use common sense. Make sure you bring plenty of water for your pup if the temps are up!

A portion of the proceeds from the sale this guidebook will be donated to Second Chance Animal Sancturary and Wildcare:

www.wildcareoklahoma.org

www.secondchancenorman.com

In closing, I would like to say that the opportunities to hike around the refuge and Quartz Mountain while working on the book were special. Sunrises were spectacular from the backcountry in the Wichitas and at Quartz. Watching a herd of buffalo, I imagined what it must have felt like to the Native American who lived on these lands. For more that 26 years the Wichita Mountains and Quartz have been a place where my family, and now my grandchildren have enjoyed. It's been as much a part of our lives as breathing our next breath, we love these wild lands. Please take care of these places and give them the respect they deserve. Good stewardship is the only way these places will remain beautiful for future generations.

I hope this book serves you well.

~Tony Mayse

Photo by Stanley Vrba

GETTING TO THE WILDLIFE REFUGE

• From Oklahoma City:

Drive south on Interstate 44; turn right at the Medicine Park exit 45, which is Hwy 49. Stay on Hwy 49 seven miles to the wildlife refuge. Drive time from Oklahoma City is about 1½ hours.

• From Amarillo, Texas:

Drive east on Interstate 40, exit on Hwy 83 south. Take Hwy 83 south to Hwy 62 east. Continue on Hwy 62 east to Lawton, exit on Hwy 115 north towards Cache, which leads to the Holy City located in the refuge. Drive time is about 5½ hours.

• From Dallas, Texas:

Drive north on Hwy 287 to Wichita Falls. Take Hwy 44 north to Lawton exiting on Hwy 62 west. Follow Hwy 62 west then exit on Hwy 115 north towards Cache, which leads to the wildlife refuge. Drive time is about 3½ hours.

CAMPING

When rock climbing at the wildlife refuge camping can be found at Camp Doris, located inside the wildlife refuge. Camp Doris has showers, electrical hook-ups, drive-in and primitive camp sites. Camp sites are reserved first come first served. Call for reservations on group sites (580)429-3221.

Camping can also be found at Lake Lawtonka, drive out of the refuge heading east on Hwy 49 turn left at Jct 58 and follow the signs to Lake Lawtonka.

WICHITA MOUNTAINS PLACES TO EAT:

Meers

The Meers Store is located on highway 115, 1.5 miles north of the Wichita Mountain Wildlife Refuge, Take I-44 to Hwy 49. Travel west about 4 miles, to Hwy 58. Turn to the north for about 5 miles to the turn-off to Meers (follow the signs).

Restaurant Hours:

Sunday–Thursday 10:30am–8:30pm

Friday & Saturday 10:30am–9pm

Closed on Tuesday. 580-429-8051 | www.meersstore.com

Riverside Café

Located about five minutes from the wildlife refuge in Medicine Park.

180 E Lake Dr, Medicine Park, OK 73557

(580) 529-2626

IMPORTANT NUMBERS

Wichita Mountains Wildlife Refuge
Headquarters - 580.429.3222

Quartz Mountain State Park - 580. 563.2238

WMCC (Wichita Mountains Climber's Coalition)
www.wichitamountains.org

The authors contact:
www.guideforaday.com

Elisha Gallegos Artwork

CLIMBING GYMS

Threshold Climbing Gym

6024 Westlake Memorial Parkway
Oklahoma City, OK 73142
(405) 470-3611
www.thresholdclimbinggym.com

Climb Up

2701 Washington Dr
Norman, OK 73069
(405) 310-4648
www.climbupgym.com

Climb Up OKC

200 SE 4th St
OKC, OK 73129
(405) 673-7448

Photo by Andrew Burr

WICHITA MOUNTAINS WILDLIFE REFUGE RULES AND REGULATIONS

The Wichita Mountains Wildlife Refuge is located on federal property. Certain rules and regulations apply to all visitors. Please stop by the Visitors Center for an updated list of regulations that govern the wildlife refuge. This will insure that your stay while visiting the refuge will be a pleasant experience. Remember this is an open range and there are hazards that are to be taken into consideration.

Some of the rules:

- No Drone Zone (The refuge is a designated wilderness area).
- Backcountry camping in designated areas (no camping below climbing areas).
- No alcohol.
- No swimming.
- Pets must be leashed at all times.
- Do not harass the wildlife.
- Pack out all trash (Leave No Trace).
- Obey the closing times for all gated areas (closed at sunset).
- See Camp Doris rules while camping there. Obey quiet hours.
- Obey speed limits in the refuge (evening speed limits are reduced).
- No bolting without permit.
- No guiding without proper permit.
- Picking wildflowers and removing cactus is illegal.

Photo by Tony Mayse

Photo by Tony Mayse

WICHITA MOUNTAINS GEOLOGY

By Mark Herndon

When you sink your hand into a crack or grab a hold in the Wichita Mountains, you might not know the incredibly long and complicated geologic history told by the rock you are touching. The granite is about 540 million years old. It is part of a long, linear mountain range, called the Wichita–Amarillo Uplift by geologists. Although the eastern outcrop of the range lies southeast of Mount Scott, in actual lava flows on Fort Sill, the westward extension continues well to the west, all the way to Baldy Peak, and the granite knobs around the town of Granite. The range then vanishes beneath the surface just west of Baldy Peak. From there, it dives deeper and continues west-northwestward beneath the surface far into the Texas Panhandle, reaching as far west as northeastern New Mexico, where geologists have easily followed it by thousands of oil and gas wells. The mountain range was at one time covered with many kilometers of now eroded sedimentary rocks. As the process of uplift and erosion were ongoing at the same time, the true past height of the Wichita Mountains is not known, but only about 15 miles north of the Wichita Mountains, a huge series of faults exist. On the northern, downdropped side of these faults lies the deepest interior sedimentary basin in the U.S., the Anadarko Basin, a major petroleum resource. Rocks that are equivalent to the Wichita Granites, that crop out at the surface in the Wichitas, are buried by over 40,000 feet of younger sediments in the basin just to the north, less than 20 miles away.

The rocks that form the Wichita Mountains were originally created in a great intracontinental rift in southern Laurentia, the predecessor continent to modern North America. The rift was part of a breakup of the ancient supercontinent Rodinia, and a large chunk of the Laurentian portion of this supercontinent was separated and rifted away. Today that rock is found in the Precordillera of Argentina. Tracing continents and subcontinents as they wander around the globe is like a moving jigsaw puzzle. With modern dating and magnetic techniques though, a rock can be dated very accurately, and the latitude at which it formed is frozen into the magnetic minerals, like little compass needles, that can be measured. Longitude is still a mystery in many cases, though.

Osage Lake | Photo by Tony Mayse

The rift, similar to the East African Rift, was formed as Rodinia broke apart, 550–600 million years ago, long before plants or animal life existed on land. Traces of the rift can be followed along the Wichita–Amarillo Uplift, northwestward to northern New Mexico, and onward into southwest Colorado and southeastern Utah. The southeastern end of the rift continued well into Texas. It is not visible at the surface.

The rift valley rapidly filled with sea water, and then began to fill with sediment from adjacent weathering rocks.

Lava then began to fill the rift, and a large amount of Gabbro, a black igneous rock, formed. The gabbro still crops out in many areas of the refuge, but gabbro weathers far faster than granitic rocks, and tends to form the gentle valleys, especially on highway 49, west of the refuge headquarters. Trees also grow well on Gabbro, but poorly on granite. If you keep on the lookout, you can see these black rocks in a few places, but they cover a large part of the refuge, just below the surface, especially on the north side of Mt. Scott and Mount Sheridan, and to the west along highway 49. They are covered by vegetation, whereas the granite outcrops are far more resistant to vegetation. Landforms are often governed by a principle: Rocks resistant to weathering tend to make hills or ridges. Rocks that weather easily tend to form valleys.

Next, granitic magma began to pool beneath the rift valley. It actually erupted at several places north and south of the refuge, creating rhyolite, which is simply erupted granite. Most of the rhyolites crop out in Fort Sill. Rhyolite is a granite that cooled quickly, so its crystal structure is very fine. Much of the magma was

Photo by Andrew Burr

injected into layers between the overlying rhyolite and underlying gabbro, however, and it cooled slowly enough to form the coarse grained Wichita Granite Group—the Wichita Granite that we all know and love.

The rate of cooling is important in any igneous rock: Magmas which cool slowly allow enough time for the crystals to grow large. If the rock cooled quickly, the crystals will be small and it will be "fine grained." The granite of Mount Scott was relatively thin, so it is finer grained, as a general rule, than granites in the southern part of the refuge, because those were thicker and therefore cooled more slowly. There are variations in the granite throughout the range, because the magma cooled at different rates.

After the igneous rocks were in place, 530 million years ago, the area continued to subside below sea level, and filled up with thick layers of marine sedimentary rocks over the next 250 million years, as oceans filled the original rift. The Wichitas didn't begin to uplift above the surface until 300 million years ago. The mountains grew during an episode of compression from the south. One of the theories is that the southern edge of Laurentia, where the Wichitas were located, collided with South America and Africa. The northern and southern margins of the Wichitas are bounded by huge faults. The mountains themselves were uplifted as more or less one block. Thousands of feet of sedimentary rocks were eroded as the uplift continued. As uplift and erosion were occurring at the same time, it is difficult to say how high the Wichitas were at their highest point, but it was probably during the Pennsylvanian to Permian Periods, 250–300 million years ago. Extensive gravel deposits, thousands of feet thick and over a hundred miles long are found in the subsurface to the north of the uplift, where many oil and gas wells have been drilled.

Later in this period of uplift, the Wichitas became surrounded by sea water yet again. This isn't unusual for a geologically active area. In southern Kansas, the ocean shoreline had advanced and retreated dozens of times during this period. The Wichitas continued to erode, and thick sections of granitic gravel was shed as the exposed granite eroded. This eventually buried the western edge of the uplift, and features interpreted as shoreline action exists in the Quartz Mountain area. One of these features can be seen at ground level on the far southeast extent of the face of Baldy Peak, as a head-high horizontal groove extending for several hundred feet. Other features of the Permian shoreline are found at higher levels within Quartz Mountain State Park.

The mountains were mostly or completely buried during Permian time beneath their own eroded gravels, and this erosional surface is visible today on the southeast side of Mount Scott. Since that time the Wichitas have been near the surface or above it on occasion. Landforms that are this old are uncommon, but present, here and there around the world.

It is fascinating to contemplate a starry night, with the Wichitas as scattered islands in a shallow ocean, before disnosaurs had begun to rule the earth. Most rocks in Oklahoma are older than the Mesozoic, the time of the dinosaurs, but they had just started to appear during the Permian period, and today we can see the Permian shoreline on the south side of Mount Scott, as well as along the base of the SE edge of Baldy Peak.

When we look at the present day Wichita Mountains, we are looking at a landscape with roots deep in the geologic past, and ancient landforms which have been recently exhumed, showing us the mountains that we see today, formed in many ways in the deep past.

CONSERVATION AND COMMUNITY IN THE WICHITAS

By Marion Hutchison

A little more than twenty years ago, hundreds of concerned climbers from Oklahoma, Texas, and Kansas crowded into the Great Plains Vo-Tech School in Lawton to hear the shocking news: rock climbing was to be banned at the Wichita Mountains Wildlife Refuge. The year was 1994, and like many climbing areas across the country, the Refuge was about to be engulfed by a growing access storm.

For several decades, climbing in the Refuge had been an out-of-the-mainstream adventure practiced by a few dozen highly dedicated and independent spirits. But in the matter of a few short years in the late 1980s and early 1990s, climbing had exploded into popular culture as an extreme sport-of-sports sought out by hundreds of everyday faces.

Suddenly, parking lots were overflowing, trails were eroding, and bolts were popping up like spring weeds. The passive years of little or no communication between climbers and refuge staff soon led to misunderstandings about the nature and value of climbing, as well as serious concerns about the impact of climbing activity on refuge resources.

Threatened with the loss of a way of life and access to a place more dear than home, local climbers joined forces together as a community of friends to save climbing at the refuge. As part of that endeavor, the Wichita Mountains Climbers Coalition was formed to work in cooperative partnership with the US Fish and Wildlife Service in managing climbing activity and protecting the natural resources at the refuge. Since that partnership began in 1996, the climbing community has provided thousands of hours of volunteer service for trail work and other conservation projects, and the dedicated work of the Advisory Bolting Committee has helped to insure that the refuge's wilderness and other natural resources are protected.

Through those efforts, local climbers discovered a sense of community that was often missing in earlier days. Thanks to our common goals and shared values, we stepped beyond our philosophical differences and found the importance of working together as a community of friends to protect that which we all treasure: climbing in the Wichitas.

That community spirit proved its worth once again in 2001 when it was learned that Baldy Point, one of the greatest climbing resources in the Wichitas, was about to be sold to a private developer. But in a matter of a few short weeks, more than one hundred local climbers collectively pledged nearly twenty thousand dollars to help fund the purchase of Quartz and assist in its transfer to Quartz Mountain State Park, thereby protecting access to one of our most cherished climbing areas.

As tomorrow dawns, the sun will be shining brightly on the future of climbing in the Wichitas. Let's savor that fact, and the knowledge that we, as a community of climbers, succeeded in saving climbing at the refuge and Quartz. At the same time, let's not forget the years of hard work and dedication that got us here. Because the word "complacency" is not found in our climbing community's dictionary. And that's important. For while our access and conservation efforts have been a success, our work to protect our climbing resources continues. As such, it remains the responsibility of each and every climber who frequents the Wichitas to support our climbing community and assist with our conservation efforts. By doing so, we insure our climbing future and that bright tomorrow.

Photo by Andrew Burr

Climbing Ethics and Ratings

With more people getting into climbing it is important to reach out to new climbers and reiterate to the experienced ones the importance of taking care of the places where we climb. One of the biggest impacts to an area is trash. Not only does it have adverse effects on keeping these wilderness areas pristine, but it is harmful to the wildlife. Remember, we are just visitors, you climb for a few days and go home, if you walk by that discarded water bottle it will be there the next time you come out, so make a difference and pick it up, yours or not. This is not a climbing gym, there is no staff to pick up your tape or sunflower seed shells, banana peels, or power bar wrappers. This activity is seeing more individuals wanting to venture outdoors to rock climb. Let's set the example as to how we interact with nature.

Removing vegetation such as trees or cacti is illegal. Once that food source is removed animals starve, and when you're done climbing all you have to do is dial up a pizza on your phone or stop off at your favorite eatery. That ringtail cat has no such luxury. I personally witnessed a climber doing this very thing at Quartz Mountain, on a popular classic trad climb, using his nut tool to remove a fruit bearing cactus at the top of the cliff. The solution was to just step around the offending cactus and redirect your rope, problem solved.

Most of the routes in the Wildlife Refuge are traditional climbs, protected with natural gear (removable protection); the routes at Quartz Mountain are mostly bolt protected. Do not add or remove anchors or bolts from any route in either of these areas. There is a bolting committee and a bolting policy in place. Do not bolt without permission. Contact the WMCC website for more information on this subject.

Chipping holds is unethical. Every area has its own style and technique. Do not bring any route in this guide down to your level by chipping or enhancing the rock. Train hard and get the red-point on your own.

Ratings

This guidebook uses the Yosemite Decimal System which is the standard for rock climbing in the United States. Routes for these areas are rated from 5.5–5.13. When the climb is rated harder than, 5.10 but not 5.11 a sub-rating is then applied with a letter from a–d. Ratings are subjective and often a matter of consensus. The only way to get a better understanding of climbing ratings is to go out and climb a variety of grades. But, here lies the caveat...all areas vary in ratings and climbing style. If you are not a strong crack climber a route like *Papa Was a Rollin' Stone* 5.9 at Lost Dome may seem much more difficult to a gym like climb *Pimpin' ain't Easy 5.11a*. Footwork intensive areas such as Quartz Mtn. seem to fall prey to the same debacle, although fear from being way above your last bolt seems to increase your "perceived" difficulty of a route in this area. Whereas if you are on toprope climbing *Last of the Good Guys* for instance it seems reasonable.

Bottom line, just go out, climb a lot of different routes and work on your weaknesses. If you struggle on climbs in a certain style work on those, and given the opportunity, watch climbers better than yourself. This seems to be one of the biggest teachers of moving smoothly and confidently over stone.

In this guidebook routes are given colored lines resembling ratings of various difficulty.

Green = 5.5–5.9

Blue = 5.10

Yellow = 5.11

Red = 5.12–5.13

Below are some examples of the standard for various grades:

5.5 = **Monkey on a Football**, Quartz Mountain.   **Tiny Big Crack**, Charon Gardens.

5.6 = **Great Expectations**, Elk Mountain.   **T-Bone**, The Narrows.

5.7 = **Ker Plunk**, The Narrows.   **Bourbon Street**, Quartz Mountain.

5.8 = **Crazy Alice**, The Narrows.   **Larry's Folly**, Lost Dome

5.9 = **S Wall**, Quartz Mountain.   **Papa Was a Rollin' Stone**, Lost Dome.

5.10 = **The Claw**, Crab Eyes.   **Amazon Woman**, Quartz Mountain.

5.11 = **Ra**, Crab Eyes   **League of Doom**, The Narrows.

5.12 = **Rap Bolters From Hell**, Lost Dome.   **Lost My Religion**, Lost Dome.

5.13 = **Tied to the Whipping Post**, Lost Dome.   **Moby Dick Direct**, Crab Eyes.

There are aid routes in this guidebook. I personally still do aid climbs, although the use of pitons is no longer accepted with modern aid gear such as hybrid cams and cam hooks which have turned piton craft into an outdated mode of aid climbing. For example, *Anorexia* (aid climb) goes entirely clean and has been led in less than 50-minutes. Please do not bring pitons on this route.

Aid Climbing Ratings:

A0 = Pulling on quick-draws to get through a move.

A1 = Aiding on bomber gear placements.

A2 = Aiding on bomber gear with a few shaky placements.

A3 = Aiding on shaky placements, then a reprieve with a bomber piece.

A4 = Body weight placements for a ways with an occasional "thank god" piece.

A5 = An entire pitch of body weight placements, no fall zone.

Danger Ratings:

This guidebook has ratings that let the climber know if there is a runout or bad fall potential. However, these ratings are subjective and come with a caution. Any runout has potential for serious bodily injury or death. An example is your belayer has extra slack out, you fall low on the route, your gear placement is crap, you feel cocky and run it out on easy ground and do not place protection, then fall etc.

R= Runout without decking.

RX= Runout with a ledge strike potential.

X= You fall, you die.

Some examples of these routes:

R = *Amazon Woman, Baptists on the Rampage, Cruisin' for a Bruzin', Ker Plunk.*

RX= *Wild Child, S Wall, Pauper, Dr. Coolhead, Snow White, League of Doom.*

X= *Jet Stream, Hook Roof, Vincent Black Shadow.*

Quality Ratings

This guidebook has stars next to the difficulty rating letting the climber know at a glance which routes are of higher quality. It's always nice to know the best routes to do on any visit to a climbing area. The star system is straight forward, the more stars given the better the route. These are like anything else, however, only an opinion. You may find these stars fall short or long from one climber to the next.

1 star = Nothing to write home about, just okay.

2 stars = Good route with one or two fun moves.

3 stars = Great route.

4 stars = Stellar, classic! *Amazon Woman.*

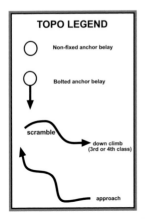

TOPO LEGEND

Non-fixed anchor belay

Bolted anchor belay

scramble

down climb
(3rd or 4th class)

approach

Photo by Andrew Burr

Roped Grades		Bouldering Grades	
YDS	French	Vermin	Fontainbleau
5.6	4		
5.7	4+	V0	
5.8	5a	V1	5c
5.9	5b	V2	
5.10a	6a	V3	6a
5.10b	6a+	V4	6b
5.10c	6b	V5	6c/6c+
5.10d	6b+		
5.11a	6c	V6	7a
5.11b		V7	7a+/7b
5.11c	6c+	V8	7b+
5.11d	7a	V9	7c
5.12a	7a+	V10	7c+
5.12b	7b	V11	8a
5.12c	7b+	V12	9a+
5.12d	7c	V13	8b
5.13a	7c+	V14	8b+
5.13b	8a	V15	8c
5.13c	8a+		
5.13d	8b		
5.14a	8b+		

THRESHOLD
CLIMBING + FITNESS

6024 Westlake Memorial Pkwy, OKC • M-F 11a-10p • Sat 9a-10p • Sun 12p-8p

📞 405.470.3611 ✉ hello@thresholdclimbinggym.com 𝐟 @thresholdclimbing

Equipment

Oklahoma rock climbing areas are, for the most part, traditional in their ethics. There are sport (bolted) routes, but the majority of the climbs are gear routes, meaning you need to carry your own protection on them.

A "standard rack" for the Wildlife Refuge and Quartz Mountain is two sets of camming devices ranging from TCUs to #4 Friend size, a set of stoppers, at least 8–10 quickdraws, and a few long runners. A 60-meter cord is preferred. Double-rope rappels are sometimes required, especially at Quartz and Elk Mountain.

I have added a gear list on the route descriptions for each climb. The rule of thumb is to bring more gear if you are unsure about the rack list described. The cams mentioned on the gear list are in inches unless specified as being Camalots. Example: a #2 cam can protect a two-inch crack. If you question the placement of any piece of gear back it up. Remember a gear placement is only as good as the rock quality and the person placing it.

Climbing Season

Climbing in Oklahoma can be a year-round experience with short mild winters and hot summers. The best climbing season is from March through early June, then late September through December. You can beat the heat by hitting the climbs early in the summer months. July and August temperatures can exceed 100 degrees. Climbing temperatures become friendlier again from the end of September through December. January and February are the coldest months. Temperatures can dip into the low 30s, but sunny days allow climbing on south-facing walls, especially at Quartz Mountain. Old Baldy is the winter playground for climbing in Oklahoma. If the winds are howling out of the north on a cold, sunny winter day head for the sunny walls of Quartz!

Climbing Dangers

The descriptions and ratings given in this guidebook are subjective and should be used as information only. This guidebook will not teach you how to climb or keep you from getting into a bad situation. Only experience and good judgment will teach you this.

Climbing magazines show professional climbers doing amazing climbs and making it appear easy. Do not be misled by this and attempt to climb beyond your immediate ability.

The traditional routes listed in this book require a fair amount of knowledge in placing gear. A route is not the location to practice placing gear. If you fall on poorly positioned protection, you may not get another chance. Physical strength is no substitute for good judgment.

The majority of the routes in this book I have climbed countless times over many years. The descriptions and ratings are described to the best of my recollection. Take each description with a grain of salt and do not attempt any route in this guidebook if it looks too scary to you or you feel uncomfortable climbing it. Come back another day when you have gained more skill.

Make sure your rope reaches the ground or belay anchors and always tie a knot in the end of your rope before you rappel. Many of the route lengths on the topos are approximate.

Belaying does not mean hold the rope! I have seen on countless occasions climbers belaying their partners with too much slack running from the belay device to the climber on lead. The leader is oblivious to this because he or she is focused on the climb and the belayer is oblivious to the dangerous situation he or she is creating by not keeping the appropriate amount of rope paid out to the leader. The leader's life is in your hands, take belaying seriously! It's a lot more than just a "catch!"

While hanging out at the base of climbing routes stay away from the "impact zone." This is where falling rock or dropped gear may hit you. If you are climbing and knock off loose rock or drop gear shout "ROCK!" This may keep someone from getting injured.

"There are specific things that I would like to accomplish—grades, routes, mountains—but all that pales in comparison to staying healthy, strong and confident. The only way to ensure these things is to follow my heart, and also work for balance—not too much play without work, not too much climbing without rest, not too much fun without suffering, not too much travel time without time at home, not too much taking without giving."

~Sam Elias

THE OKLAHOMA STONE MASTERS

The climbing in Oklahoma is rich in history and the accounts of routes that were established back then are legendary.

The rock is granite, some of the best stone on the planet, and when it's mentioned to the prolific climbing legend Doug Robinson, he says it with the biggest grin "it's the kind." In fact, it really is the kind. This stone has allowed climbers to create a climbing arena that is as good as anything found in Colorado or the western United States in the high desert of Joshua Tree, or Tahquitz in California.

Quartz Mountain and the Wichita Mountains Wildlife Refuge are very different in terms of climbing style. The Wichita's have vertical and overhanging roof cracks, heads-up trad climbing, and steep bolted routes. Whereas Quartz Mountain, about an hour north and west of the Wildlife Refuge, is a granite dome with superb slab climbing.

These areas were shaped by a group of young men that had a vision as to how the climbs should be established and a desire to climb the unclimbed. In the 1970s and well into the 1980s the ground-up style of climbing was the way it was done. This meant you walked up to a stretch of rock that looked like something you wanted to climb and set out on the adventure. If it was a crack you could put in gear and keep moving up, if the crack faded out and no other protection availed you stood on a stance and drilled a bolt while on lead. Balancing and hand drilling that bolt which was a ¼" x 1.25" Rawl button head, then continue climbing to the top to set up the belay and then walking-off or scrambling back down the cliff to the base. This was the way.

Duane Raleigh climbing Are You a God? 5.12c X circa 1980s. | Photo from Doug Robinson Collection

The main driving force behind Oklahoma rock climbing was Duane Raleigh who was arguably the best climber of that time and probably the best climber to come out of this state. Duane was the master climber who set the tone as to how the climbs were laid out. His first ascents are countless and they span the years from the 1970s up to the late 1980s, including climbs like *Chicago Bound, Master Race, Master's Roof, Earth Man, Jet Stream, Last of the Good Guys,* and *Amazon Woman* just to name a few of the Quartz climbs. In the Wichita Mountains, there are classics on the Lichen Wall, *League of Doom, Space Balls, Nuclear Combat* and *Nubian Dance.* In the Charon Gardens backcountry Duane climbed the huge rock domes behind Pear and Apple, Secret Agent Dome. These climbs were led up to sixty-feet before the first and only bolt was drilled off a small stance creating *Secret Agent Man, Vincent Black Shadow, Matt Helm,* and *Agent 99.* The dome's name is inspired by the popular song named "Secret Agent Man."

Out at Crab Eyes, Duane climbed *Are You a God?,* ground-up, taking falls and pushing the limits as to what was possible on a blank face with overlapping cracks. Duane also climbed the bold and intimidating aid lines of the day like *Yellow Jacket* and *Blade Runner.* Then he went on to lead *Ra, Power Series,* and *Where the Buffalo Roam,* a deceptively steep dihedral that at first look doesn't seem intimidating at all steep until you step back and look at it from a side view, revealing this alarming vertical test piece. At Quartz Mountain, he climbed the classic *Anorexia* on aid which climbs a thin seam and crack on a tilted headwall above a slab. Time was not on his side for this one however, as he moved out of state to Colorado before he was able to free climb it. Out at Hidden Dome, Duane also climbed *Serpentine,* a hard face climb and still committing, even today, with bolts now protecting the climbing, but back then it was done sans bolts, just a couple fixed pins and gear. Lost Dome was also climbed without bolts on routes like *Drop Dead, Steep Show,* and *Slime of the Century.*

It is a difficult task trying write about the level of skill that Duane had in establishing these routes. The only way to truly understand the talent he possessed is to step up to the base and venture out on any one of these climbs without rehearsing them on toprope.

Duane was not alone during those days. He created lots of routes with partners like Bill Thomas and Stuart Stanford, Jon Frank and Jimmy Ratzlaff, and many others, just look at the long list of first ascents, he climbed with everyone.

Steve Gillam, Mike Hankins, Rick McCusic, David & Mike Panciera, Jay Lowell, Keith Egan, Jack Hill, Bill Ward, Karl Bird, Carl Murray, Bernie Wire, Jack Wurster, Stewart Stanford, Rick & Bill Thomas, Donnie Hunt, Bob Pearson, Marvin Hayes, Ken Rose, Kenny Stern, Chris Mohr, Diane Fisher, Marc Johnson, James Hollingsworth, Larry Fuson, Bob Hopkins, Sandy Stewart, Laura Vaughn, Kurt Shier, Steve Harwell.

Jimmy Ratzlaff was also a driving force back in those days, towering over the other climbers with a 6'6" frame. Jimmy was a masterful climber. He made many of the first ascents at Quartz and the Wichita's. His name spans the guidebook with hard routes many of which are bereft of any opportunities for protection.

One weekend after a restless night camped in the Main Boulder field below Old Baldy at Quartz Mountain, mosquitoes were getting the best of him, so, he got up early and headed up the south face of Baldy, climbing on to a seemingly holdless, steep wall and started hand drilling the first bolt on the blank

Jimmy Ratzlaff stepping out into the void on the intimidating and heady Scream Dream 5.11 X circa early 1980s. | Photo from Jimmy Ratzlaff Collection

Jon Frank climbing Master Race 5.12 RX in the early 1980s. | Photo from Doug Robinson Collection

stretch of rock without a belay. Just a rope tied to his waist and the remainder of the rope running down the cliff. Duane heard the unmistakable tinking of the hammer down at the campsite and quickly jumped up, then ran to the base putting Jimmy on belay just in time for him to clip the first and only bolt on what would become *Scream Dream* 5.11 X on the Scream Wall.

On another first ascent adventure, Jimmy teamed up with Duane for a new, steep, and daunting line up Quartz Mountain's headwall. This new route involved committing moves way above your bolt, offering stances from which to bolt, but they were far and few, which invariably meant this climb would be hard and run out. At the time, Jimmy was dating a girl who lived in Chicago. *Chicago Bound* was now the name of this Quartz soon-to-be-classic test piece climb.

Jimmy seemed to have a penchant for the bold routes. He was also the first to climb *McBride's Mind* on Zoo Wall, taking a whipping fall while he was hand drilling the first bolt, flying through the air with drill still stuck in the rock, only to climb back up and finish the route. This was the early makings of what would become the classic Narrows climb, *Dr. Cool Head.*

Mark Herndon making the second ascent on the classic aid line Anorexia circa early 1980s. | Photo from Jimmy Ratzlaff Collection

If you look at Lichen Wall's first ascents you will notice a face climb named *Jesus Lives* rated 5.11b. This one-hundred-foot pitch climbs the stretch of rock just to the right of *League of Doom's* first pitch; you will also take note that there is no protection.

Jimmy was all over the refuge, running up routes sans rope on Elk Slabs, finding the short crack gems at the *Dream Boat Annie* area named Area 1 back then. Jimmy's enthusiasm also pushed him towards climbing in Yosemite Valley California. One summer Jimmy left for Yosemite Valley with $60 in his pocket. He bought 5 pair of climbing shoes in Bishop for $10 each, then he sold them in the Valley for $40 a pair to climbers in Camp IV, giving him enough money to make it for a month!

One of Jimmy's main climbing partners was Jon Frank. Jon along with Jack Wurster and Duane Raleigh produced the second and third guidebooks for the Wildlife Refuge and Quartz Mountain with *Oklahoma on the Rocks* and *Oklahoma on the Rocks II*. These were the modern guidebooks of the day.

Jon Frank's name was synonymous with power. Physically he is one of the strongest climbers to set foot on Oklahoma rocks. He could do seven one-arm pull-ups with his right arm and five with the left arm, four one-arm pull-ups on the 1/4" door frame and a one-arm, one-finger pull-up! Duane even challenged Jon to a one-arm, one-finger pull-up contest in the fire cave at Quartz. Duane had a dowel just outside of the cave with a sling. Duane could do a single one-arm, one-finger pull-up and Jon not having warmed up used two-fingers, so Duane won that challenge. The classic story of one-arm pull-ups which has now reached legend status was when Jon challenged Bart Conner, the world famous Olympic Gold Medalist gymnast, to a one-arm pull-up contest. While at an OU gymnastics tournament Jimmy Ratzlaff walked over to Bart and asked him how many one-arm pull-ups he could do? Bart seemed annoyed by this and replied "I don't know?" The next year at the same meet Jimmy sees Bart again, but this time, Bart seemed a bit more relaxed, almost smug, or maybe just a little confident. There is a sense of pride in his voice as he says to Jimmy "hey I remember you from last year, how are you doing?" Bart says this like he had accomplished something. Bart then quips "Well, ever since you asked me about the pull-ups I started working on them, I can do six." Bart waiting for Jimmy to be pleased with his performance and maybe as happy as he with this accomplishment, but, Jimmy says without the slightest hesitation, "that's pretty good, but he can do seven", and then pointed over to Jon! For a brief instance, they both thought Bart was going to throw down the challenge right then and there, but he just walked away, maybe thinking yeah right or maybe thinking, "I need to train harder?"

Jon's power was not just on the door jams and pull-up challenges, he was equally as strong on the rock. Jon's first ascents included *Desperate Reality's* 5.12 roof crack, *Aerial Anticipation*, *Critical Mass*, *Sloth*, and *Wild and Crazy*, the steep and committing overhanging face climb on the more than vertical side of Leaning

Tower, and the roof crack sitting on top of Lichen Wall, *Same Reality*.

Jon once climbed *Desperate Reality* without shoes! I mentioned this to Jimmy who quickly said "When you can do one-arm pull-ups, you don't need to use your feet!"

Mark Herndon was the intellect of the group and the one who excelled in aid climbing and would often rope up with Duane on free climbing first ascents. Mark was the book of knowledge. During the evening campfire conversations, all subjects were on. Sometimes the most mundane of subjects would be brought up. He would often argue some things that came up during the evening chats, like which types of wood burned hotter, oak or cherry? Duane would utter cherry and the game was on! Not a "know it all" by any means, Mark had the respect of those that knew him, he was a smart guy with a wit about him, earning an intellectual scholarship to the University of Oklahoma. Mark was also, probably the only person to question Duane, the master climber, on climbing subjects as well. One time, Mark had a photo of the Great Roof on the *Nose*, Duane disagreed that it was the *Great Roof* in the photo on the basis that he had climbed the *Nose* with Jimmy and they were stuck on its face during and ice storm. Duane never gave in as to being wrong, but then again, this was in fact a game of wits and baiting your opponent was fair game. You must remember this was way before the internet. Mark could do this as he and Duane were the best of friends and all this banter was in the spirit of comradery and the utmost respect. Duane and Mark traveled to Europe together and climbed in the French Alps of Chamonix. Mark was an expert skydiver who jumped off El Capitan and has the distinction of having a low B.A.S.E. number of 104.

Terry Andrews was another force of power and skill during this Golden Age of Oklahoma rock climbing. Terry was often seen bouldering on some of the most difficult problems on the slick limestone crags at Chandler Park in Tulsa. Jon Frank commented that he couldn't touch some of these things that Terry could routinely lap! Terry's finger strength was well known in the climbing circle, he could hang onto the tiniest of holds and his fingers were said to be like "little steel hooks." Terry's excellent footwork and the fact that he could hold onto anything was the reason that routes like *Rap Bolters from Hell*, *Moby Dick* with a 5.13 Direct start, *Made in the Shade*, *Ra*, and others like *The Claw*, *Babes on Harleys*, and the *Cave Route* in The Meadows were some of his first ascents. He's still climbing hard to this day.

Another intellect of the day was Marion Hutchison, arguably one of the first climbers to explore the new route potential at Quartz Mountain as well as scoping out the many possibilities of the day in the Wichita's. On an exploratory outing Marion ventured up a steep 100 foot face with barely any gear... this was the early makings of the now classic *League of Doom* in the Narrows. Marion has always had a keen eye for finding new routes to climb. Marion and Terry Andrews were the first climbers to get the ball rolling with their initial exploration of the slick and polished steep face with committing moves towards the top now known as *Foolish Behavior*. It now sees more attempts than onsights reflecting Marion's climbing skill back in the day.

Terry Andrews on an early ascent on one of the most iconic routes in Oklahoma, Amazon Woman 5.10b RX circa 1970s | Photo from Jimmy Ratzlaff Collection

Marion was also instrumental in organizing the climbers of the early 90s to keep the Wichita Mountains Wildlife Refuge open to rock climbing. During that time the refuge manager was not in favor of climbing. Marion rallied the climbing community and created the Wichita Mountains Climbers Coalition, thus opening a line of communication with the refuge and its officials. Then, in early 2000, Marion was called to this post once again to help negotiate a land purchase deal where climbers organized in conjunction with the Access Fund. Baldy Point at Quartz Mountain was purchased and then donated to the Oklahoma State Department of Tourism, with the understanding that climbing will remain at Quartz as long as the sun rises in the east and sets in the west.

Another super athlete to line the pages of Oklahoma rock climbing history was Eric Forney.

Eric was built like Adonis and was a master at pole vaulting, holding records at Oklahoma State University, competing at a professional level, and traveling around Europe with the best pole vaulters on the planet. Eric went on to compete in the Olympic Trials jumping a height 18'6." His wife Kathy was also a super athlete in her own right, being the first woman in the United States to score a perfect 10 in gymnastics. Eric rock climbed during his years of pole vaulting but then committed to climbing once his competition days were behind him. Eric teamed up with Jon Frank to establish the Narrows classic *Aerial Anticipation* and the sketchy *Vegetarian Delight*. Notably, Eric has also put his fitness to work outside the state of Oklahoma with countless steep, cutting edge routes in Arkansas. Eric is also well traveled with recent trips to the strict-ethics climbing area of Elbsandstein in Germany and the sea cliffs of Sardinia, Italy.

Jack Wurster was a good free climber with the steel mind of Duane Raleigh. He was known to not bat an eye after a long fall on any given route and then get right back up there again and again. Most climbers would have turned to mush after the first big whip.

Greg Schooley was an army brat and a classic 70s climber. Greg was the first climber to put up a bolted route at Quartz Mountain establishing the mega-classic *Bourbon Street*. He had spent some time climbing in California learning the craft of bolting slab routes which he quickly shared with the young hard chargers of the day, Marion Hutchison and Terry Andrews, who were still on the strict ethic of Eldorado Canyon climbing where installing bolts was considered taboo!

His dad flew as a Flying Tiger in WWII. One summer, there were helicopter rides just down the road form Old Baldy, at the theme park. Greg's dad was an aerospace inspector and quickly discovered that the helicopter pilot was operating without a license as well as not having the proper credentials to fly people in his machine. He quickly shut the operation down!

The best story teller out of all the gang was Sam Audrain. Sam was an incredibly gifted athlete, winning skate boarding events. He was a super strong boulderer as was the case for most Tulsa climbers. Sam was really handsome and had no problem picking up any girl he wanted, but mostly, he wanted to hang out with people. Everyone was, in a way, a Sam clone back then.

Chris Rowins was a good free climber but excelled at aid climbing. Chris was a former military guy. He was only on the Oklahoma climbing scene a couple of years. He was well known for having a Volkswagen turbo Jetta with the passenger seat taken out. He would rip across the countryside at 90

Marion Hutchison on Steak Dinner Boulder circa 1981. | Photo from Marion Hutchison Collection

Eric Forney climbing Desperate Reality 5.12b. | Photo by Chris Lenox

to 100 miles per hour with his "fuzz buster" on the dash! Chris had an Alaskan driver's license and if he got pulled over he would pull it out and hand it to the officer then throw the ticket away if he received one! Back then, Alaska didn't seem to care if you got a ticket outside of the state, as they didn't keep records. On a road trip to Hueco Tanks with Jon Frank, Jon's fears were realized when Chris was pulled over! Jon was sitting on the gear box with the seat belt wrapped-around him as there was no passenger seat! Things worked out as they always seemed to for Chris. On another trip, Chris drove to Yosemite, did some boulder problems then headed home to Oklahoma. It actually happened! He loved to drive!

In the early 1990s many of the lines seemed to have been picked. But, sometimes the best lines are the ones that are right in front of you but have gone unnoticed. Here, two climbers from Oklahoma teamed up and set out to push the level of difficulty even further. Russell Hooper and his climbing partner Tony Wilson. At Lost Dome, they established *Tied to the Whipping Post*, maybe the first 5.13 in the refuge. This route climbs in the middle of Lost Dome's south face up a water streak. *Tied to the Whipping Post* is "the" test piece route in the Wichita Mountains. Then, just uphill on the west side of Crab Eyes the Hooper/Wilson duo freed an old aid line named *Blade Runner*, the freed line now a hard and committing test piece named *Yellow Beard* 5.12c RX. To this day, it is rarely climbed. In The Narrows, Russell and Tony finished a project route named *Isabelle* 5.12d. This is the hardest face climb on Lichen Wall and climbs a technical corner up a shallow dihedral on the upper part of the wall. Further out west in the backcountry of the refuge, Big Whiskey Peak was the next destination for this duo. This would be *Elk Horn Special* 5.13, another hard face climb with thin holds and demanding footwork.

The stars lined up back then for Oklahoma climbing with a talented group that were driven and inspired, and the result was hard, high-end routes that demanded nothing less than the same determination and mentality to climb them.

The future for Oklahoma climbing looks just as bright. The young generation of new climbers is just as excited to venture out and push themselves to the limits of what is possible.

> "It is not the critic who counts; not the man who points out how the strong man stumbles, or where the doer of deeds could have done them better. The credit belongs to the man who is actually in the arena, whose face is marred by dust and sweat and blood, who strives valiantly; who errs and comes short again and again; because there is not effort without error and shortcomings; but who does actually strive to do the deed; who knows the great enthusiasm, the great devotion, who spends himself in a worthy cause, who at the best knows in the end the triumph of high achievement and who at the worst, if he fails, at least he fails while daring greatly. So that his place shall never be with those cold and timid souls who know neither victory nor defeat."
>
> ~Theodore Roosevelt

The late Russell Hooper styling on Ra 5.11d |
Photo by Chris Corbett

FIRST AND LAST CLIMB IN OKLAHOMA

By Jon Frank

I am holding onto wrought iron bars outside the Quail Creek Golf and Country Club pool. I am on the outside because my family is not a member. I am watching everyone splashing around, going up to the concession stand, putting food orders on their unlimited tabs, and generally trying to make the most of an Oklahoma summer. I didn't come to torture myself but to check out a really cute girl that was at the pool with her friends. As I scanned the pool for my future wife, up walks Jimmy Ratzlaff. He is very tall (6'6"), thin, ruggedly handsome, and full of brevado. As another non-member, he stands next to me, also grabbing the bars and peering in. I ask, "What's up?" He replies, "I came to check out Stacy, she is hot." I nonchalantly said "huh" but what I was thinking is, "So everyone has noticed my future wife, this is not good." As we stood there Jimmy starts to enthusiastically tell me about his recent trip to Colorado. He went with Charlie Hayes and got to have a rock climbing course at the fabled Boulder Mountaineer Guide School. He tells me about climbing the Bastille Crack in Eldorado Canyon, the sheer walls, the rope work, and grabbing small holds. This all sounded interesting enough but I wasn't getting to Colorado anytime soon and there weren't any mountains in Oklahoma. Jimmy goes on to tell me that he went climbing last weekend and he is going this weekend. Then he asked me if I wanted to come along. I released the bars, turned to Jimmy, and said sure. Jimmy, like most beginning enthusiastic climbers, had made it all sound so FUN while leaving out the smaller details of terror, work, and suffering. At the time I didn't know it but this chance encounter with Jimmy would change my life. I also said yes because this would get Jimmy away from Stacy and I could measure myself against the competition.

Jimmy Ratzlaff styling on Crazy Alice 5.8 in the 1970s. | Photo from Jimmy Ratzlaff Collection

That Saturday, Jimmy picked me up in his 1967 metallic blue Mustang. Jimmy looked the part of a European Mountain Guide. He had knickers that went down just below the knees, wild colorful socks that went up to the knees, his Yvon Chounard climbing shoes, a multicolored rugby t-shirt, and to top it all off, a Jackie Stewart racing-type hat. I had never seen him dress like this. Did I need to dress this way to grab the affections of Stacy away from Jimmy? I doubted it, since she hadn't noticed either of us drooling on the wrought iron bars. Jimmy had asked a few others to come along and his shocks were a little bottomed out with all the climbing gear and the five of us. We headed down the H.

E. Bailey Turnpike. Jimmy would get the toll booth change ready down to the nickel and throw it in the basket five feet away never stopping for the green light. On the drive down Jimmy invented the first-ever cruise control. He took a stick and rammed one end on the accelerator and the other end against the seat. Boy howdy, we were moving. I had a lot of questions about what it was going to be like climbing and everyone patiently answered the ongoing barrage. My inquiry was interrupted by flashing lights behind the Mustang. Jimmy's prototype cruise control had betrayed him. The officer pulled Jimmy over and asked him to step out of the car. As Jimmy swung open the door the officer was first greeted by Jimmy's climbing shoes. The officer probably thought they were stolen bowling shoes. Next his socks, then the knickers, the colorful rugby shirt, and finally the racing hat. I think the racing hat was what made the officer give him the maximum fine. I mean if he would have been pulled over in the Swiss Alps he would have probably gotten off, but outside Chickasha, he was done for. We all felt awful as the officer made Jimmy stand outside as passing motorists rubbernecked the Reinhold Messner look-alike being ticketed.

Back on the road we see Mt. Scott growing in the distance and the excitement matches the growing mountain. Now in the refuge, Mt. Scott rolled by and we took a right heading towards Meers. Before we get to Meers, J.R. pulls over on the side of the road next to a mountain with a rock outcrop at the top. At this point I am nervous as I look upwards to the crag. We pile out of the car and go across the road to a barbed wire fence with a sign that says, "No Trespassing Keep Out Violators Will Be Prosecuted." I felt like I was back at the Quail Creek Country Club and asked the others about the fence. Everyone to the last man told me that nothing would happen and that no one cared and that they had done this many times.

Gee, if these words didn't sound familiar. I had helped some friends break into an elementary school one time, having said the same thing, got caught, and spent two weeks cleaning the school on summer break. The penalty was to last longer but we did such a bad job the janitors let us off on the premise that it took too long to teach us idiots anything and they were tired of redoing our work.

We climbed the fence and bushwhacked our way up a faint trail. Arriving at the base was strange to me. I had never bushwhacked in a forest before or stood nose to nose with a near vertical cliff. Thinking about actually climbing it made me feel excited and nervous. Jimmy found the route and flaked the rope but he didn't lead it. The route was lead by Scott McBride, the most experienced climber in the group. Yes, this is the *McBride's Mind* on the Zoo Wall Jimmy named after him. The first pitch went up thirty feet to a large sloping ledge and then went a little right to a splitter hand crack going up the face and then traversed left to a good ledge behind a flake. Scott went up, got to the first ledge, put in gear, and finally got up and traversed left at the 80ft level behind the large flake yelling, "Off belay." Next up went Jimmy, then Marvin, then it was my turn. Charlie tied me in, gave me a thirty second hand jam lesson, and up I started. All I remember about the climb was clinging on hard to the rock, doing a lot of pull ups, and hearing a continual mantra of, "Use your feet." I got to the anchors, traversed left, room was made for me behind the flake, and there I squatted. I liked being behind the flake because I didn't have to look down. After they said I was tied in and safe, "I hadn't been safe to this point?" I took a look. I was afraid coming up but now that I stopped my motion, I became terrified. The approach up to Mt. Sheridan is a steep 900ft gain in elevation and then you start up the rock. At this point we were 1000 ft above the road and I felt like I was in an airplane. My mouth was dry and my muscles sore. Scott started to lead the next pitch before Charlie came up. It is hard to fit five guys on any belay ledge. Scott was leading and I was watching him. I was thinking I can't do this, no way, the next section is scary and even more exposed. Right then a small dot of a car pulls up next to Jimmy's Mustang. Charlie pointed out that it looked like a ranger car but Scott yelled down that it was probably someone just watching our magnificent ascent. An even smaller dot of a man got out and then starts talking through a bull horn. "You guys are trespassing and if you are still here when I get back your car will be towed." The man got back into the car and left. We talked the situation over trying to figure out how to get everyone down as quickly as possible. The plan was to get Charlie and me down fast with the car keys and drive around

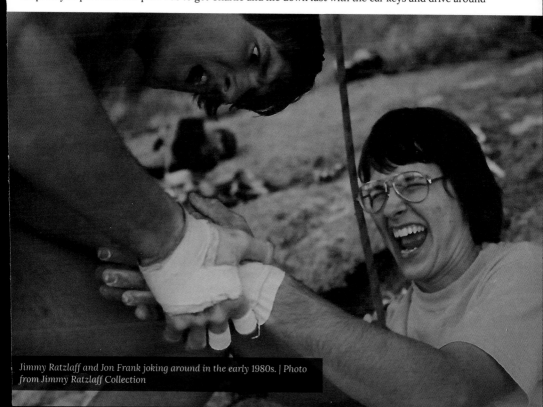

Jimmy Ratzlaff and Jon Frank joking around in the early 1980s. | Photo from Jimmy Ratzlaff Collection

until everyone else got down from the cliff and to the road. Jimmy lowered Charlie down since he was still on belay. Then I was lowered. This scared the crap out of me. When I got to the ground I was overwhelmed with gratitude to be alive. Charlie and I took what we had and crashed our way down through the forest. We arrived back at the road in 10 minutes, put the keys in the ignition and waited for the ranger car to come over the hill at which point we would start the car up and drive off. A problem with the plan was neither Charlie nor I had a legal driver's license, just permits. Neither of us were willing to drive away from a ranger so we sat nervously awaiting Jimmy. We waited, and waited for over 50 minutes when Jimmy, Marvin, and Scott emerged from the woods. Jimmy was carrying Scott piggy-back style. Marvin was carrying the rest of the gear. Jimmy began yelling for help and we hurried over grabbing the gear. "What happened?," we asked. Jimmy told us to get Scott and the gear in the car and get out of there. Scott, unable to walk, was gently placed in the car, groaning, the trunk with the gear, was slammed shut and off we went. After clearing the refuge boundaries Jimmy started to tell the tale of their delay. Jimmy and Marvin had rappelled down and Scott was still up top. Scott rearranged gear for the final rappel then weighted the rope. What happened next was anyone's guess as Scott became airborne. He fell feet-first fifty feet onto the first ledge, laid there for a second, then rolled off of it, and fell the other thirty feet, decking in front of Jimmy and Marvin. Scott sat there moaning in a fetal position as Jimmy and Marvin stared on in shock at what they had just witnessed. After a while Scott began to move. Jimmy and Marvin assessed him for broken bones and found he could move all his limbs. Miraculously, nothing seemed broken. Jimmy and Marvin managed to get Scott on Jimmy's back, and Jimmy, in a herculean effort, carried Scott down the 900 ft slope. We all talked in hush tones on the drive back trying to figure out what to tell and not tell our parents. We arrived at Scott's house. His parent's weren't there. We carried him into his bed, laying him down gently. Scott said his parents would be back sometime later, so we went back to the car, leaving him to deal with his mom and dad. When I got home my mom asked me how it was, and I said it was fine leaving out pretty much everything that happened that day. If I would have fessed up that would have been the end of my climbing career and I would have had to go back to doing time behind the bars of the Quail Creek Country Club.

Looking back on the day, I felt so free, so alive, cheating death, and the rangers. The experience was nothing that I could have imagined and I had turned a new chapter in my life that would take me to wild places with wild people. As a postscript Scott McBride couldn't walk for ten days but didn't break anything. This was also the last climb he ever did that I know of.

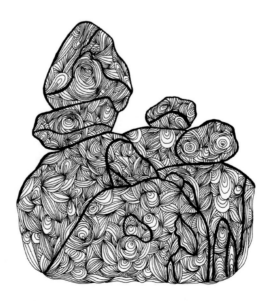

Artwork by Molly Hennesy

ROPING UP WITH A MAD MAN

By Jon Frank

I am thirty feet up on the first pitch of *Baptism* and Duane yells down not to fall; he says the anchors are a little shaky. Duane is such a joker, hold on, wait, Duane doesn't joke. Well he does but it is usually some sort of hyperbolized sarcasm. Now I have to think. Is his last statement hyperbolized sarcasm? He has never said this before so I check for understanding. "So you said the anchors aren't any good?" Duane yells down, "They are fine if you don't fall." He has always been this way since I have known him, straight forward in his speech, optimistic, and prone to bend reality like a pretzel maker twists dough. Most of the time his lack of frictional contact with the space-time dimensional granite of the universe suffers no consequences, but there is always a first. With my keen mind I simulate a fall scenario and realize that at this point I will live skidding down thirty feet of Quartz granite and his life will come to a painfully cruel death falling 90 feet and smashing into the boulder pile below. This will serve my idiot partner right belaying me with poor anchors. There is a chance though that I would fall and hit the ground before he does, then he would land on me elongating his impact time like an air bag killing me and saving his life. With my luck this would probably be the scenario. I tip toe my way up the first pitch figuring that the anchors really are not THAT BAD and at the same time knowing that they probably are. Arriving at the belay I realize who the real idiot is, ME for roping up with a mad man. These anchors are not just a little shaky but more like someone having a grand mal seizure, someone with full Parkinson's, someone in an electric chair cranked to full. Duane has a stopper that he keeps replacing, and a dished out friend. I look at the set up and see why he is not hanging on the anchors. I clip into the imaginary belay and glance at Duane. He is totally focused on the water streak to our left and is unconcerned about the crappy belay.

Duane's goal is to do every first ascent Quartz has to offer and this is just another slice in a rather large and uneaten pie. He didn't bring a bolt kit because he figures the last pitch would only have a 40 foot run out so why bother. Duane starts out left over a bulge with his left foot on the bulge and his right foot on the slab above me. He grabs some micro holds and pulls. His right foot comes off the slab and is stabbing at blank rock. He holds this position for about a minute and then says he is going to fall. I am thinking, "No you aren't," as I imagine the both of us taking the wild ride into the talus below. Off he comes!

Duane Raleigh climbing solo on Jet Stream circa early 80s | Photo from the Doug Robinson Collection

The first time I ever saw Duane was in the Narrows. I was climbing with Jimmy Ratzlaff and we had just done the first free ascent of *Critical Mass*. While coming down we saw Duane coming up to the Zoo Wall with his partner Bill Thomas. This was the first time I had ever seen another climber in the Narrows besides Jimmy, or the other three climbers we knew. Duane looked lean and really strong. We didn't say "hi" because by the time we walked down he was already on the *Dihedral*. Jimmy and I thought a lot of ourselves and figured it was some gumby. It took little time for us to be corrected on this point. He led the dihedral putting in no gear. Then to our surprise, Duane went through the overhang at it's top (later known as the *Flying Nun*). He did the whole route with two pieces of gear. It looked intense and we wondered how hard it was. Duane and Bill came down and Jimmy and I had roped up and been working on *Scrotum Roof*. Jimmy had put in a bolt the week before and we thought it would be easy but turned out to be ridiculously impossible. We backed off this Rubik's Cube puzzler and said "hi" to Duane and Bill. Just "hi," and nothing else. Duane asked us about *Critical Mass* and we told him it was 5.10. This would be the first 5.10 in the Narrows. His eyebrows went up slightly and then he proceeded to try *Scrotum Roof*. He slung a chicken head for a directional anchor twenty feet to the left of the route. Duane started up, got to the lip, clipped the bolt, and went for the crux mantle. He fell off, the rope tightened, and the chicken head broke off, leaving enough slack for Duane to deck. In an astonishing move, Duane grabs the rope going through the bolt at the lip of the roof and catches himself with his feet swinging in space. Bill, Jimmy and I are stunned looking at a pile of rope at Bill's feet. Duane, dangling in mid air, proceeded to lower himself off the bolt. When his feet hit the ground we all had a formal introduction.

On the new route Duane's fall is no less spectacular. With cat-like precision, he off-loads himself from the bulge and jumps onto the slab right above me, sticking the landing. I think he just ropes up with partners as witnesses to the first ascents because it doesn't seem like he ever needs a belayer. To say he falls is not really correct as he never hangs from the rope. He does this one more time and then takes a break. We talk a little about the sequence and Duane comes up with a funny solution. He back-steps his way onto the bulge with his right foot and then casually steps through and accesses another foot hold out to his left. I doubt that he could reverse the sequence but there is no need to worry. He calmly makes his way up what looks like a holdless slab. As he moves upward I internally calculate the fall forces and know at ten feet out the belay probably won't hold. At twenty feet out it surely won't hold and at forty feet out it is anchors away. The tables are turned now. If he falls he might go up to 45 feet before shock loading the system which would make his fall another 45 feet to the ground after getting some relief from the total energy dispersion in the shattered belay. I, on the other hand, will be 90 feet up when everything goes. I keep trying to put the nut in that continually falls out and imagine a position that I could somehow hold the fall and keep myself on the rock but this is pure fantasy. After a while I don't see him anymore and then I hear the sweet sound of OFF BELAY!

Seconding, I manage the disco step past the crux and finish off the rest of the route. I ask him what he is going to name it and he says *Desire*. I think in my mind, "Good name because I have no desire to repeat it."

I also remember belaying him on *Jet Stream*. You really aren't belaying the leader ten feet above the first bolt. I got really nervous watching him going up wondering about my moral obligation to spot him 60 feet up or just step aside if he falls so he wouldn't kill me. He truly was the best partner I, or anyone else, could have had.

Duane ended up making a career out of belaying himself. He was so good that no one could keep up with him so he had to belay himself. He related many stories of self belaying but here are the top ones that have stayed in my mind. He was soloing *Cosmos* on El Cap and had completed pitch six. This pitch consists of basically a complete sideways pitch of expanding flakes and hooks (A4). He gets to the belay and starts to back-clean the pitch to the belay at pitch six. Now at the anchors at six he looks horizontally across over 100 feet to the anchors of pitch seven without a stitch of pro between the two fixed points. He puts a hook onto the ledge less belay six, cleans and unclips from everything else. Next he grabs the anchor slings, unhooks the hook, and is left holding onto slings with his feet dangling looking at a 200 foot swing. He said he just keeps holding on until his strength gave out. As he let go he let out

Duane Raleigh on Ra circa early 80s | Photo from the Doug Robinson Collection

a horrible scream ripping through the air with his eyes closed. He said he opened them briefly just in time to watch a blur of granite pass by then headed up the other side of the pendulum. Then back down, and then back up. This went on for several minutes. After stopping he just continued up and finished the route.

Another was when he was soloing *Lost World*. There is a pitch that is just a chimney and he hadn't put in any pro for twenty feet and was a foot from the anchors. He reached out and fell, going upside down and backwards. As the rope drew taunt Newton's 1st law of motion took over, "An object in motion will continue to stay in motion until an outside force acts upon it." Well, his gear slings continued in motion right off each shoulder. Upside down he just watched the slings with most of his gear head earthward. He barely had enough gear to make it back to the ground.

The strangest of all stories was told one time when I ran into Duane in the Narrows. He was subdued, thoughtful, none of the driving energy he usually had, just really reflective. He had just gotten back from soloing desert spires. Then he tells me about his last solo. He was on a desert spire and had topped out at night. He had a sling around his neck. Attached to the sling was carabiner with a rope clipped into it. The rope was not coiled but just hanging the full length from the carabiner. Duane is all set up and starts to rappel, the next thing he knows he is flying through the air. He is for sure dead. What could save him? When he stops he figures he has hit the ground. His ribs are in pain and he is having trouble breathing. He says to himself, "So this is what it is like to die, it will only be a few moments and then I will breathe my last breath." After a few seconds he starts to feel his way around where he landed. There is nothing to feel. It is just air. Then he realizes he isn't on the ground but hanging from the rope attached to his gear sling. Somehow the rope that was clipped into the gear sling going over his neck had caught in a crack. Before Duane loses consciousness he clips his jumars into the rope. He has no idea if the rope is going to stay wedged as he starts to climb up it. When he arrives at the attachment point he finds a lot of melted rope stuck in the crack. Somehow he cuts away a 60 foot section of it and makes it down to the bottom, sleeps, drives back to Oklahoma, and is alive to tell me the story.

Duane is still at it but it is starting to catch up with him. A few years ago he ripped his shoulder out doing a self arrest right before heading off a cliff. He needed major reconstructive shoulder surgery. From the days of the self-belay the first time I meet him at *Scrotum Roof*, to sticking the landing on *Desire*, until the present, no partner should ever worry about bad anchors with Duane. If he invites you along to climb he probably just wants company, he really never needed a belay partner anyway.

Old Baldy

*"In all the splendor of solitude... it is a test of myself, and
one thing I loathe is to have to test myself in front of other people."*
~Naomi Uemura

WE KNOW
SHOES

WE KNOW
GEAR

NOW WE'VE GOT BOTH

ROCK and RESOLE

WWW.ROCKANDRESOLE.COM | 303.440.0414

Get your edge back

WORDS FROM THE PUBLISHER

By Fred Knapp

In an odd sense, Oklahoma climbing has been on my radar since my youth. As a teenager I devoured climbing media, and I distinctly remember an article (in *Outside* magazine, I believe) about a prodigy who made breakthrough ascents on El Capitan, the Utah desert, and on difficult free routes—and whom few appreciated. Duane Raleigh, the story explained, honed his craft on a small dome jutting from the patchwork and furrowed fields of Oklahoma. The story stuck with me, as inspiration perhaps.

Years later, after moving to Boulder, I befriended a transplanted Oklahoma climber, Jimmy Ratzlaff, who retold the stories of his early Oklahoma days. Most stories centered around the gripping climbing at Quartz and adventures with Duane. The place, it seemed, left a mark on those who climbed there.

It would be decades before I actually journeyed to "the other granite state," inspired to climb with Tony Mayse—an author who I enjoyed working with, though we'd only corresponding via emails and phone calls. With the upcoming publication of this new guide, I took the opportunity to travel with Sharp End's designer, Sarah, to the midwest.

Quartz Mountain was, much as I suspected, an area stuck in the past. The routes are bold and slabby, meandering through sculpted weaknesses in near-perfect granite. Hillsides of granite boulders reside between farmland and small towns that smacked of rural America. We stopped at a grocery/diner where old men in overalls talked and played cards. In the midst of this Norman Rockwell setting sits Quartz.

The Wichita Mountain Wildlife Refuge caught me more off guard. This area was not part of my subconscious, as Jimmy and Duane left before the prominent development of the refuge—a massive expanse of preserved land, punctuated with reservoirs and streams, and overlain with a massive amount of granite detritus. My first thought was that this would be a mecca for bouldering. On our early morning drive, the first visitors we saw were, in fact, pad people approaching Mt. Scott via foot as fog closed the road.

Sculpted stone juts sporadically from the purlieu of the frontier setting. Long approaches on flat trails lead to granite walls, topped by hoodoos and pigmented with lichen. The climbing is not concentrated and the setting lonely (at least in the heat of early summer). The hardiness of pioneers seems to emanate from the landscape, and a certain hardiness is expected from the locals. This isn't Rifle or Wall Street. The stone I experienced from Crab Eyes to the Narrows was impeccable and not suited to stereotypes. Steep sport climbs, splitter cracks, mixed routes following incipient cracks, and bold face climbs are intermixed at the crags.

Oklahomans are blessed to have these wonders, and fortunate to have someone like Tony—so enamored by these places, stones, and history. As we were guided crag to crag, moving from dawn to dusk, his enthusiasm and passion were undeniable, genuine, and moving. Tony's superlatives and excitement overrode the dank heat. The Wichitas won us over.

Team Colorado Sarah Nicholson & Fred Knapp sampling Oklahoma granite on Fun Ride 5.12a. | Photo by Tony Mayse

VERTICAL MIND

By Don McGrath & Jeff Elison

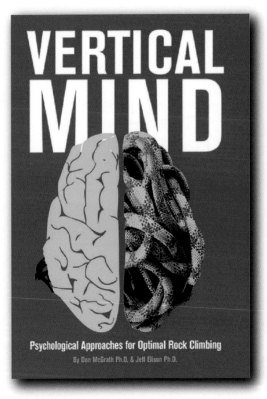

In Vertical Mind, Don McGrath and Jeff Elison teach rock climbers how to improve their mental game so they can climb better and have more fun. They teach how the latest research in brain science and psychology can help you retrain your mind and body for higher levels of rock climbing performance, while also demonstrating how to train and overcome fears and anxiety that hold you back. Finally, they teach climbing partners how to engage in co-creative coaching and help each other improve as climbers.

With numerous and practical step-by-step drills and exercises, in a simple to follow training framework, your path to harder climbing has never been clearer. If you are a climber who wants to climb harder and have more fun climbing, then Vertical Mind is required reading. Well, what's stopping you? Pick it up and get training today!

Curious about our latest books? Follow us:

○ ☐ @sharpendpublishing

www.sharpendbooks.com

Elisha Gallegos climbing the classic Narrows route The Dihedral 5.6 on Zoo Wall. | Photo by Tory Mayse

These areas can also be approached from the Sunset parking area.

Photo by Andrew Burr

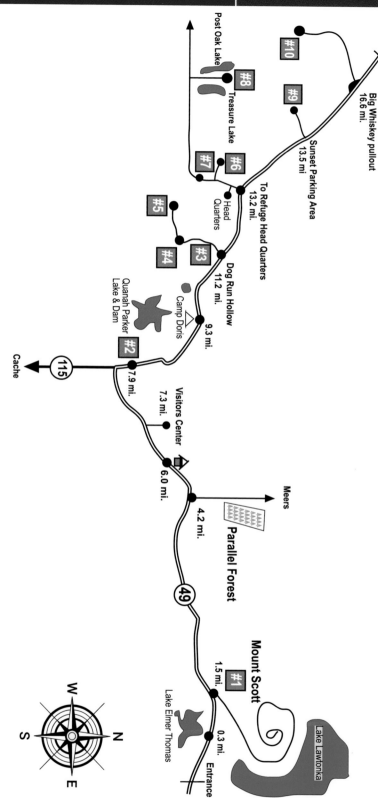

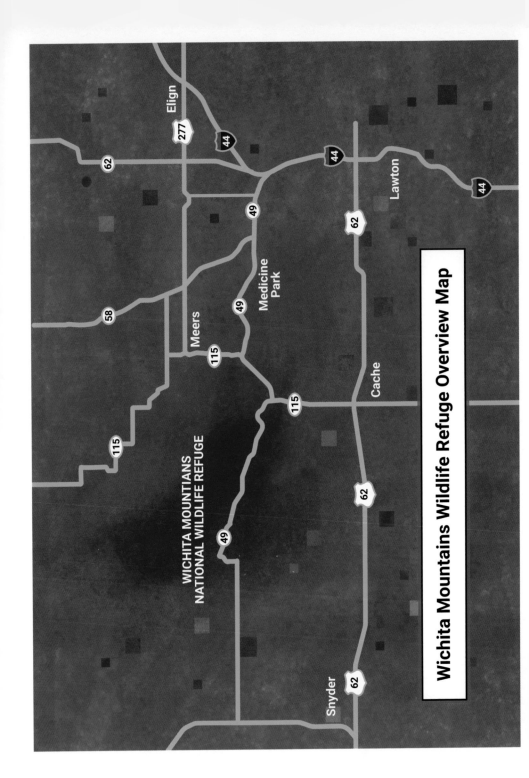

Wichita Mountains Wildlife Refuge Overview Map

MOUNT SCOTT

Mount Scott has been a popular place to visit ever since the road to the top was constructed in 1938. On any given morning you can see runners, hikers, and people making their way towards the summit on the almost 3-mile-long steep, winding road with a breathtaking view overlooking the lakes and open prairies of the Wichita Mountains. Like any area with a peak there are always challenges to see who can get to the top the fastest, Mount Scott is no exception.

Mount Scott is also a popular past time among cyclists. In May of 2003 Steven Cate of Moore Oklahoma rode his bicycle up Mount Scott in 11 minutes 34 seconds. This record is no easy feat. Steven is an accomplished Pro Cyclist winning his first National Championship title in the U23 Road Race after racing for the US National Team in Europe. In 2000, he earned his second title with a win at the Amateur National Road Race Championships in a sprint finish after 126 miles in the May heat of Natchez, Mississippi.

For rock climbers Mount Scott offers challenges typically found off the beaten path. Mount Scott has four climbing areas: Lower Wall, Jugi Fruit Area, Upper Wall and Dream Boat Annie Area. The majority of the routes require gear but there are some bolted climbs as well. A relatively easy approach and a variety of different grades make this area very popular. All the routes are located by driving uphill from the gate which opens at 9:00 am and closes at sunset. Zero-out your odometer at the gate and reference the overview map for the climbing areas.

Lower Wall faces east and north, it goes into the shade later in the day. Jugi Fruit Area faces to the west and makes for a good morning spot in the summer or later in the day in winter. Upper Wall faces east and shades later in the day. Dream Boat Annie Area is north facing.

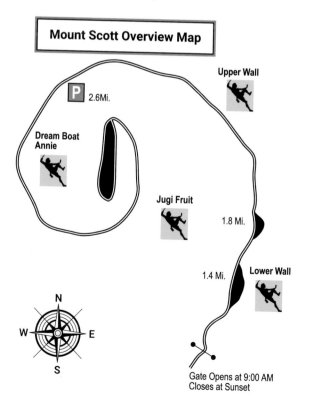

MOUNT SCOTT LOWER WALL

Lower Wall is a 1.4-mile drive from the bottom of Mt. Scott. Park along the guardrail on the prominent pullout that usually has three or four cars parked in it (see overview topo). Walk back down the road to the end of the guardrail to pick up the trail. Walk east (towards the lake), on a well-marked trail that leads to the top of the cliff. From the top of the cliff head north (left) to the switchbacks, which lead to the bottom of the wall. There are two walls, one faces east and the other faces north. Morning sun and PM shade.

Approach: 5–8 minutes

Between 1980–1983 Keith Egan and Jack Hill were the first known climbers to explore and establish most of the early lines on the Lower Wall. Unfortunately their ascents were not documented.

"I always loved climbing in Oklahoma, the smell of sage, the great granite, and the climbing community all adding to the fun and satisfaction. After moving to Boulder, the adventure opportunities grew but the overall experience over Oklahoma did not. We were just in the right place, right time at the right age in OK."

~Keith Egan

1. Pablo 5.10 ★

Located just left of *Blank Check* down by the trees that touch the wall's base. Climb the short face to an overhanging crack.

FA: *Chuck Lohn, et al. 1990s*
Gear: cams to #2 Camalot
No anchor   40ft

2. Blank Check 5.11c ★★

Located a few feet right of *Layaway Plan*. This is a bolted face climb that rarely gets climbed.

FA: *Russell Hooper 1990s*
Gear: quickdraws
No anchor   60ft

3. Layaway Plan 5.11a/b ★★★★

This route climbs the face to the left of the arête. Five bolts mark the line for *Layaway Plan*. Technical face climbing on a steep wall using both the face and the arête to make your way to the top. Lori first spotted this route around Christmas time, around the same time I had a Christmas gift for her in layaway.

FA: *Tony & Lori Mayse, Carl Murray 1994*
Gear: quickdraws
2-bolt anchor   60ft

4. Teacup Arête 5.10c ★★★

Ten feet right of *Layaway Plan* is a broken rock band with a short overhang that leads to a nice hand crack. Continue up the crack to a stance by a pillar. Climb out left on exposed moves to the arête and a bolt. Continue up the arête to a ledge up top.

FA: *Jimmy Forester, Tony Mayse 1994*
Gear: cams to #3 Camalot, quickdraws
No anchor   60ft

4a. Crack Finish 5.8+★★

From the top of the pillar step right and up into a wide crack that leads to the top. (Bring wide gear for this section).

5. Mr. Clean 5.8+ ★★★★

Twenty yards uphill from *Tea Cup Arête* is a dihedral with a short roof at the top. Climb this dihedral up to the roof; turn the roof on lie back moves continuing up and left to a ledge. One of the best 5.8 climbs in the refuge.

FA: *Eric Forney*
Gear: cams to #3 Camalot
No anchor   60ft

Mount Scott
Lower Wall

Mount Scott
Lower Pullout

6. Stole Your Face 5.11b ★★
A few feet right of *Mr. Clean* is a steep arête and face climb. From the patio climb up the arête and slightly to the left protected by a line of bolts. The route was bolted then remained unclimbed until someone else climbed it, thus the moniker.

FA: *Todd Ward, Mike Johnson 1995*

Gear: quickdraws

No anchor   60ft

7. Birthday Boy 5.6 ★★
Up and to the right of *Stole Your Face*. Located on the same wall and far to the left of *High Anxiety*. Follow the crack and use some face holds to the top.

FA:*1990s*

Gear: cams to #2 Camalot, stoppers

No anchor   65ft

8. High Anxiety 5.7 ★★★★
Face and crack climb 30 feet to the right of *Birthday Boy*. From a ledge climb up just to the left of the corner making your way up to a short roof. Move around the roof onto the face next to the arête. Continue up the steep wall, crack and face climbing. A variation to the start begins directly below the route, climbing on face holds.

FA: *Eric Forney*

Gear: cams to #2 Camalot, stoppers

2-bolt anchor   60ft

9. Final Exit 5.11b/c ★★
Bolted line to the right of *High Anxiety*. Side-pulls at the start and barn door moves getting past the second bolt. From here continue up and right following the line of bolts to the top. Use the anchors on *High Anxiety* at the top.

FA: *Unknown 1990s*

Gear: quickdraws

2-bolt anchor   60ft

10. Repeat After Me 5.10c ★★★★
Located 15 feet around the corner from *High Anxiety*. This route follows a series of short roofs protected by bolts. Bring a small #1-size cam for the move getting to the first bolt. The moves past the last bolt can be done by exiting left, or climb out right for a (5.11) finish.

FA: *Mike Johnson, Todd Ward 1995*

Gear: 0.75 - #1 cams, quickdraws

No anchor   60ft

11. Full Cavity Search 5.7 ★
Located in the dihedral just right of *Repeat After Me*. Climb the corner up through a small roof. The name came from the day Chris was removing some loose blocks prior to climbing it. Apparently, the Rangers were called out to see what the commotion was all about.

FA: *Chris Corbett 2003*

Gear: small to med. size cams

No anchor   60ft

Max Munchinski climbing Layaway Plan 5.11b, on Mount Scott's Lower Wall. | Photo by Molly Hennesy

Jugi Fruit

Downhill view Mount Scott
(1.8 miles from Entrance Gate)

JUGI FRUIT AREA

From the entrance gate of Mount Scott drive uphill 1.8 miles. There will be an obvious pullout on your right, park here. Walk across the road and pick up the trail leading up hill. *Jugi Fruit* climbs a 45 foot corner crack located on your left. The cliff faces the west. As of this writing, the pullout has been getting trashed out with graffiti and garbage. Please help keep this place clean. (See overview map).

1. Jugi Fruit 5.11+ ★★★★

Steep corner crack. Hard moves with slick footholds leads to strenuous but more secure layback moves up higher, ending with a 3" crack at the top.

FA: Mike Galoob 1990s

Gear: TCUs to #3 Camalot

No anchor   *45ft*

Jugi Fruit

1

Mount Scott
Upper Wall

Mount Scott Upper Wall Overview

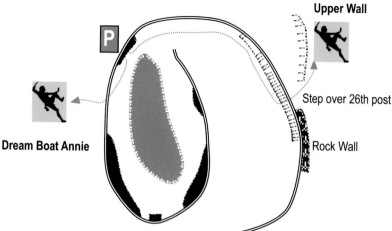

Upper Wall

P

Step over 26th post

Dream Boat Annie

Rock Wall

MOUNT SCOTT UPPER WALL

Mount Scott Upper Wall has several short routes on low-angle rock. Most of the climbs can be toproped. There are a few bolted routes like the *Toprope Route* and *Frankly Scarlet*, which give the area some variety. Upper Wall can be reached from parking at the top of Mt. Scott then walking back down the road following the guardrail. Follow the guardrail for about 100 feet or count 26 guardrail support posts. Step over the guardrail to gain access to a ramp, which leads over loose rock to the bottom of the climbing area.

This is a popular area so please pack out all trash, yours or not.

1. Marc Johnson Face Route 5.9 ★★ Toprope

First climb just after the walk-down. A flat spot at the base of the climb just before you head down the talus field. Almost a pure friction climb except for a few ripples in the rock. Thin face climbing leads to easier climbing up higher.

FA: *Marc Johnson 1980s*

Gear: toprope

No Anchor   50ft

2. Atomic Knee Drop 5.6 ★★

Just to the right of *Marc Johnson Face Route*. A nice hand crack leads to a small roof.

FA: *1980s*

Gear: cams to #2.5

No Anchor   50ft

3. Chuck's Boulder Problem 5.10 ★

Short problem right of *Atomic Knee Drop*.

FA: *Chuck Lohn 1990s*

Gear: boulder problem or toprope

No Anchor   25ft

4. Pile Driver 5.6 ★★

Large flake marks the start of this route. Climb up the left side of the flake.

FA: *Unknown 1980s*

Gear: cams to #4 Camalot

No Anchor   50ft

5. Spinning Back Kick 5.4 ★

Short crack climb just to the right of *Pile Driver*.

FA: *Unknown 1980s*

Gear: cams to #2 Camalot

No Anchor   50ft

6. Down for the Count 5.6 ★★
Fifteen feet right of *Pile Driver*, climb the fist crack moving right then up to easier climbing.

FA: Unknown 1980s

Gear: cams to #3 Camalot

No Anchor   *50ft*

7. The Sleeper 5.6 ★★
Ten feet right of *Down for the Count*, climb the hand crack or move out to the right and lieback the flake to the top.

FA: Unknown 1980s

Gear: cams to #3 Camalot

No Anchor   *50ft*

8. Arm Bar 5.6 ★★
Climbs the arête a few feet left of *Foolish*. Climb the face then follow the crack to the top.

FA: Unknown 1980s

Gear: cams to #3 Camalot

No Anchor   *60ft*

9. Foolish 5.8 ★★
Crack climb in the dihedral to the right of *Arm Bar*. Climb the dihedral then traverse right onto the face; continue in the crack to a ledge.

FA: Unknown 1980s

Gear: cams to #3 Camalot, stoppers

No Anchor   *60ft*

10. Foolish Behavior 5.9+ ★★★★
This route is 10 feet right of *Foolish*. Start up the crack exiting left to a stance with a bolt. Continue up the polished face past the second bolt moving up on small edges to the top. This route has sustained crack and face climbing on good rock. A Mount Scott classic!

FA: Duane Raleigh, Terry Andrews, Rick Thomas, Marion Hutchison 1982

Gear: cams to #3 Camalot, stoppers

No Anchor   *60ft*

Discovered by Marion Hutchison and Terry Andrews. Terry came back and bolted the line but too tired to lead it after a cold day of bolting... Later it was discovered that Duane nabbed the first ascent. Best route on Mount Scott!

11. Toprope Route 5.11b/c R ★★★★
Bolted face climb to the right of *Foolish Behavior*. Once a toprope climb now protected with modern hardware. This route has sustained, steep face climbing on polished rock. The hardest route on the Upper Wall.

FA: Duane Raleigh, Jimmy Ratzlaff 1982

2nd Ascent Keith Egan, Jack Hill

Gear: quickdraws

No Anchor   *50ft*

12. Frankly Scarlet 5.9 ★★★
Face climb on the arête to the right of *Toprope Route*. Climb up the arête reaching out left to clip the two bolts. You can climb the face to the left of the arête and clip the bolts but this makes the route seem contrived. (No topo photo of this route).
FA: Jon Frank 1982
Gear: quickdraws, small stoppers
No Anchor   50ft

13. Groove Rat 5.10d ★
Right of *Frankly Scarlet* and before you get to *Yee Haw*. The route is marked by an overhanging block above. Nice lieback and stem problem leads to a short slab before topping out. (No topo photo of this route).
FA: Chuck Lohn et al. 1990s
Gear: cams to #3 Camalot
No Anchor   60ft

14. Yee Haw 5.6 ★★
Wide crack climb. Continue down the wall walking to the right of *Frankly Scarlet* to a wide crack. This route takes cams up to #4.
FA: Unknown 1980s
Gear: cams to #4 Camalot
No Anchor   60ft

15. Hern, Frank Thing 5.10d RX ★★
A dicey proposition on a lichen-covered wall. Just to the right of *Yee Haw* is a lichen-covered face with no gear for 30 feet until you reach the crack that leads to easier climbing. Jon Frank was working on the *Oklahoma on the Rocks* guidebook when he ran into "The Hern" on this day...
FA: Mark Hendon, Jon Frank early 1980s
Gear: cams to #3 Camalot
No Anchor   60ft

16. Mr. Green Slings 5.8 ★★
Climb up to a slick slab below the short roof. Past the roof the climbing gets easier once again (No topo photo available).
FA: Jack Hill, Marc Johnson 1981
Gear: cams to #3.5
No Anchor   60ft

17. Wolfman's Route 5.9 ★ Toprope
Named after Ron Teague, a fixture from the early years of Oklahoma climbing. Face climb to the left of *Two Trojans*. A moss-covered face leads to thin face climbing just right of the water streaks above. (No topo photo available).
FA: Ron Teague 1990s
Gear: toprope
No Anchor   50ft

18. Two Trojans 5.8 RX ★
This climb is located approximately 20 yards to the right of *Mr. Green Slings*. Crack climb with an overhanging boulder above.
FA: Keith Egan, Jack Hill, Marc Johnson 1981
Gear: cams to #3 Camalot
No Anchor   60ft

19. Roof Crack 5.9+ ★★★
Roof crack in a huge boulder. Great hand jams and good protection lead to the roof, pull the roof and continue in the crack on easier climbing. This route is a good introduction to roof climbing.
FA: Mark Herndon early 1980s
Gear: cams to #3 Camalot
No Anchor   60ft

20. Roof Corner 5.10 ★★
Climb the corner a few feet right of *Roof Crack*. This route starts in an overhanging crack up to a roof continuing on its right side. The climbing is a little more strenuous than *Roof Crack*.
FA: Mark Herndon early 1980s
Gear: cams to #4 Camalot
No Anchor   60ft

21. Wendy's Salad Bar 5.9 Toprope

Face climb starting just left of *Locomotive Breath* then climbing up towards the bolts on *Baldielox Bulge*.

FA: Chuck Lohn et al. 1990s

Gear: toprope

No Anchor   *50ft*

22. Locomotive Breath 5.10b/c RX ★★★

Located to the far right of *Roof Corner*. This route has thin face climbing and there is no protection on the lower part of the route. From a ledge just right of a boulder sitting below the route, climb up the face past a large hole and 20 feet to a bolt; after clipping the only bolt on the route continue up on sustained face climbing.

"I had just purchased a bolt kit and was dying to use it!" ~Keith Egan

FA: Keith Egan, Jack Hill early 1980s

Gear: quickdraw

No Anchor   *50ft*

Locomotive Breath

23. Baldielox Bulge 5.11d R

A mixed climb with two bolts right of *Locomotive Breath*. Starting from the right side of the wall climb up and to the left to a bolt just above the lip, continue up five more feet to the second bolt. From here continue up protecting the climb with crack protection up higher.

FA: Chuck Lohn et al. 1990s

Gear: cams to #2 Camalot

No Anchor   *50ft*

Artwork by Elisha Gallegos

ROMPER ROOM AREA

Romper Room Area is located ten feet to the right of the route *Baldielox Bulge*. A room with cracks and chimneys. Most of the routes are crack and chimney climbs except for one toprope face climb named *Inshallah*. There are five routes listed for the Romper Room Area from 5.7–5.10. There is a 2-bolt anchor above the climb *Simply Red*.

Approach: From the climb *Locomotive Breath* drop down to ground level and walk around the large boulder on it's right side, then scramble up to the ledges by a large tree. Romper Room routes are located in the back room. The tops of the routes in the Romper Room Area can be accessed by scrambling up rocks 15 feet to the right of the large tree that guards the Romper Room ledges. This is also the descent from the climbs.

24. Simply Red 5.8 ★★★

This is the first climb in the Romper Room. Look for a dihedral on the back wall (not the wide crack on the left wall). *Simply Red* climbs a hand-size crack to a chimney directly overhead. Continue up to a 2-bolt anchor under a boulder on the top.

FA: Chuck Lohn et al. 1990s
Gear: cams to #4 Camalot
2-bolt anchor　　　　　　*50ft*

25. Kingfisher Caravan 5.8 ★★

Chimney climb on the back wall starting just to the right of *Simply Red*. There is a bolt that is hard to spot above the overhang. Continue up, then move left to the anchors on *Simply Red*.

FA: Chuck Lohn et al. 1990s
Gear: cams to #4 Camalot
2-bolt anchor　　　　　　*50ft*

26. Hour of Power 5.10 ★★

This climb is across from the route *Simply Red*. Look up and you will see a slightly overhanging wall with a hand sized crack a foot away from it's edge. Climb up eight feet to gain the crack and gear opportunities, continue up, stepping over into the chimney of *Kingfisher Caravan*. Continue up the chimney to the two-bolt anchor. One of the more challenging routes in the Romper Room Area.

FA: Chuck Lohn et al. 1990s
Gear: cams to #4 Camalot
2-bolt anchor　　　　　　*50ft*

27. Mild and Wild 5.7 ★★

Located to the right of *Kingfisher Caravan's* chimney. This climb is located outside the chimney routes and climbs the dihedral just left of the face climb *Inshallah*. Follow the dihedral to the upper ledge. Belay here, bring #1 and #2 cams for the belay. Walk down to your right or rap station of *Simply Red*.

FA: Chuck Lohn et al. 1990s
Gear: cams to #2 Camalot
No Anchor　　　　　　*50ft*

28. Inshallah 5.10 Toprope

Face climb 5 feet to the right of *Mild and Wild*. Climb the middle of face ending at the same belay ledge as *Mild and Wild*.

FA: Chuck Lohn et al. 1990s
Gear: cams to #4 Camalot
No Anchor　　　　　　*50ft*

UPPER MOUNT SCOTT BOULDER

This boulder is located just behind *Foolish Behavior* and sits on a slab of rock shaded by trees and has been the main hangout spot for countless climbers for many decades. This boulder with it's prominent horizontal finger crack on a steep and slightly overhanging face is good one to learn finger-locks.

1. Unknown 5.10 ★★★

Start on the boulders left side with fingers locks in a horizontal crack moving to the right and finishing on a vertical crack to the top. Challenging problem at the base of classic Upper Mount Scott climbs.

2. Unknown 5.10 ★★

Face line starting on the jug right of the finger crack problem. Move up from the starting jug to small holds, exiting left and up.

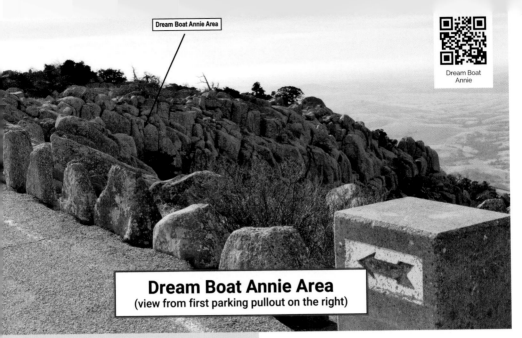

Dream Boat Annie Area

Dream Boat Annie Area
(view from first parking pullout on the right)

DREAM BOAT ANNIE AREA

To get to this area drive to the top of Mount Scott and park in first set of parking lanes to the right. Walk up the road for 30 yards and look for a trail on your right (west) side of the road which leads to the top of the climbs, 25 yards from the road. Drop down into a wide slot with a boulder putting you at the base of the climbs. There is a short vertical wall with three cracks starting from the bottom and ending at a ledge up higher. The routes are only about 25 feet long and can easily be toproped. This area is a good place to come if you're short on time and want to get in a few climbs.

When Jimmy Ratzlaff found this area he said, "It made my heart jump!" All these routes were first toproped, and later Jimmy came back and then did them all free-solo.

1. White Lightning 5.6

This is the left route on the wall. Climb the wide crack with a weird exit.

FA: Jon Frank, Jimmy Ratzlaff   July 14, 1979
Gear: #2, #3 Camalot
No anchor   25ft

2. Dream Boat Annie 5.10d ★★★★

The finger crack in the middle of the wall. Climb up the crack for about 10 feet, then lieback to the top exiting out left. Often toproped but has been led and bouldered. Excellent route!

FA: Jon Frank, Jimmy Ratzlaff   July 14, 1979
Gear: TCUs, cams to #2.5, stoppers
No anchor   25ft

3. Red Wine 5.8 ★★

Hand crack to the right of *Dream Boat Annie*. Climb the crack moving right to the top.

FA: Jon Frank, Jimmy Ratzlaff July 14, 1979
Gear: cams to #3.5 Camalot
No anchor   25ft

THE MEADOWS

The Meadows was referred to as Osage Lake Area in the older guidebook. The area was climbed in the 1970s by Jay Lowell establishing *Lampoon* 5.7. The locations of these ascents were not very clear and some routes such as this one have gone into obscurity. The area is now referred to as The Meadows with several climbs ranging from 5.5–5.13.

This area is a nice place to climb to beat the summer heat as some of the formations face north. Most of the routes are bolt protected with a few crack climbs. With a quick approach this area is a good place if you are short on time or not wanting a long approach to go climbing. All of the routes follow Quanah Creek which snakes it's way west and south.

The Meadows is a memorable place for me. In May 1996 while hiking with my dogs Sugar and Scooby, I got off trail and was struck in the lower leg by a rattlesnake. Be advised, a rattlesnake bite is quick and painless but then after five to ten minutes the pain will be an unforgettable experience! This encounter landed me in Comanche Memorial Hospital for 4 1/2 days and bed ridden for a month once I got home. Be aware of your surroundings when you are off-trail. Not to deter you from visiting this area, this place is no more prone to snakes than others in the refuge.

Approach: Drive to the Quanah Parker Dam on Hwy 49 and park there. From the Wichita Mountains entrance cattle-guard crossing it is 7.9 miles to the turnoff leading to The Meadows parking. From the parking area pick up the trail just to the left of the kiosk. Walk south over the rocks then down into the woods on a good trail. Continue making your way up and over a rocky outcrop. Walk down the granite slabs and head to the right (west) where you will see a dry creek bed in front of you. The first wall is directly south of the creek bed and is behind the trees. Pick up a faint trail for about 50 yards heading south; the gray-colored north-facing cliff is Smashing Hornets Wall.

From Smashing Hornets Wall follow Quanah Creek west, you will see Thunderdome Wall just downstream. Take the trail on the right side of the creek as you walk towards Thunderdome.

The Meadows Climbing Area exit
(view looking to the north)

The Meadows Pullout

The Meadows Area parking
(view looking to the south)

THUNDERDOME WALL
To get to Thunderdome Wall follow the creek west from Smashing Hornets Wall. The approach time from Smashing Hornets Wall is less than 5 minutes.

1. Creek Show 5.10c/d ★★★
This route is located 15 yards to the left of *Dying Time*. Walk across the rocks in the creek to access the wall. Climb the short overhanging face protected by two bolts. Sustained, steep face climbing just above the creek. The top of the route can easily be accessed from the right side.

FA: Mike Galoob 1995
Gear: quickdraws
2-bolt anchor   *50ft*

2. Dying Time 5.10c/d
Route with a large block, located to the left of *Blockade*. From the first bolt on *Blockade* move left over the huge block to another bolt. From the second bolt climb left to the crack that leads to the top.
FA: Mike Galoob 1995
Gear: med to large cams, quickdraws
2-bolt anchor   *70ft*

SMASHING HORNETS WALL
This is the first formation just off the creek. It is a gray wall and faces north. From here, all formations listed are located west and to the south just off the creek. Hike time 10 minutes.

1. Smashing Hornets 5.10 ★★
Face climb protected by three bolts. Climb up on face holds to a bolt below a roof, continue up steep rock with face climbing to the top.
FA: Aaron Gibson, Andy Magness 1990s
Gear: quickdraws
2-bolt anchor   *50ft*

Smashing Hornets

Thunderdome

3. Blockade 5.11b R ★

Face climb with four bolts that climbs right of a huge block. Climb up a slick black slab making your way to a bolt below a large block. Continue climbing up and over a small roof to the second bolt. From the second to the third bolt is about 15 feet, this is the hardest climbing on the route with sharp holds and sometimes questionable rock. There is one bolt at the top for an anchor.

FA: Peter Holcomb 1995
Gear: quickdraws
1–bolt anchor   70ft

4. Barter Town 5.11a ★★★

Steep face with six bolts. This climb is fun from the starting moves. Climb up and left to the first bolt making your way over a short roof protected by a bolt, continue climbing up and right on good holds. The best climb on the cliff.

FA: Mike Galoob 1995
Gear: quickdraws
2–bolt anchor   70ft

5. Atomic Cafe 5.8 ★★

Diagonal crack to the right of *Barter Town*. Follow the diagonal crack with a few face climbing moves at the top. You can belay off the anchors of *Taco Time*.

FA: Unknown
Gear: bring a variety of cams, stoppers
2–bolt anchor   70ft

6. Interceptor 5.7

Located just to the right of *Atomic Cafe*. Climbs the right-facing flake that intersects with *Atomic Cafe*. (No topo photo.)

FA: Unknown
Gear: bring a variety of cams, stoppers
2–bolt anchor   70ft

7. Taco Time 5.6 ★★★

Face climb with four bolts. This route starts near the tree about 15 feet right of *Atomic Cafe*. Climb the face protected by four bolts. (No topo photo.)

FA: Aaron Gibson 1990s
Gear: quickdraws
2–bolt anchor   70ft

8. Welcome to Sniveldome 5.10 RX

Right-facing dihedral just behind a large tree 20 yards to the right of *Taco Time*. Protected by one bolt.

FA: Andy Magness 1990s
Gear: quickdraws, small wires
No anchor   50ft

Tar Baby

Briar Patch

CREEK BOULDER PROBLEM

From *Tar Baby* continue southwest following the creek for about 200 yards. A large boulder in the creek resembling George Washington's profile. Walk past the boulder and look back to the north to best see the profile.

1. The Schnoz 5.9 (BOULDER PROBLEM)

Traverse in from the left and continue moving right over the water. Move up once below the roof, continue straight up to the top from here.

FA: Mike Galoob et al. 1990s

ATLANTIS WALL

From *The Schnoz* continue southwest following the trail alongside the creek. Atlantis Wall faces north-northeast. It sits in the creek directly in front of the approach trail. There are two routes on this wall.

1. Over Sea and Sky 5.9 ★★

Traverse in from the left making your way up to a dihedral. Climb up the broken dihedral and continue in a second dihedral formed by a huge boulder at the top.

FA: Jason & Andy Magness 1990s

Gear: stoppers, cams to #2 Camalot

No anchor   65ft

2. Watered Down 5.10a ★ Toprope

Starting on the far right of the Atlantis Wall. Traverse left from the right side for 50 feet just above the water. Climb to a right-angling crack to the top.

FA: Aaron Gibson

Gear: toprope

No anchor   65ft

BRIAR PATCH WALL

From Thunderdome Wall walk south following the trail on the right (west) side for about 100 yards. Briar Patch Wall has one climb. This wall faces southeast and is identified by its black and yellow streaks; it overhangs about 30 degrees. A significant amount of briars protect the base. It is best to approach the wall from the north walking around the briars to a faint trail leading to the starting ledge. To the right of the starting ledge you can access the top by climbing easy terrain up and to the far right.

1. Tar Baby 5.11d ★★★

Overhanging face climb protected by three bolts. The first bolt can be clipped easily by stepping left from the starting ledge. Technical moves past the first bolt lead to incut holds and steep climbing to the top. Pumpy.

FA: Mike Galoob 1990s

Gear: quickdraws

2-bolt anchor   40ft

The Schnoz

Atlantis

SHIT FOR BRAINS WALL

Follow the creek west for 200 yards from the Atlantis Wall. An obvious prow sticks out just above the trees on this east-facing formation. The lower part of the wall is covered by vegetation and trees. Skirt in from the right to access the base avoiding some of the thicker vegetation. There are two separate bolted lines on this wall about 6 feet apart. Both projects have two bolts, both date from the early 90s. Starting from the ground just feet away from the trees the climbing is steep and reachy. This formation looks like it has potential but the upper half of the wall has bad rock. The upper roof just below the summit has bad rock, belayer beware.

Bring #4 Camalots for the top anchors.

1. Shit for Brains 5.12? (PROJECT)

Left route with two bolts down lower on the wall. Climb steep rock with reachy moves over a small roof, and then continue up small holds leading to blocks and flakes up higher. The upper roof system below the summit has loose blocks.

FA: 1990s
Gear: quickdraws, #4 Camalots for anchor
No anchor   65ft

2. Unknown 5.12? (PROJECT)

Located a few feet right of *Shit for Brains*. Two bolts protect the start of this proposed line.

FA: 1990s
Gear: quickdraws, #4 Camalots for anchor
No anchor   65ft

MIDDLE WALL

This formation is located 30 yards from Shit for Brains Wall and faces to the east.

There is one bolted route with anchors on this wall.

1. Princess Di's Tragedy 5.10b/c★★

Located 30 yards to the left of Shit for Brains Wall, this face climb is protected by 3 bolts. Steep, with rock quality becoming questionable towards the top just above the last bolt. Even with questionable rock this route is still fun to climb.

FA: Dave Kramp 1997
Gear: quickdraws, .5-.75 cam
2-bolt anchor   50ft

AQUAMAN WALL

Located 25 yards to the left of Middle Wall.

1. Aquaman 5.12 ★★

Located 50 yards left of Middle Wall. Bolt protected face climb just above the creek. A rubber raft maybe useful for the start of this one! From just above the water climb the overhanging wall moving up and right following the bolts to a bolted belay anchor.

FA: Andy Magness, Aaron Gibson 1990s
Gear: quickdraws
2-bolt anchor   50ft

2. Chocolate Rocket 5.12 Toprope

Climbs a vertical line just to the right of *Aquaman*.

FA: *Aaron Gibson 1990s*

Gear: toprope

No anchor   50ft

Mike Galoob climbing Aquaman 5.12 circa 1990s. | Photo by Cyril Le Fredon

THE CAVE

Approach: Follow the creek south from *Aquaman*. The approach time is about 16 minutes to the base of The Cave. The large cave is on the west side of the creek and sits high above the canyon and faces to the east. This thing is quite the spectacle and is worth visiting. Hike up the slope and follow the trough up making your way to the base. You can access the top by scrambling up the left side just before the entrance to the cave. There is a bolted belay in the back of the cave near a ledge with fixed pins, a fixed draw and a bolt just below the lip. The top anchor takes a variety of gear from #1 to #4 Camalot. Bolted in the 1990s. There is a large refrigerator-size block hanging in the middle of the roof.

1. The Cave Route 5.12? (PROJECT)

Climb up to a ledge with two bolts for a belay. Climb out to the lip and continue in the wide crack climbing right over the mouth of the cave and continuing until you reach the other side of the horizontal crack and then up the vertical crack to the top. Equipped by Russell Hooper, Tony Wilson, Terry Andrews and Aaron Gibson in the 1990s.

FA: *Unknown*

Gear: cams to #4 Camalot, quickdraws

No anchor   100ft

2. The Cave Route 5.13? (PROJECT)

Same start as the *Cave Route*. Clip the fixed draw and continue up the overhang on face holds to the top.

FA: *Unknown*

Gear: same as the Cave Route

No anchor   100ft

The Cave

Ice Box Crack

Road view looking east

ICE BOX CRACK

Ice Box Crack faces north and can be reached by parking in the pullout just before the gate leads to Dog Run Hollow area.

Approach: From the pullout walk past the gate heading down the road until you reach the 25 MPH sign. 200 yards past the sign you will see a large boulder on your left next to the road. This boulder has a large eyebolt sticking out of the top. Pick up the trail directly behind the boulder walking east. Ice Box Crack formation is directly in front of you. It is also possible to approach from the bottom. The walk is just a few minutes off the road.

Burford Lake
Boulder Picnic Area
Lost Lake Picnic Area
Dog Run Hollow Trail
←

**Exit for: Ice Box Crack/The Narrows &
Forty-Foot Hole Climbing Areas**
(view looking to the west)

1. Ice Box Crack 5.9 ★★

From a moss covered ledge climb the fist crack for 12 feet leading to better hands up higher. The belay accepts a variety of cam sizes from #1 to #4 Camalot. Please do not belay off the cedar tree.

FA: Jon Frank, et al. 1979

Gear: cams to #3 Camalot

No anchor   40ft

Ice Box Crack

"Before the deed comes the thought. Before the achievement comes the dream. Every mountain we climb, we first climb in our mind."

~Royal Robbins

THE NARROWS

The main climbing area in the wildlife refuge is The Narrows. To reach The Narrows, drive west via Hwy 49 for 11.2 miles from the refuge entrance cattle guard, exit on Dog Run Hollow Trail Rd. (If you are camping at Camp Doris drive 1.9 miles west to the exit of Dog Run Hollow Trail Road).

Approach: Drive past the entrance gate 2.1 miles to the Boulder Picnic area, park here. Walk past the gate and restrooms on your left and continue past the Boulder Cabin (see overview map for The Narrows).

A nice trail designed by Jim Angel of Oregon and built by the climbing community leads across the creek to a canyon with 200 foot walls towering on each side of Cache Creek. It's a spectacular setting reminiscent of climbing areas found in Colorado. The hike into the main climbing area of Zoo Wall takes about 15 minutes from the parking area. The Narrows is a great summer spot to climb. With its shaded walls, climbers can seek refuge from the Oklahoma sun.

> *"In the mountains there are two grades: you can do it or you can't!"*
>
> ~Rusty Baille

Narrows Pullout

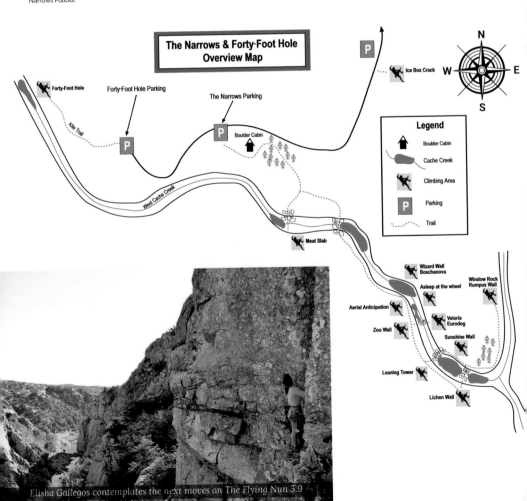

Elisha Gallegos contemplates the next moves on The Flying Nun 5.9

The Narrows & Window Rock Climbing Areas
Trailhead is just past the gate and left of the Boulder Cabin

The Boulder Cabin was built by Armsby Dave Lawrence, his wife Winnifred C. Lawrence and their two sons Robert and Arthur Lawrence in 1912 for their enjoyment of the Wichitas and to passing travellers for shelter, and is still to this day serving that purpose.

Narrows Trail Head

MEAT SLAB

Meat Slab faces east. With an easy approach, just a few minutes from the parking area, it is ideal for beginning climbers learning how to rock climb. These three topropes are a great place to work on your friction skills.

Approach time: 10 minutes

1. Rump Roast 5.5 ★★
Farthest left water streak.
FA: Unknown
Gear: toprope
2-bolt anchor   40ft

On his first day rock climbing, Logan Boren works his way up Rump Roast 5.5. | Photo by Lori Boren Mayse

2. T-Bone 5.6 ★★
The middle water streak and the longest route on the Meat Slab.
FA: Unknown
Gear: toprope
2-bolt anchor   40ft

3. Bed Rock 5.7 ★★★
Rightmost route on the Meat Slab.
FA: Unknown
Gear: toprope
2-bolt anchor   40ft

WIZARD WALL

This is the dark-colored wall approximately 250 yards north of *Aerial Anticipation* on the east side of Cache Creek. From *Aerial Anticipation* walk north on the east side of the creek skirting the base of the wall. A 40-foot slab that starts in the water leads up to a tree below a black wall; this is the start of *The Wizard*.

1. The Wizard 5.11c R ★★★

Thin crack climb on a black and yellow-colored wall. Climb up a short slab 40 feet (5.6) to a ledge with a tree (belay here). Small wires (and a blind #1 cam placement in the crack up and to the right) protect the (5.11) moves leading to the hand crack. From here continue with good gear up the crack on hand jams to a 2-bolt anchor. On the first ascent the route was toproped before it was lead.

FA: Cosby, Frank, and Raleigh 1982

Gear: TCUs, cams to #3, stoppers, offset wires
2-bolt anchor   *50ft*

2. Boschanova 5.11 ★

Located approximately 30 feet right of *The Wizard*. This is a bolted climb that follows the dihedral up a line of bolts. A bolted belay is at the base of the dihedral marking the start of the climb.

FA: Chuck Lohn et al. 1990s

Gear: quickdraws
2-bolt anchor   *50ft*

ASLEEP AT THE WHEEL

Asleep at the Wheel is located 100 yards east and directly across from *Aerial Anticipation*. Walk across the canyon to a wall with a large tree at its base. *Asleep at the Wheel* climbs a west-facing bolted line on a dark-colored rock behind a tree.

3. Asleep at the Wheel 5.11 ★★

Climb up a bolt protected face on a steep wall. Steve Hunt on his way to the refuge for some weekend climbing was falling asleep at the wheel. The name stuck.

FA: Steve Hunt, Jimmy Forester 1990s

Gear: quickdraws
2-bolt anchor   *50ft*

Wizard Wall

Asleep at the Wheel

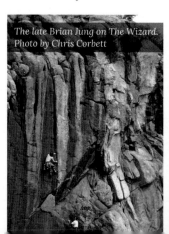

The late Brian Jung on *The Wizard*. Photo by Chris Corbett

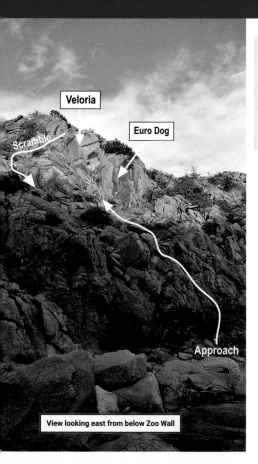

Veloria

Euro Dog

Scramble

Approach

View looking east from below Zoo Wall

VELORIA AND EURO DOG

These two climbs are located across the creek (east) of Zoo Wall. There are two bolted routes (5.9–5.10) just uphill from the creek. (See topo for approach and descent). Bring cams to #3 Camalot for the anchors.

Approach time: 20 minutes

1. Veloria 5.10 ★

Climb up a short, steep section with a hand-size crack to get established below the first bolt (there is some crunchy rock around the first bolt). Rock quality is somewhat better higher up. Continue up the 2 roofs protected by bolts and a ledge for the belay up top.

FA: Chuck Lohn et al. 1990s

Gear: cams to #3 Camalot, quickdraw

No anchor 60ft

2. Euro Dog 5.9 ★

Located twenty feet to the right of *Veloria*. Face climb on a dark slab of rock protected by two bolts.

FA: Chuck Lohn et al. 1990s

Gear: quickdraws

No anchor 40ft

Veloria and
Euro Dog

THE RESCUE

By Jimmy Ratzlaff

It started off like any other trip to the Wichitas, in my '67 Camaro, cruising down the turnpike. It was just another carefree weekend climbing with a friend. There was neither internet, nor social media, nor cell phones, nor worries. Only a band of brothers that lived for climbing. This trip would take Joel Dyer and me to "The Narrows" an area where I loved to climb. After a long, brutal hike we arrived at our destination. I was never sure, back then, why the road to get to The Narrows was closed. It was blocked off, leaving what seemed like miles of hiking down a perfectly good road. I hated hiking down it because I knew I should be driving down it. The only time I didn't mind was when I was climbing with my friend Sam Audrain, and he had just got the new Sony Walkman. I put those headphones on and I couldn't believe that I was listening to music and hiking at the same time; at the time the experience was surreal. This particular day no one else was there so Joel and I had the canyon all to ourselves. We ticked off a few routes and were taking a break, and then something different started to take place. Joel and I heard clanging and muffled voices, and we wondered what was going on. Soon, a line of people came in single file down the trail and headed straight to where we were. From a mountaineering club, around 15 people had come to sample the rock. Joel and I stood back and watched, as piles of rope and gear came out of the packs and the people began to rope up. Listening to them I could tell most of them were beginners. Some of them had no clue what

they were doing. It reminded me of my climbing beginnings where my friends and I climbed. There were never any other climbers around to show us what to do. By the grace of God we didn't get hurt, or worse, while learning how to climb. Joel and I watched multiple parties rope up and began to climb. I watched a man lead the corner on the left side of the Zoo Wall. He had only placed a couple of pieces of gear on his way up. This was normal if you were an experienced climber but he was not. As he neared the top his arms were giving out on the layback section and I realized he was in trouble. He realized it also and began yelling that he was coming off. Now "coming off" or falling at this point was going to be disastrous. He moaned and yelled and as his arms, then fingers, began to straighten out, I yelled, "Just one more move you can do it," then ping, he was off.

Jimmy Ratzlaff at Zoo Wall circa early 80s.

In slow motion he descended and hit an angled ledge where a muffled "ouffff!" noise came out of him and then he cratered at our feet. It was silent for a moment as everyone tried to absorb what had just happened but reality quickly woke us up. As I looked down, I saw the man had multiple fractures and his head was split open and bleeding. Joel was hit by the man's rack of climbing gear, but was not seriously injured. Luckily, I had been a boy scout so I knew some first aid. We did some preliminary first aid to stop the bleeding, then made him comfortable. The woman belaying him thought she had pulled him off and was crying. It was a chaotic scene of people scrambling around with a variety of emotions coming from the mountaineering group.

In those days we didn't have cell phones so I said I would run and get help. I was in excellent running shape thanks to my basketball coach who loved to torture us by running all kinds of drills in the Oklahoma heat with no air conditioning. With no pack and incredible motivation I took off like a track runner and headed for my car. I was hot and tired but, aware of the condition of the climber who had fallen, I never slowed. After arriving at my car I knew where the ranger station was and I was sure I could find some help there. If you have ever traveled in "The Refuge" you didn't dare go over 35 mph or you would get a ticket, pronto. But this time, I wanted to see a ranger and I had a good excuse, if I got caught, why I was speeding. I was hitting 75 mph through the refuge on the way to the station. I had never driven at this speed in the refuge and I have to admit I was enjoying it. To my surprise I didn't see a single ranger. When I got to the ranger station no one was there.

At this point I began to panic. All I could think about was the man bleeding to death in the canyon. Then I remembered where the rangers lived. I rushed to the houses and began knocking on doors. No one answered my knocks on the first house. I ran to the next one, with the same result. As I arrived at the last house someone heard my frantic knocking and sheepishly came to the door. The woman who answered the door looked afraid of me. She stood back and would not open the door, but peered at me through the screen. While receiving her frightened stare, I realized that I had blood on me and was dripping with sweat. She probably thought I had just killed everyone in the last three cabins. I explained what had happened and she said she would contact the rangers to meet me at the gate to The Narrows. She never actually came close to the door, just in case I wasn't telling the truth, probably thinking I was going to bust through the door and assault her. I got back in my car and was cruising at 75 and still didn't have contact with a ranger. I waited by the gate to the Narrows for what seemed like an eternity when finally the ranger showed up. He unlocked the gate and we drove down the road that I had run earlier. It seemed like light speed compared to running down the road. We got out of the car and started to head to the canyon. I noticed as the ranger got out of the car he was, let's just say, "out of shape." With a strenuous hike I knew he could not keep up, and I thought he was going to have a heart attack and have to be rescued also. After a millennium he made it to the scene alive. The ranger got on the radio and said the nearby Fort Sill was sending a rescue party. At this time I was beginning to relax a little, knowing that the rescue was at hand; but I found out differently. Eventually, a Huey helicopter could be heard in the distance and was getting closer. It was like a scene from a Vietnam movie as the chopper came through the canyon. But the pilot didn't stop and continued to fly right past us. The ranger with us got the bright idea of "popping smoke" and pulled out a smoke bomb from his pack and touched it off to try and get the pilot's attention. Yet, the problem was he did this right beside the man we were trying to rescue, and he was gagging from the smoke. I picked up the smoke bomb and tossed it down the canyon while burning my fingers in the process, but I didn't care. Again, the chopper flew by without seeing us. This time the ranger said he had a flare gun and would shoot it off as the chopper went by. On the helicopter's third trip we heard the thump from the engines echoing off the walls, you could feel the thump in your chest as he came down the canyon. Then the ranger, instead of shooting the flare up, decided to shoot it at the chopper and almost hit it. Needless to say it got their attention, while almost shooting it down. In an amazing feat of flying the pilot stopped and angled in toward us. The pilot's skill was amazing. But after lowering a basket from a rescue line, they said it was the wrong kind of basket so they would have to bring in a new one. I was dumbfounded. Why could they not use that one? So we waited and waited, and finally we could hear on the ranger's radio that the rescue crew with the new basket was lost in the woods and couldn't find us. I had an idea where they were located so once again, I sprinted off to find them. I finally found them and they were lost and moving at a snail's pace. I was fed up with their slow pace and, to their disapproval, took the basket from them and proceeded to run back to the rescue site without them. The chopper came back to the scene of the accident. To make a long story shorter, the rescue team pulled the injured climber up the rescue line in the new basket and got him in the chopper. From there they quickly flew to the hospital. It had been about four hours since he had fallen and I wondered if he would survive. I told Joel if I was to ever fall, to drag me and do whatever he needed to get me out because it would be quicker than a rescue team trying to rescue me. However, I'm sure today the rescue methods have improved greatly from these early years.

I heard later that the injured climber in the accident had lived, but was seriously injured and it would take a long time for his recovery. It was just another exciting Oklahoma weekend, climbing with my friend.

Army helicopter flying close to Zoo Wall. | Photo from the Jimmy Ratzlaff Collection

4th class

SUNSHINE WALL

Located across from Lichen Wall. Faces the southwest, which makes it a good winter climbing area.

This much-overlooked wall has some of the best face climbing in The Narrows. There are four routes on this wall from 5.8–5.10; however these are not beginner lead routes. *Cool Dude, Shuttle Booster,* and *O-Ring* share the same belay; *Rocket Sled* climbs up and to the right at a separate belay location.

Approach and Descent: To get to the base of the climb traverse the rock just above the water (see approach photo); easy scrambling and a bit of 4th class terrain will get you to the base. Bring some #2, #3 cams for the anchor up top.

To descend the routes walk off to the east and follow the gully or downclimb the approach.

Approach time: 30 minutes

1. Cool Dude 5.8 Toprope ★★★

Face climb on the left side of the wall. Climb up the hand–fist crack to a stance, step left then up on featured rock. From the first ledge and horizontal crack below the summit, climb to a short section of fist-size crack to gain the summit ledge (bring #2-#3 size cams for the belay).

FA: Chris Mohr 1986

Gear: toprope

No anchor   60ft

Tony Mayse & Joe Romero enjoying the alpenglow on the Sunshine Wall. | Photo by Chris Corbett

2. Shuttle Booster 5.10a RX ★★★

Same start as *Cool Dude* but continues up the flake then steps right to face climbing with sculpted holds and featured rock to the top. Same exit cracks as *Cool Dude* (bring #2–#3 size cams for the belay).

FA: Jon Frank, Diane Fisher 1986

Gear: stoppers, TCUs, cams to #3 Camalot

No anchor   60ft

3. O-Ring 5.8 RX ★★★

Located ten feet to the right of *Shuttle Booster*. Climb up the slab start to featured rock, climbing past horizontal cracks with gear opportunities. Same exit cracks as *Cool Dude* and *Shuttle Booster*.

FA: Jon Frank, Jimmy Ratzlaff 1978

Gear: TCUs, cams to #3 Camalot

No anchor   60ft

4. Rocket Sled 5.10d RX ★★★★

The hardest route on the Sunshine Wall. Face climb to the right of *O-Ring* protected by two bolts, #2 or #3 Camalot out to the right before the first bolt and a #3 cam protects the exit moves at the horizontal crack after the second bolt. Sustained (5.10d) climbing.

FA: Diane Fisher, Jon Frank, Chris Mohr 1986

Gear: TCUs, cams to #3 Camalot

No anchor   60ft

"Expose yourself to your deepest fear:

after that, fear has no power,

and the fear of freedom shrinks

and vanishes. You are free."

~Jim Morrison

Sunshine Wall

AERIAL ANTICIPATION

This is the first wall on your right (west) as you make your way down into The Narrows. After you cross the creek walk about 50 yards south. There will be a wall with a right-facing dihedral and three prominent roofs (usually with chalk on them) and a set of chains at the top of the route. Aerial Anticipation faces to the east.

Approach time: 20 minutes

Zoo Wall

1. Dallas Morning News 5.10a ★ Toprope

Toprope to the left of *Aerial Anticipation*. Climb the face up to a short roof, and then traverse right to easier climbing and the chain belay on top of the wall above a ledge.

FA: Jon Frank 1986

Gear: toprope

2-bolt anchor   60ft

2. Shake Your Groove Thing 5.6

Start in the dihedral of *Aerial Anticipation* then continue up and left, then follow the broken cracks trending up and right to the bolted belay anchors.

FA: Unknown 1980s

Gear: cams to #2 Camalot

2-bolt anchor   60ft

3. Aerial Anticipation 5.11c ★★★★

Sport route on the west side of Cache Creek. This five-bolt route climbs past three roofs on good rock. Climb up an easy dihedral (5.6) then step right to a bolt (you can protect the moves to the first bolt with a small cam in the dihedral). Continue up through the three roofs protected by bolts. (Consider using long quickdraws down low).

One of the best climbs in The Narrows.

FA: Jon Frank, Eric Forney, and Duane Raleigh (Direct finish) 1986

Gear: 0.75–#1 Camalot, quickdraws

2-bolt anchor   60ft

On the first ascent Jon Frank and Eric Forney rappelled the route and put in "really bad bolts." During the first lead they took the line to the left after the roof. Duane was called out and climbed straight up, putting a direct finish on *Aerial Anticipation*.

In October 2016 Climbing Magazine listed *Aerial Anticipation* as one of "America's 100 Best Sport Climbing Routes." "Although no single move is harder than about 5.10+, the steep roof is unrelenting on blood filled forearms, and each hold grabbed will leave you expecting big air..."

"You have to try hard if you want to be a climber girl!" ~Kali Jo Boren (6 years old)

Elisha Gallegos climbing Aerial Anticipation. | Photo by Tony Mayse

Aerial Anticipation

Daniel Schuerch climbing the overhanging Narrows route Aerial Anticipation 5.11c. | Photo by Tony Mayse

ZOO WALL

The most popular area in The Narrows with several good classic crack climbs. This wall is on the same side of the trail which leads into The Narrows. Walk past Aerial Anticipation then head uphill to Zoo Wall (see topo photo). The wall is divided into two sides: Zoo Wall (Right) and Zoo Wall (Left).

Zoo Wall (Right)

1. Master Mind 5.10 X

Located to the left of *The Dihedral*. Climb up the unprotected face to a horizontal crack with a pin; continue up intersecting with *Masters of Reality* as it traverses under the roof. Finish on *Masters of Reality*.

"Kinda spooky." ~Jimmy Ratzlaff

FA: *Jimmy Ratzlaff, Jon Frank 1980s*
Gear: TCUs, cams #2–#3.5, med. wires
2-bolt anchor   70ft

2. Masters of Reality 5.10d RX ★★

From the anchors on *Crazy Alice* step down (placing gear high) then traverse across the face (5.10a/b R), move underneath an overhang, #3 or #4 Friend works here. Keep traversing until underneath a thin left-facing corner with a fixed copperhead. Use TCUs and medium-size wires. Pull the roof into a corner then angle up and left around an arête to a bolted anchor. A short 5.7 pitch leads to the top, or rappel 70ft from the anchors.

FA: *Jimmy Ratzlaff on aid 5.10A2 climbed July 24, 1981*
FFA: *Jimmy Ratzlaff, August 15, 1981*
Gear: TCUs, cams #2–#3.5, med. wires
2-bolt anchor   70ft

3. The Dihedral 5.6 ★★★★

Probably the most climbed route in Oklahoma! Climb the dihedral on polished rock exiting out right below a short roof to a ledge with a 2-bolt anchor. Bring a variety of gear and some long runners.

FA: *Unknown*
Gear: cams to #4 Camalot, long runners
2-bolt anchor   80ft

4. Squeeze Play 5.9★ Toprope

Climb the polished face to the right of *The Dihedral*.

FA: *Jimmy Ratzlaff, Jon Frank 1979*
Gear: toprope
2-bolt anchor   80ft

Zoo Wall

5. Crazy Alice 5.8 ★★★★

Mega Classic! This is the prominent crack in the middle of Zoo Wall. Climb up to a short ramp, step left to reach the crack. Continue up on good jams and some lieback moves through the middle part of the climb. This is a very popular Narrows route.

FA: *Mike Panciera, Greg Schooley 1976*
Gear: cams to #3 Camalot, stoppers
2-bolt anchor   80ft

6. The Flying Nun 5.9 ★★★

Climb *The Dihedral* then continue up the corner to a short roof. Turn the roof and belay here. A great finish to *The Dihedral*. Walk down 3rd class to the anchors on *Crazy Alice*.

FA: *Duane Raleigh, Bill Thomas 1978*
Gear: TCUs, cams to #3 Camalot
No anchor   90ft

7. The Sloth 5.10a ★★

The first route rated 5.10 in Oklahoma. Hand-sized roof crack directly above *The Flying Nun*. Wide hands lead out the overhanging roof. Jimmy Ratzlaff and Jon Frank toproped this route then came back for the lead.

FA: *Jon Frank, Jimmy Ratzlaff 1979*
Gear: cams to #3 Camalot
No anchor   25ft

8. McBride's Mind 5.10a R ★★★

A nice varying route to test your crack and face technique on. Face climb 15 feet right of *Crazy Alice* to a bolt. Climb 10 feet past the bolt, then step right into a left-angling hand crack following it on up. *McBride's Mind* was the early makings of *Dr. Coohead*.

FA: *Jon Frank, Jimmy Ratzlaff, March 1979*
Gear: small cam, quickdraws
2-bolt anchor   40ft
* *Southern Exposure.*

9. Dr. Coolhead 5.10d RX ★★★★

Five feet right of *Crazy Alice* is the start of this face climb with two bolts. (See description for *McBride's Mind*). Climb 15 feet up the face to where the wall steepens (a small cam (0.75-#1) protects the moves getting to the first bolt). Climb past the first bolt on thin edges and polished rock to the second bolt. From here continue up on sustained 5.10 climbing to the top.

FA: *Duane Raleigh, Bill Thomas, Rick Thomas 1980*
FSA: *(First solo ascent) Mike Hankins late 80s*
Gear: small cam, quickdraws
2-bolt anchor   80ft

10. Resurrection Factor 5.11 ★★ Toprope

Hard face climb up the steep face to the right of *Dr. Coolhead*. The lone bolt is not part of this route.

FA: *Jimmy Ratzlaff 1984*
Gear: toprope
2-bolt anchor   70ft

Elisha Gallegos onsighting Leap Frog 5.10a on the Zoo Wall. | Photo by Tony Mayse

11. Richard Pryor Route 5.8 ★

Ten feet to the right of *Resurrection Factor*. Climb the steep crack, working your way to a small alcove. Step right then continue up on easier climbing to a stance below a slab. Continue up and to the right, following the crack system to the top of Zoo Wall.

FA: Bob Marvin, Scott McBride 1976
Gear: cams to #3 Camalot, stoppers
2-bolt anchor   *70ft*

12. Leap Frog 5.10a ★★★

Climb *Richard Pryor Route* and continue in the diagonal crack that angles left onto the headwall of Zoo Wall. Climb the diagonal crack finishing on face holds that lead to the top and 2-bolt anchor.

FA: Bob Marvin (toprope), Jon Frank, Jimmy Ratzlaff 1978
Gear: cams to #3 Camalot, stoppers
2-bolt anchor   *70ft*

13. Larin Has Balls 5.7 R ★

Just a few feet right of *Richard Pryor Route*. Look for a short dihedral. A few "ballsy" moves lead to easier climbing. Finish on any number of routes above.

FA: Larin 1978
Gear: cams to #2 Camalot
2-bolt anchor   *75ft*

14. Too Much Fun 5.10b ★★

Located to the right of *Richard Pryor Route* is an overhang. On the left end of the overhang climb up and traverse right. Continue the traverse underneath the overhang to easier climbing, or continue up to actually make a climb out of it.

FA: Frank, Hayes 1981
Gear: cams to #2 Camalot, stoppers
No anchor   *30–60ft*

15. Scrotum Roof 5.11 ★★

Located a few right and down from *Richard Pryor Route* is an overhang with a bolt. Climb up and over the overhang and continue on easier climbing to the top.

FA: Bob Hopkins, Sandy Stewart 1982
Gear: quickdraws, cams to #3 Camalot, stoppers
No anchor   *70ft*

16. Conflict in Terms 5.12a ★

Located 10 feet to the right of *Scrotum Roof*. Hard start leads to easier climbing above.

FA: Jon Frank 1983
Gear: small gear to #2 Camalot
2-bolt anchor   *40ft*

17. Extended Alter Call 5.9★

Below and at the far left end of *Critical Mass* roof lies a left-leaning crack. Climb the crack and continue on a summit route to the top.

FA: Jon Frank, Fletch Taylor 1981
Gear: cams to #2 Camalot
2-bolt anchor   *75ft*

18. Sweet Jesus 5.6 ★

Same start as *Critical Mass* but takes the easy hand crack to the left, avoiding the *Critical Mass* roof crux.

FA: Jon Frank, Jimmy Ratzlaff 1982
Gear: cams to #2 Camalot
2-bolt anchor   *75ft*

19. Critical Mass 5.10b ★★★

Climb up the low-angle face to the roof; protect the roof with a variety of gear. Climb over the roof to a wide low-angle crack continuing on easier climbing to the top. This route was originally done on aid.

FA: Jon Frank, Jimmy Ratzlaff September 29, 1979 (later free soloed by Jimmy Ratzlaff)
Gear: TCUs to # 4 Camalot
No anchor   *70ft*

20. Unfinished Piece 5.6 ★★

Climb the start of *Critical Mass*, then move right into a low- angle crack system that leads to the summit of Zoo Wall.

FA: Unknown 1980s
Gear: cams to #2 Camalot
2-bolt anchor   *75ft*

21. Yellow Corner 5.7 ★★★

Left-facing yellow-colored corner near a cedar tree to the right of *Critical Mass*. Climb up the corner on sometimes questionable rock. Good gear can be found on this route.

FA: Unknown
Gear: bring a variety of cams, stoppers
No anchor   *100ft*

22. Triple Decker 5.8 ★★

Long route to the right of *Yellow Corner*. Follow a series of short overhangs (some loose sections) with occasional ledges breaking up the climb. This route eventually tops out at the same place as *Yellow Corner*.

FA: Jon Frank, Jimmy Ratzlaff 1977
Gear: bring a variety of gear, stoppers
No anchor   *110ft*

23. Time the Avenger 5.10a ★ Toprope

Left of *The Big Flush* is a prominent roof marking this route. Climb the face up to the roof, then continue and over roof leading to face climbing above.

FA: Jon Frank 1983.
Gear: toprope
No anchor   *60ft*

24. The Big Flush 5.7 R ★

Large corner crack/chimney system to the immediate right of *Time the Avenger*.

FA: *Unknown*

Gear: large cams

No anchor   70ft

25. Straight Face 5.9+ ★ Toprope

Climb the face to the right of *The Big Flush*.

FA: *Unknown 1980s*

Gear: toprope

No anchor   60ft

26. My Name is Nobody 5.9 R ★

A classic 70s western movie! *My Name is Nobody* climbs the crack system below *The Big Flush*.

FA: *Jon Frank Charlie Hayes 1979.*

Gear: cams to #2 Camalot

No anchor   60ft

Zoo Wall (Left)

To reach Zoo Wall Left scramble through the cave to the left of *The Dihedral* route. This area has some enjoyable moderate routes and is usually not as crowded as Zoo Wall Right. Some of the routes have runout potential. To descend the routes walk off to the south and scramble down on easy terrain.

1. Side Saddle 5.6

Climb the low-angle slab with the thin crack, using the crack for protection.

FA: *Scott Kimball, Lober 1982*

Gear: small cams, stoppers

No anchor   60ft

2. Slap Roof 5.6

Climb the crack to the left of *No Stone Unturned*. Funky first move.

FA: *Unknown*

Gear: cams to #3 Camalot

No anchor   60ft

3. No Stone Unturned 5.9 ★★★★

Climb the crack/face to the left of *Shake and Bake*. Make your way up to an overhang (the move can be protected with a cam out right) before clipping the bolt. Surmount the overhang and continue up with moderate climbing to the top.

FA: *Kimball, Lober 1982*

Gear: cams to #3, stoppers, quickdraws

No anchor   60ft

4. Shake and Bake A2 ★

Aid route to the left of *Fantasy Roof*. This route has the obvious improbable-looking horizontal roof. Climb to the roof aiding your way out the thin crack.

FA: *Hayes, Jimmy Ratzlaff 1978*

Gear: variety of gear including pins

No anchor   60ft

Jimmy Ratzlaff on the first ascent of McBride's Mind circa 80s. | Photo from the Jimmy Ratzlaff Collection

Martin Ferguson belayed by Brian Strangeland on the classic No Stone Unturned. | Photo by Drew Nevius

"When we pick out anything by itself, we find it
hitched to everything else in the universe."

~John Muir

5. Fantasy Roof 5.8 ★★★★

A few feet left of *Sundown Dihedral*. Start in the
dihedral below the roof. Pull around the feature
resembling a diving board, and then continue in the
crack or the face to the top. Bring a variety of gear.

FA: *Fantasy Ridge Guides 1982*

Gear: TCUs, cams to #2 Camalot, stoppers

No anchor   60ft

6. Sundown Dihedral 5.8 R ★★★

Located on the right just after passing through
the cave. Climb up the dihedral on steep, slightly
off-vertical rock to the top with an interesting exit
move.

FA: *Kimber, Lober 1982*

Gear: TCUs, cams to #2 Camalot, stoppers

No anchor (#3, #4 cams)   60ft

Artwork by Elisha Gallegos

Jon Frank climbing Critical Mass 5.10b with belayer Jimmy Ratzlaff circa 80s. | Photo from the Jimmy Ratzlaff Collection

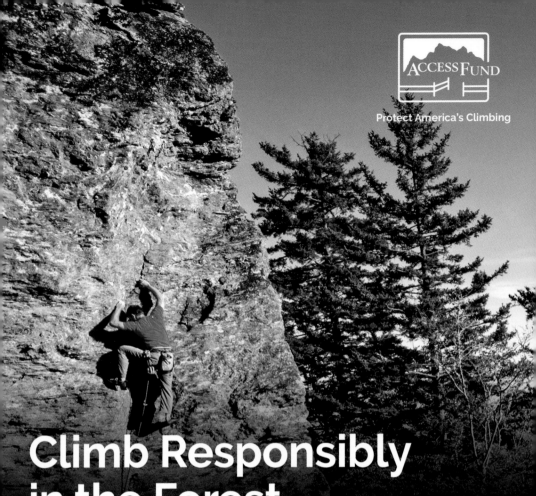

Climb Responsibly in the Forest

Many forested climbing areas are located near densely populated metropolitan areas and demand special minimum impact behaviors.

Honor seasonal cliff-dwelling raptor closures by climbing elsewhere.

Minimize erosion by containing gear and pads to durable surfaces.

Keep a low profile by minimizing noise. Keep music to yourself.

Forest soil can biodegrade human waste in a properly dug cathole, but use a toilet or pack it out in high-use areas.

Learn more at: www.accessfund.org/forest

Leaning Tower

LEANING TOWER

The Leaning Tower is 200 yards down the canyon on the same side of the creek as Zoo Wall. Follow the trail that winds its way through the trees to reach the base of the tower. The routes on Leaning Tower offer longer climbs with nice exposure. The left side of the Tower is where most of the easier climbing is to be found. All of the routes can be descended by walking off to the south of the tower or the rap station on top of LTD. (Bring 2 ropes for the rappel).

Approach time: 25 minutes

1. The Crucifix 5.6 ★
Twenty feet left of *Tight Rope*; follow the dark-colored corner up and left.
FA: *Unknown*
Gear: cams to #3 Camalot
No anchor   50ft

2. Tight Rope 5.6 ★
Low-angle corner to the left of *No Name*.
FA: *Unknown*
Gear: cams to #3 Camalot, stoppers
No anchor   60ft

3. No Name 5.6 ★
Short finger crack to the left of *Second Hand*.
FA: *Duane Raleigh, Hunt 1978*
Gear: small cams, stoppers
No anchor   60ft

4. Second Hand 5.7 ★
Climb the corner crack 15 feet left of *The Y*.
FA: *Unknown*
Gear: cams to #3 Camalot, stoppers
No anchor   70–80ft

5. The Y 5.7 ★
Gully located 25 feet left of *Arrowsmith*. Climb up the gully through a short roof, to easier climbing up top. This route eventually intersects with the top of *Arrowsmith*.
FA: *Unknown*
Gear: cams to #3 Camalot, long runners
No anchor   70–80ft

6. Arrowsmith 5.7 ★★
This is the first route on the left side of the tower. Follow the very prominent left-facing dihedral up through a corner, and continue up the dihedral to easier climbing out right. There are various options for topping out on this climb.
FA: *Ken Rose, Kenny Stern 1974*
Gear: cams to #4 Camalot, long runners
No anchor   100ft

7. Neckline 5.8 R ★
Start in the dihedral with loose rock at the base. Climb up the dihedral to a ledge, belay here. Continue up and left under *Love Potion #9*, continuing left on more moderate terrain to the top.
FA: *Donnie Hunt, Duane Raleigh, Bill Thomas 1980*
Gear: stoppers, cams to #2 Camalot
No anchor   130ft

8. Dream Landscape 5.8+ R ★

Just to the right from the start of *Neckline*. Climb the face with a few protection opportunities to the obvious ledge. Continue on *Neckline* or any number of routes to Leaning Tower's summit.

FA: Jon Frank, Bob Pearson 1984

Gear: stoppers and cams to #2 Camalot

No anchor   50ft

9. Funky Finger Crack 5.10a R ★★★

Located down and about 30 yards left of LTD. Climb the finger crack and make your way to a large ledge. From here continue on any of the routes that lead to the top of the tower.

FA: Diane Fisher, Jon Frank 1984

Gear: small stoppers, cams to #2 Camalot

2-bolt anchor   80–90ft

10. Love Potion #9 5.10c RX ★★★

This route is located to the left of *Wild n' Crazy*. There are anchors down low on the route which also makes for a good belay station for *Funky Finger Crack*. Bolts on this route were replaced in the mid-2000s.

FA: Tony Cosby, Jon Frank 1984

Gear: cams to #2 Camalot

No anchor   100ft

11. Wild and Crazy 5.11 R ★★★★

Overhanging face climb to the left of LTD. This route can be climbed by doing the first pitch of LTD. From the belay climb left under the overhangs, move up and over a roof to a hidden bolt. Follow the bolts to the top on airy and exciting climbing. This route has had the bolts replaced. Bring some cams along with longer draws. Save small cams for the finish.

FA: Jon Frank, Jack Wurster 1986

Gear: TCUs, cams to #2 Camalot

No anchor   130ft

12. Leaning Tower Direct A.K.A. LTD 5.9 RX ★★★★

"The Classic" Tower route! This route starts on a ledge with a tree.

Pitch 1: Climb the slabby corner on thin edges. Continue up on easier climbing to a stance below the chimney (belay here).

Pitch 2: Climb through chimneys and overhangs. Leave the chimney system exiting out to the right on a ledge with a 2-bolt anchor.

FA: Rose, Stern 1974

Gear: TCUs to #3 Camalot, stoppers

2-bolt anchor   130ft

13. Lycra Sheath 5.10c/d R ★★★

Bolted line on the vertical face right of LTD's second pitch. Climb LTD's first pitch and continue up the line of bolts on a vertical face to the right. This route does not follow the natural line of the wall; the bolts force you to climb on harder sections of the face. There is a bit of route finding which adds to the adventure. After the third bolt, TCUs protect the climbing. Airy!

FA: *Gary Ballard, Mike Yarbrough 1988*

Gear: TCUs, cams to #2 Camalot, quickdraws

2-bolt anchor   130ft

14. Captain Crunch 5.7 ★★★

Located around the right side of *LTD* is a lower-angle ramp in a corner. This is the start of *Captain Crunch*. Climb up the corner to a roof with some loose blocks, a nice airy finish for this grade climb. Bring some long runners to eliminate rope drag at the top.

FA: *Ken Rose, Kenny Sterns 1978*

Gear: cams to #3.5, stoppers

No anchor   120ft

15. Crunchberries 5.10a ★★★

Bolted line to the right of *Captain Crunch*. Climb up the ramp to a face on the right-hand side with three bolts.

FA: *Chuck Lohn 1990s*

Gear: quickdraws

No anchor   60ft

16. Tenderfoot 5.10c R ★

Start down and to the right from *Crunchberries*, next to a cave. Work your way through some overhangs and to a bolt higher up. Belay on a ledge just above the belay ledge for neighboring climbs.

FA: *Chuck Lohn 1990s*

Gear: cams to #2 Camalot

No anchor   70ft

17. Dr. Kildare 5.9+ R ★★

Thirty yards to the right of *Crunchberries* is a dihedral with a piton fixed in the crack. This route has historical significance. The first Oklahoma climbing guidebook *Southern Exposure* was written when Duane Raleigh took some time off after a bad fall on this route.

FA: *Duane Raleigh, Jon Frank, Mark Herndon, Jimmy Ratzlaff, Feb. 21, 1980*

Gear: TCUs, cams to #2.5, stoppers

No anchor   60ft

"It doesn't have to be fun to be fun."

~Barry Blanchard

Dr. Kildare

Joe Romero enjoying some exposure on the spectacular Lycra Sheath 5.10d. | Photo by Tony Mayse

LICHEN WALL

Lichen Wall is the tallest wall in The Narrows. Continue walking past Leaning Tower to the end of the canyon. The wall has water at the base, which makes for a nice setting. Although some of the routes have lichen on them, the climbing is quite spectacular. To descend the routes walk off to the gully on the west side of Lichen Wall. The routes on Lichen Wall are divided into three sections: Lichen Wall Left, Center and Right.

Approach time: 30 minutes

Lichen Wall Left

1. Riverside Attraction 5.11b/c ★★
Face climb to the left of *Ker Plunk*. Traverse left over the water then climb up the face past two bolts.
FA: *Keith Milne, Donny Scott 1987*
Gear: quickdraws
No anchor   *60ft*

2. Ker Plunk 5.7 R ★★★★
Mega classic route that follows the ramp on the left side of Lichen Wall. Start to the right of the water.
Pitch 1: Face climb then move left, eventually making your way up the corner to a ramp. From here continue on edges protected by crack gear. Belay at the tree.

Pitch 2: Climb the gully up and to the right, making your way to the anchors just above a ledge. A 60-meter rope barely gets you to the ground from the anchors. This route gets its name from the first ascent when a block was pulled off, landing Charlie in the water.
FA: *Charlie Oydston, Panciera 1975*
Gear: TCUs, cams to #3.5, stoppers
2-bolt anchor   *100ft*

3. Monkey's Way 5.7 ★★
Crack climb to the right of *Ker Plunk*. Same start as *Ker Plunk* but continue right, pulling around a huge flake. From here follow the offwidth crack to the top.
FA: *Unknown*
Gear: cams up to #4 Camalot
2-bolt anchor   *80ft*

4. Jay's Gully A3
Gully to the right of *Monkey's Way*.
FA: *Jay Lowell 1970s*
Gear: aid rack
No anchor   *160ft*

Lichen Wall

5. Old #7 5.7 ★★

Crack climb to the right of *Monkey's Way*. Climb up the dark-colored crack to a ledge, belay here. Continue up the gully or traverse left to the ledge with a 2-bolt anchor.

FA: Jay Lowell, Kenny Stearns, Ken Rose 1974
Gear: bring a variety of cams, stoppers
2-bolt anchor   *80ft*

Lichen Wall Center

6. League of Doom 5.11c RX ★★★★

Located to the far right of *Old #7*.

Long, exposed and very challenging, this route has it all, which makes it one of the classic climbs in Oklahoma.

Pitch 1: Climb up broken rock to a corner with a short roof above it, traverse to the right below the roof onto a polished face stepping back left over the overhang. Continue on runout climbing on a lichen-covered slab, ending on a sloping ledge with a bolted belay (5.9 RX).

Pitch 2: Step left and up the (5.10) face 20 feet to the first bolt. You can find gear placements but the rock quality is questionable. Clip the bolt then move up to a short horizontal crack (gear), continue up the clean face to another bolt then traverse out right and up to a stance. Continue up the wide (5.8) crack to a ledge with a 2-bolt anchor belay.

FA: Jon Frank, Duane Raleigh 1980
Gear: TCUs, cams to #4, quickdraws
2-bolt anchor   *120ft*

6a. The 3rd Huber Direct 5.11b/c ★★★

A roof climb finish to *League of Doom*. From the top of *League of Doom's* second pitch continue up the corner on lieback moves to a 12-foot roof. From here step out onto a steep face below the roof, pull the roof on sustained gymnastic moves making your way to a ledge. From here, join the bolt-protected face of *Space Balls*. This is currently a toprope climb pending a bolt application.

FA: Tony Mayse 2017
Gear: finger-size cams
2-bolt anchor   *120ft*

Attempted by Jon Frank & Jimmy Ratzlaff in early 1980. A bolt was installed but pulled out when Jon fell off the roof, taking a 20-foot whipper! (When bolted, this pitch will offer 100 feet of sustained (5.11) climbing connecting League of Doom with Space Balls). Permit pending.

7. Jesus Lives 5.11b X ★

Just to the right of *League of Doom*. Climb the unprotected face making your way to the belay anchors of *League of Doom*.

FA: Jimmy Ratzlaff 1983
Gear: free solo
2-bolt anchor   *80ft*

8. Fantastic Voyage 5.11a X ★★★★

Located 10 feet to the right of *League of Doom's* start.

Pitch 1: Climb a diagonal crack, and then continue on unprotected face climbing to a 2-bolt anchor.

Pitch 2: Climb right from the anchor then up the black face protected by bolts. Continue up the crack making your way to the balcony and a 2-bolt anchor shared by *League of Doom*.

Pitch 3: Continue up and traverse left below the bolts on *Space Balls* making your way to a bolt out left. Continue up of on face holds to a short dihedral before reaching the top.

FA: Duane Raleigh 1983
Gear: same as *League of Doom*
2-bolt anchor   *200ft*

9. Spaced 5.8 RX ★

Located 15 feet to the right of *League of Doom's* start. A wide angling crack gets you to unprotected face climbing following the line of least resistance up to a 2-bolt anchor. From here traverse right on a lichen-covered ramp, continue right, then angle left to the top.

FA: Jon Frank, Jimmy Ratzlaff
Gear: cams to #2 Camalot, long runners
2-bolt anchor   *200ft*

10. Vegetarian Delight 5.10d RX

Climb the first pitch of *League of Doom* or any route which gets you the belay station. Traverse to the left on a ledge with two bolts protecting the climbing. Continue up the crack system to a ledge, belay here. Climb the crack then move out to the left on the vegetated slab which leads to the top.

FA: Jon Frank, Bob Pearson, Eric Forney 1985
Gear: same as *League of Doom*
2-bolt anchor   *200ft*

11. Nuclear Combat 5.11b RX ★★★★

Pitch 1: Climb *League of Doom's* first pitch.

Pitch 2: Climb left on a ledge to bolt then up the thin face to another bolt; face climb left to a dihedral and easier crack climbing leading to a 2-bolt anchor.

Pitch 3: Continue up and left with moderate face climbing to the top.

FA: Duane Raleigh 1983
Gear: same as *League of Doom*
2-bolt anchor   *200ft*

12. Nubian Dance 5.12c RX ★★★

Climb *League of Doom's* second pitch, then move left at the horizontal crack below *Isabelle*. The crack has a fixed piton and bolt at the end of the traverse. Continue up the dihedral to a 2-bolt anchor. From here continue up on moderate terrain to the top. Prior to becoming a free climb the name was *Wet Dream* (5.11 A2) climbed on aid by Duane Raleigh & Rick Thomas in 1980. *"Established during a very rainy weekend siege."* ~*Southern Exposure*

FA: *Duane Raleigh 1987*
Gear: same as League of Doom
2-bolt anchor   *65ft*

13. Isabelle 5.12d R ★★★★

Short dihedral with three bolts located to the left of the upper section of *League of Doom's* second pitch. Follow *League of Doom's* second pitch to its final bolt. Here, instead of heading right, move left and climb the thin dihedral marked by three bolts to a bolted belay. Rappel here or continue on routes which lead to the top (see topo).

FA: *Russell Hooper, Tony Wilson 1990*
Gear: same as League of Doom
2-bolt anchor   *80ft*

In 1987 the ground-up style was still in full-swing in Oklahoma and throughout most of the U.S. Belayed by Tony Wilson, Duane Raleigh led off from the anchors atop of League of Doom's *first pitch and climbed up the blank section of rock which was the early makings of* Isabelle. *Duane led up the dihedral and placed the first bolt hanging off a hook. Not wanting to drill a bolt ladder he came down. A few years later, Russell Hooper and Tony Wilson added the other bolts on rappel and climbed the pitch naming it* Isabelle.

14. Space Balls 5.11 ★★★★

Overhanging bucket blast above the second pitch of *League of Doom*, this is the standard finish to *League of Doom*. From the belay step right then traverse up and left to the first bolt. From here it's a continuation of overhanging jug pulling past the five bolts to the top. The third clip creates rope drag; consider a long runner here. It is possible to run pitch two of *League of Doom* with *Space Balls* for a long pitch. One of the better pitches in The Narrows.

FA: *Tony Wilson, Duane Raleigh 1987*
Gear: quickdraws
2-bolt anchor   *60ft*

15. The Naked Hedge 5.10a R ★★

Pitch 1: Climb the first pitch of *League of Doom*.
Pitch 2: Traverse right on the slab making your way to the obvious dihedral right of *Fantastic Voyage's* second pitch. Continue climbing until you reach a wide crack system that leads to the bolted belay station of *League of Doom*.

Pitch 3: Step right to a (5.9) crack then easier climbing to the top. (See topo).

FA: *Duane Raleigh, Rick Thomas 1980*
Gear: cams to #2 Camalot
2-bolt anchor   *100ft*

16. Munge 5.8

To the right of *The Naked Hedge* is a large flake that curves its way up the wall. From the top of *League of Doom's* first pitch climb the slab out to the right making your way to the right of *The Naked Hedge*. Continue up the crack/flake of *Munge* then easier climbing to the top.

FA: *Chris Mohr, Jack Wurster 1986*
Gear: cams to #2 Camalot
2-bolt anchor   *100ft*

17. Same Reality 5.9 ★★★

Roof crack located to the right of *Space Balls* top out. Excellent roof crack pitch!

FA: *Jon Frank, Jimmy Ratzlaff 1980*
Gear: cams to #4 Camalot
No anchor   *60ft*

Lichen Wall Right

18. Large Corner Girdle 5.6 R ★★

Large corner on the left side of the descent gully. Climb the "Girdle" moving up then left to a large ledge. From here continue on nondescript climbing or exit out to the right taking the line of least resistance to the top.

FA: *Unknown*
Gear: cams to #4 Camalot
No anchor   *100ft*

19. Tra Hex 5.6 ★

Located to the right of *Large Corner Girdle* and before the route *Rage*. Climb a left- angling crack system that leads to a ledge.

FA: *Unknown 1970s*
Gear: cams to #3 Camalot
No anchor   *70ft*

20. Rage 5.13 ★★ A.K.A. Practice Aid Crack

Climbs the slightly overhanging finger crack from a ledge located uphill and left of the decent gully. Climb to a short roof, move right from the roof to gain the finger crack above. Finger locks lead to better jams up higher. On the first ascent this route was climbed free with a point of aid at (5.12a/b A1).

FA: *Duane Raleigh, Bill Thomas 1979*
FFA: *Marcus Garcia 1999*
Gear: small cams to #2.5, stoppers
2-bolt anchor   *70ft*

Rage

Tony Mayse on 3rd Huber Direct 5.11b/c | Photo by Joe Romero

21. Rock Bottom 5.11b ★ Toprope

Climbs the arête right of *Rage*. Climb up the face to a stance just left of the arête; step right on thin face moves to the arête, continue up the face to a short hand crack (5.9) to the top. Named by Bob Scheier who's climbing hit *Rock Bottom* that weekend...

FA: Bob Scheier, Tony Mayse 1995

Gear: #3, #4 cam for the anchor

No anchor   *60–70ft*

22. Fool's Aid 5.7 R ★

Climbs the dihedral immediately right of *Rock Bottom*. This line in the hidden corner has fallen into obscurity over the years. Climb the dihedral to a ledge then a lieback crack to the top.

FA: Unknown 1970s

Gear: TCUs to #2 Camalot

No anchor   *60ft*

RUMPUS WALL

On the same side of the canyon as Window Rock (west) is a gray-colored wall with a couple routes. This wall is pretty easy to spot once you see Window Rock. (See topo).

1. Project Delphi 5.11 Toprope

Located 30 feet left of *Tyro Rumpus*. Climb up through the overhanging rock onto the face and anchors shared with *Tyro Rumpus*.

FA: Chuck Lohn et al. 1990s

Gear: toprope

2-bolt anchor   *120ft*

2. Tyro Rumpus 5.9 R

Climb up the thin crack to a ledge and a bolt above. Continue climbing the face staying left and avoiding rotten sections of rock to a ledge with a 2-bolt anchor. There is a variation start to the right which accepts larger cams.

FA: Chuck Lohn et al. 1990s

Gear: stoppers, cams to #4 Camalot

2-bolt anchor   *120ft*

WINDOW ROCK AREA

From Lichen Wall continue hiking east for a short distance, then, as the trail forms a "Y" go left (north) following the trail for approximately five minutes. Window Rock is just ahead and sits on the west side of the canyon. It's a beautiful tower of rock with yellow lichen and a window near the top. For many years there was only one route on the wall, *Tuberculosis*, established in the mid-70s.

1. Horn of Plenty 5.8 R

A longer face route on the left side of the buttress. Climb sometimes questionable rock.

FA: *Chuck Lohn et al. 1990s*

Gear: cams to #2 Camalot

No anchor   140ft

2. Bone Collector 5.9 R

This climb must be accessed from the top and rappelled in order to get to the base. Located to the right of *Horn of Plenty*. Rappel to the base and climb the face with runouts in between the two bolts.

FA: *Chuck Lohn et al. 1990s*

Gear: cams to #2 Camalot

No anchor   80ft

3. Grave Digger 5.10 R

Same start as *Bone Collector* to the first bolt then move out right to the line of bolts taking you to the top.

FA: *Chuck Lohn et al.1990s*

Gear: cams to #2 Camalot

No anchor   80ft

4. Tuberculosis 5.8

Start on the unprotected face to the right of the dihedral. Climb up the slab then traverse left to gain the crack after the roof. Continue up the crack on loose sections and questionable rock to the window and chimney taking you to the top or step left to solid rock avoiding the chimney section. Descend to the right.

FA: *Ken Rose, Jay Lowell, Kenny Stearns 1974.*

Gear: cams to #4 Camalot, stoppers

No anchor   100ft

5. Afterburner 5.9 R ★★

Same start as *Tuberculosis*. Climb up the face to a crack then move out to the right under a roof and a bolt. Continue up to a ledge with a 2-bolt anchor.

FA: *Chuck Lohn et al. 1990s*

Gear: cams to #2 Camalot

2-bolt anchor   80ft

Forty-Foot Hole Pullout

FORTY-FOOT HOLE

This area is a big attraction for hikers and refuge visitors. There are a handful of climbs and they are worth doing if you don't mind the crowds. To get to the Forty-Foot Hole continue driving past The Narrows parking area to the end of the road. Park here. The trailhead is hard to miss and the approach is relatively short, about 10 minutes from the car. The majority of the climbs face west. A nice area in the summer with morning shade and PM sun. Please be aware, rappelling is a popular past time here. Please remove any duct tape from the top of the cliff. Tape seems to remain in place long after the rappel crowd has left.

1. Bombs Away 5.11b/c★★★

Sport climb with three bolts. This is the best climb at the Forty-Foot Hole area. Steep bullet-hard rock with sustained moves makes this route the one to do! In the early 90s this route had ring angle bolts, now updated with modern hardware. Bring small stoppers or TCUs for the start.

FA: Unknown 1980s

Gear: TCUs, stoppers, quickdraws

No anchor   *60ft*

2. It's a Family Affair 5.12 ★★ Toprope

Located between *Bombs Away* and *Old Dog's New Trick*, this thin face climb goes right up the middle of the aforementioned climbs. Expect 5.11c climbing with little reprieve. No move is harder than 5.11, but due to its sustained nature it's graded harder.

FA: Tony, Aubry Mayse 1991

Gear: toprope

No anchor   *60ft*

3. Old Dog's New Trick 5.7 ★★

The easiest route on the wall. Climb the crack just right of *Family Affair*. Moderate route with good gear opportunities.

FA: Vinny Deangolo 1990s

Gear: cams to #2 Camalot, stoppers

No anchor   *60ft*

John Tarkington climbing Bombs Away 5.11b/c with Sierra Tarkington belaying. | Photo by Tony Mayse

4. New Tricks 5.8 ★ R

Crack climb to the right of *Old Dog's New Trick*. From the polished slab climb up on blocks for 15 feet to a good stance and gear. Work up and left (marginal gear placements) leading to better rock and good gear opportunities higher up. Continue up the crack and to the top on easier climbing joining *Old Dog's New Trick* or climb out to the right (variation) on face holds to a short headwall.

FA: Unknown

Gear: cams to #2 Camalot, stoppers
No anchor   *60ft*

5. Scary Okie 5.10b ★★ RX

Climb the left leaning blocks under the roof just right of *Old Dog's New Trick*. Climb up 15 feet on blocks and good holds to a stance, then continue left on barn-door moves below the roof, exiting on positive holds up and to the right finishing on a ledge.

FA: Jimmy Forester, Ryan Ray 2004

Gear: cams to #2 Camalot, stoppers
No anchor   *60ft*

5a. Okie Dokie 5.11+ Toprope

This variation finish continues left and up onto the short, steep headwall. From the exit moves of *Scary Okie* move left to the obvious holdless stretch of rock leading to the top.

FA: Tony Mayse 2016

Gear: toprope   *30ft*

Forty-Foot Hole: Continuation

The following routes are not on the main wall. The locations are described in the routes description (no topo for these climbs).

Head Banger 5.8 ★★

Crack climb 15 yards downstream and across the creek from *Bombs Away*. There is a fixed pin lower on the wall marking the routes location. This route has 2 fixed pins and a bolt. Rock quality gets better towards the top.

FA: Chuck Lohn et al. 1990s

Gear: cams to #2 Camalot
No anchor   *60ft*

Littlest Mermaid 5.8 ★★

Crack climb located upstream from *Bombs Away*. There is a shallow pool just below, marking the route's location. This route faces the northwest. Climb a thin crack, passing a ledge higher up on the climb.

FA: Chuck Lohn et al. 1990s

Gear: cams to #2 Camalot
No anchor   *60ft*

Wylie Coyote 5.9

Crack climb with one bolt to the left of *Littlest Mermaid*.

FA: Chuck Lohn et al. 1990s

Gear: cams to #2 Camalot
No anchor   *60ft*

"This is the essential thing, simply being away, struggling with a wall in the best way we can, finishing what we started, then looking back and remembering the place and the meaning."

~Tom Higgins

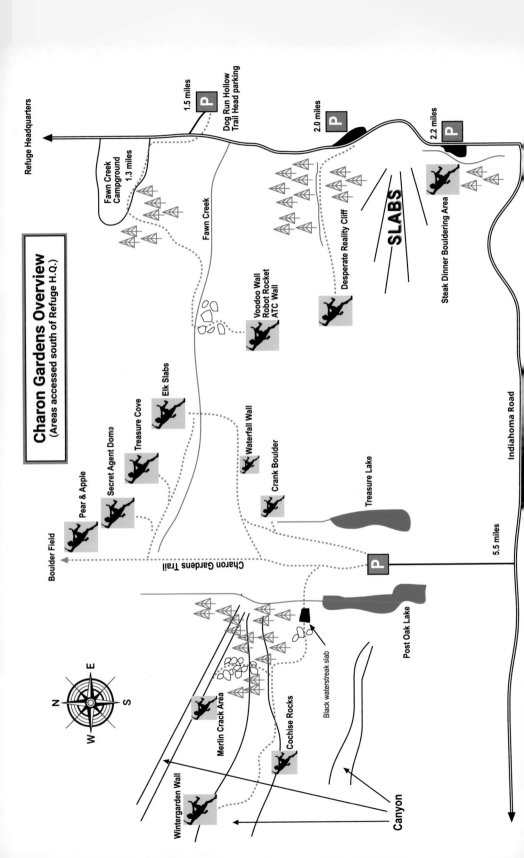

Charon Gardens Overview
(Areas accessed south of Refuge H.Q.)

Refuge Headquarters

1.5 miles
Dog Run Hollow
Trail Head parking

Fawn Creek
Campground
1.3 miles

Fawn Creek

2.0 miles

Desperate Reality Cliff

SLABS

2.2 miles

Steak Dinner Bouldering Area

Voodoo Wall
Robot Rocket
ATC Wall

Elk Slabs

Treasure Cove

Secret Agent Dome

Pear & Apple

Boulder Field

Waterfall Wall

Crank Boulder

Treasure Lake

Charon Gardens Trail

Post Oak Lake

Black waterstreak slab

Merlin Crack Area

Cochise Rocks

Wintergarden Wall

Canyon

Indiahoma Road

5.5 miles

N
W   E
S

Dog Run Hollow Trailhead Parking View
(view looking west)

Voodoo Wall

VOODOO WALL

Voodoo Wall is to the north and west of Desperate Reality Cliff, but has a different approach. This area has three separate walls: Voodoo Wall, Robot Rocket, and ATC Wall, all in close proximity to each other. Once you find Voodoo Wall all other formations will be easy to find, they are within 5-10 minutes of each other. All routes in this area are bolt-protected with the occasional extra piece of gear in between bolts. A light rack and quickdraws should suffice for routes described here. The cliffs face southeast, south, and west; they are a good winter destination or early summer climbing areas.

Approach time: 30-40 minutes

Exit Hwy 49 driving south past the refuge headquarters on Indiahoma road. At 1.5 miles, Dog Run Hollow Trailhead parking will be on your left (east); park here. From this parking area the Voodoo Wall can be seen to your west (see overview photo). Mount Lincoln is the largest and furthest formation as you are looking west. Voodoo Wall is in the small canyon just east of Mount Lincoln (do not hike to Mount Lincoln, it is mentioned as reference only). Leave your car parked at Dog Run Hollow Trailhead parking.

From the parking area, walk back out to the main road and turn right (north), walk 0.2 miles to the Fawn Creek Youth Campground. The gate will be closed as it is for reservation-only camping. Walk down the gravel road staying left. Continue walking past the restrooms, keep walking west. The road will turn north (right), but do not follow it around, instead stay left, going towards the last campsite on your left. Pick up the trail behind the last campsite on your left. Follow the trail south, which then turns west into the field. Continuing west, the trail leads towards trees alongside a creek. Follow this for a short ways and look for cairns on your left marking the spot to cross the creek.

Walk alongside the creek for approximately ten minutes before heading up the slabs to your left (south). The slabs will take you out of the gully. Voodoo Wall will be visible from the top of the south side of this gully.

Approach breakdown: Drive to Dog Run Hollow Trailhead parking, park here.

Walk to the main road you drove in on, turn right towards Fawn Creek Youth Campground on your left. Walk past the closed gate on the gravel road until the road turns, pick up the trail behind last campsite on your left.

Follow trail through the open field eventually turning towards trees. Continue until the trail takes you to a creek crossing.

Cross the creek and continue west following the creek up the gully (west) for approximately 10 minutes. Don't worry if you feel like you've gone too far or not far enough...

Make your way up the slabs on your left (south), Voodoo Wall will be in your line of sight.

Look for cairns.

Hike time from your vehicle is 30-40 minutes.

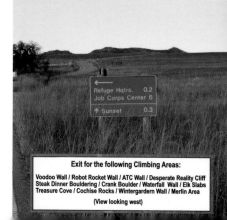

Exit for the following Climbing Areas:

Voodoo Wall / Robot Rocket Wall / ATC Wall / Desperate Reality Cliff
Steak Dinner Bouldering / Crank Boulder / Waterfall Wall / Elk Slabs
Treasure Cove / Cochise Rocks / Wintergardern Wall / Merlin Area

(View looking west)

Voodoo Wall

DO NOT
BLOCK
GATE

Fawn Creek Youth Campground
Approach for Voodoo Wall/Robot Rocket/ATC Wall
1. Walk to end of gravel road staying left.
2. Follow trail behind last campsite heading SW.

1. Unknown Voodoo 5.6 ★

There are two crack climbs on the far left side of the Voodoo Wall. They are both about the same in difficulty.

FA: *Chuck Lohn et al.* 1990s

Gear: cams to #3 Camalot

2-bolt anchor   50ft

2. Bodi Voodoo 5.7 R ★★

The first bolted line next to the *Unknown Voodoo* cracks. Moderate face climbing on the Voodoo Wall.

FA: *Chuck Lohn et al.* 1990s

Gear: quickdraws

2-bolt anchor   50ft

3. Deep Voodoo 5.10b R ★★★

This route is just right of *Bodi Voodoo*. Follow the line of bolts to the top. It is possible to clip the first bolt off the ledge which protects a more direct start.

FA: *Chuck Lohn et al.* 1990s

Gear: quickdraws

2-bolt anchor   50ft

4. Voodoo Child 5.9 R ★★★

Face climb up and over the large flakes to the right of *Deep Voodoo*. Marginal gear placements behind flakes.

FA: *Chuck Lohn et al.* 1990s

Gear: quickdraws

2-bolt anchor   50ft

Robot Rocket Wall

ROBOT ROCKET WALL

Robot Rocket Wall has historical significance. It is the site of an airplane crash. On November 30, 1968, George C. Boyd and his wife Anna, were onboard a Cessna B310 with the tail number N3603D. They were en route to Las Vegas, Nevada for an aviation convention when they encountered poor weather conditions. The aircraft went missing but was not discovered for two days.

There are still aircraft parts strewn around the Robot Rocket Wall area from this accident. Please do not disturb these artifacts out of respect to George and Anna Boyd who lost their lives here.

Robot Rocket Wall is located just to the south of Voodoo Wall. The wall has two bolted routes on a steep south-facing wall. Although the routes are short they are outstanding climbs on solid rock.

Approach: As you face the Voodoo Wall, Robot Rocket Wall is approximately 100 yards to the south and just slightly east. The easiest way to get to this hidden wall is to walk east and around the large boulders that sit just east of Voodoo Wall. From here walk to the south then go up and right (west) to where you will see Robot Rocket Wall. This is a 2-3 minute approach from Voodoo Wall.

1. Spaceman Spiff 5.10 R ★★★
The left route. Climb up the crack. A hand-size cam protects moves getting to the first bolt and finger-size cams before the second bolt.
FA: Chuck Lohn et al. 1990s
Gear: cams to #2 Camalot, quickdraws
2-bolt anchor   40ft

2. Crash Landing 5.10 ★★★★
Bolted route to the right of *Spaceman Spiff*. Climb up the dike with incut steps; continue up to the flake and second bolt leading to a rap-station.
The climbing is reminiscent of a Joshua Tree classic named *Pinched Rib*.
FA: Chuck Lohn et al. 1990s
Gear: quickdraws
2-bolt anchor   40ft

The site from the November 30, 1968 small aircraft crash. Wreckage can still be found throughout the area. | Photo by Tony Mayse

ATC WALL

ATC Wall has 2 bolt-protected routes on a west-facing wall. The wall is approximately 100 yards to the south and west of Robot Rocket Wall.

Approach: Walk south from Robot Rocket Wall about 100 yards down the slabs and then cross the gully heading to the west. After crossing the gully hike uphill towards a large boulder. This boulder has two rap-rings; this is the top of ATC Wall. An easy rappel gets you to the base. A 60-meter rope will be sufficient for these two climbs. You can also scramble down to the base just right (north) of the rap station.

1. Horizontal Hop 5.9

To the left and up in the gully from the base of *A Trivial Contrivance*. Climb up past four horizontal cracks that lead to a bolt-protected face. Shares the anchor with *A Trivial Contrivance*.

FA: *Chuck Lohn et al. 1990s*
Gear: cams #1–#3 Camalot, quickdraws
2-bolt anchor   *50ft*

2. A Trivial Contrivance 5.9

Face climb up the slab protected by a line of bolts, leading to a rap station. This route is actually more of a traverse that leads up a left-sweeping slab of granite. It is possible to place gear before the first bolt minimizing the runout.

FA: *Chuck Lohn et al. 1990s*
Gear: cams to #2 Camalot, quickdraws
2-bolt anchor   *110ft*

DESPERATE REALITY CLIFF

Desperate Reality is a 25-foot horizontal roof crack, which sits on top of the cliff and can be seen from the road. To reach the area drive in from Indiahoma Road, go 2.0 miles past the refuge headquarters and park at the paved pullout on the east side of the road. Walk back north 50 yards on the road, then pick up the faint trail on your left (west) that winds its way through the trees (if you get off-trail just follow the stream west towards the rock formations). Follow the trail until you reach the huge slabs, continue southwest eventually making your way over a seasonal creek; the cliff will be visible to your west. There are several cairns marking the way to the cliff.

Approach: 20-25 minutes

Climbs #1 through #6 are located behind and to the left (south) about 60 yards from *Desperate Reality*. To get to them, walk up to *Desperate Reality's* roof and continue walking into the narrow corridor turning to the left. Follow this to a grassy slope. From here walk downhill and look to your right (west). This gray wall holds climbs 1–6, starting with *Slab Route*, which begins at a small ledge down hill.

ATC Wall

Desperate Reality Cliff

Desperate Reality Pullout

Desperate Reality Area parking
(view looking north)

Desperate Reality Cliff
(view from Indiahoma Road)

1. Slab Route 5.9 ★
Located 10 feet down and to the left of *Fist Fighter* is a short slab with two bolts. Climb the slab up to a ledge then continue in the crack to the top of Desperate Realty Cliff.

FA: Unknown

Gear: cams to #3 Camalot

No anchor   70ft

2. Fist Fighter 5.11+ ★★★
Located just a few feet to the left of *The Warm-Up*. Climb a vertical five-inch lieback crack up to a short roof with a bolt out to the right. There used to be an old pin in a hole protecting the crux face moves; it was replaced with modern hardware. Continue up the wide crack on fist jams to a ledge up and to the right ending at an anchor. Comparable to wrestling a gorilla!

FA: Unknown 1980s

Gear: cams #1 to #4 Camalot

2-bolt anchor   65ft

3. The Warm-Up 5.11- ★★★
Located just to the right of *Fist Fighter*. The route climbs a large, arrowhead-shaped rock with a balcony at its base. Steep face climbing protected by four bolts ending at a ledge.

FA: Tony Mayse 2003

Gear: quickdraws

2-bolt anchor   60ft

4. Rope-a-Dope 5.11b ★★ Toprope
Located 8 feet right of *The Warm-Up*. Bouldery start leads to more positive climbing, moving onto the arête after the flake at the top. Shares the same anchors as *The Warm-Up*.

FA: Tony & Buster Mayse 2017

Gear: toprope

2-bolt anchor   55ft.

The "Czech Machine" Stanley Vrba on one of the hardest cracks in the Wichitas, Desperate Reality 5.12b. | Photo by Tony Mayse

5. Fight Club 5.10c ★★

Located about 50 feet right of *The Warm-Up* is a block ledge leading to a black water streak and wavy hand crack above. There is one (hard to spot) bolt on this route.

FA: *Chris Banks, Steven Charles 2010*

Gear: finger-size cams up to #2 Camalot
No anchor   *50ft*

6. Black Crack 5.10 ★★

Located approximately 100 feet to the right of *The Warm-Up*. Make your way up a high-angle ramp traversing right, then up and left (a #2 Camalot will protect the traverse). Climb broken rock down low leading to more solid rock up higher.

FA: *Eric Forney, Mike Hankins 2005*

Gear: finger-size cams up to (2) #3, (2) #4 Camalots
No anchor   *60ft*

7. Desperate Reality 5.12b ★★★★

Twenty-five foot roof crack. Begin in the corner below the roof. Wide hands (#4 Camalot) gets you started. From here climb out the roof on good hand jams which turns to thin hands to a short section of fingers before moving out to the lip of the roof to better jams. Yosemite Valley has a world-famous roof crack named *Separate Reality*, not as hard as *Desperate Reality*.

FA: *Jon Frank, Duane Raleigh Jan. 23, 1981*

Gear: (2) #1, (2) #2, (2) #3, (1) #4 Camalots
2-bolt anchor   *30ft*

8. Hand Crack 5.9 ★★

Located behind and to the right of *Desperate Reality*. Short crack, starting on a shelf and ending at a large ledge.

FA: *Unknown*

Gear: cams to #2 Camalot
No anchor   *20ft*

"Learn to jam, learn to bleed, learn to hand over the lead."

~Rex Pieper

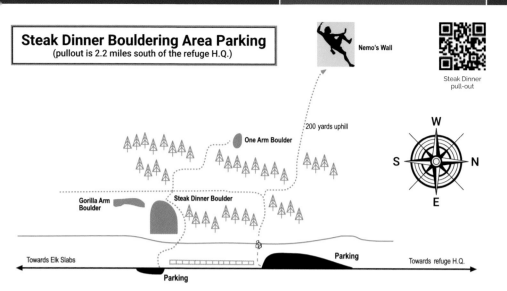

STEAK DINNER BOULDERING AREA

Steak Dinner Area has historical significance to Oklahoma climbing, namely the Wichita Mountains Wildlife Refuge. This area is located just down the road from Desperate Reality parking area and the Bat Cave (a large hole in the rock visible from the road as you head south from the Desperate Reality pullout). Steak Dinner Area has several fun boulder problems and is a good spot to hit at the end of the climbing day or if you're short on time. The approach takes about a minute from your car. The main boulder which is the namesake to this area is Steak Dinner. This is the largest and hardest of the boulder problems. *Steak Dinner* is the *Midnight Lightning* of the Wichita Mountains. *Midnight Lightning* is a world-famous boulder problem found in the Camp IV campground in Yosemite Valley, California.

The story behind the Steak Dinner Boulder is that Duane Raleigh was promised a steak dinner if he could climb it. The rest is history. This problem is about 20-feet tall and an intimidating prospect, even today with sticky-rubber shoes and crash pads. Back in the early days of climbing these highball problems were climbed sans crash pads, just a good spot and encouragement from your buddy. Steak Dinner Boulder has several problems: *Rat Crack*, *IF* and *Sticky Fingers* to name a few. Just a few yards over is the One Arm Boulder and uphill from there is a short south-facing wall named Nemo's Wall. This wall has a couple easy lines and a highball problem named *Nemo's Seam* which climbs a vertical water streak with a thin seam up the middle. All these lines were established in the late 70s and early 80s. The area still has lots of potential to climbers who are motivated to explore.

STEAK DINNER BOULDER

Approach: Drive west on Hwy 49, turn south toward the refuge Headquarters. Continue on Indiahoma Road for 2.1 miles from the turn-off from Hwy 49. At 2.1 miles you will come to a pullout on the right (west) side of the road, park here. Walk towards the guardrail and then pick up the faint trail just in front of it, continue walking to the west. Walk 50 yards on this trail, passing a creek. When the trail splits, walk left (south) for 34 yards, here you will find Steak Dinner Boulder, just off the trail.

Approach time: 1–2 minutes

Steak Dinner Boulder has several problems. The classic problem for this well known boulder is the boulders namesake, *Steak Dinner*.

1. Rat Crack 5.10 ★★★

Slighlty overhanging hand crack located on the north side. Finger locks, crimps, and sidepulls on polished rock for 13 feet lead to the hand crack above.

FA: Bill Thomas 1978

2. IF 5.10 ★★

Climb the arête 10 feet to right of *Rat Crack* (and a few feet to the left of the *Steak Dinner* problem) using both sides of the corner. Strenuous climbing leads to a mantel at the top. IF means, "If you can get to that hold..."

FA: Duane Raleigh 1979

3. Sticky Fingers 5.12 ★★★

Just a few feet to the right of *IF* and to the left of *Steak Dinner*. Begin on knobs and make your way up the steep, thin face.

FA: Duane Raleigh 1979

Preston Pettigrew on Steak Dinner 5.12. | Photo by Molly Hennesy

"A very high step for both the body and the mind."

~ *Southern Exposure*

4. Steak Dinner 5.12 ★★★★

Climb the middle of the boulder with the obvious cresent-shaped hold about 4 feet above ground level. Continue up on smears and small edges to the top. Committing propostion.

FA: Duane Raleigh 1979

5. The Hole 5.10 ★★

Located on the southwest side of Steak Dinner Boulder. Jump (or static move) to the obvious hole. Continue up on bullet-hard, polished rock to the top.

FA: Duane Raleigh 1979

GORILLA ARM BOULDER

The obvious boulder with a wavy lip, located just to the right a few yards from the base of Steak Dinner Boulder.

1. Gorilla Arm Traverse 5.8

Traverse the lip and mantel over the top once you reach the end.

FA: Jay Lowell 1979

ONE ARM BOULDER

Approach: From Steak Dinner Boulder, walk out to the main trail and look towards the northwest. One Arm Boulder is 50 yards away, nestled in the trees with a good trail leading to it.

1. Toe Hole 5.10
Start in the obvious hole to the left of *One Arm Route*. Step up and continue on edges to the top.
FA: *Duane Raleigh* 1979

2. One Arm Route 5.10
Dyno for a jug left of *The Pocket*, mantel to the top.
FA: *Duane Raleigh* 1979

3. The Pocket 5.8
Dyno to a pocket and finish over the top with a mantel. Located to the left of *Heel Hook*.
FA: *Bill Thomas* 1978

4. Heel Hook 5.9
Located to the left of *South Face*. Heel hook then traverse left and up to top out. No photo.
FA: *Bill Thomas* 1979

5. South Face 5.9
Climb up to a horizontal hold on crystals. Can also be done wth a dyno. Not pictured.
FA: *Bill Thomas* 1978

NEMO'S WALL

Approach: Cross the creek as if you were heading to Steak Dinner Boulder. Where trail splits, turn to the right (north), walk six yards and pick up the faint trail which angles towards the northwest. Nemo's Wall sits high above the boulder field and faces south. It is easily recognized by the dark water streak. The problems are 15-20 feet high.

1. Left Side 5.9 ★
Climb the face just to the left of the dark water streak of *Nemo's Seam*. A good warm-up.
FA: *Duane Raleigh* 1979

2. Nemo's Seam 5.11 ★★★
Climb up the dark water streak with the seam cutting up the middle. Best problem on the wall.
FA: *Nemo* 1978

3. Right Side 5.8
To the right of *Nemo's Seam*. Climb the crack to the top.
FA: *Bill Thomas* 1978

One Arm Boulder   Nemo's Wall

John Tarkington on Nemo's Seam 5.11. | Photo by Sierra Tarkington

Secret Agent Dome

The Treasure Cove

Elk Slabs

Wintergarden Wall

Elk Slabs / Treasure Cove

Parking for the following climbing areas:
Crank Boulder/Water Fall Wall/Elk Slabs/Treasure Cove/Secret Agent Dome/Pear & Apple/Tiny Bubbles/Cochise Rocks/Wintergarden Wall/Merlin Crack Area

COCHISE ROCKS

See the approach for Wintergarden Wall. Cochise Rocks are large boulders up and to your left (south) as you make your way into the canyon. Cochise Rocks sit up on a hill, and face to the north and are located just east and south of Wintergarden Wall. You will pass these large rocks on your way towards Wintergarden Wall. The routes are located on the north and the east face with six climbs ranging from 5.9–5.11.

To descend, walk off to the east from the top.

Treasure Lake
Post Oak Lake
Trail Head
→

Cochise Rocks (East Face)

1. Naiche 5.11 ★★ Toprope
Face climb to a right-angling finger crack leading to the top. Downclimb to the south from the top, then scramble down the gully (east) back to the large ledge at the base. (Bring #4 Camalots for the anchor).
FA: Chuck Lohn et al. 1990s
Gear: toprope
No anchor   50ft

2. Geronimo 5.10b ★★★
Face climb to the right of *Naiche*. Start from the ledge and climb to a large flake with a stance. Step left onto the face, protected by two bolts, trending left to the top. (Bring #4 Camalots for the anchor).
FA: Chuck Lohn et al. 1990s
Gear: #1, #2 Camalots, quickdraws
No anchor   50ft

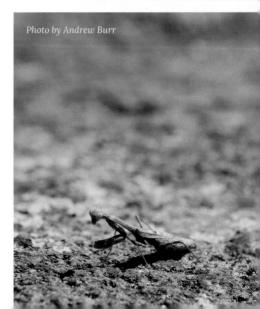

Photo by Andrew Burr

3. Devoured Cultures of America 5.9 ★★

Start in the offwidth back in the cave. Walk back 20 feet into the cave. Walk up a narrow corridor to your left and enter the offwidth crack. Climb up 15 feet, then past two diagonal cracks lèading to the top. Step over the gap at the top. Belay off to the east at the same belay as *Geronimo*. (Bring #4 Camalots for the anchor).

FA: *Chuck Lohn et al. 1990s*

Gear: fingers to hand-size cams

No anchor   *50ft*

4. Bows and Arrows 5.9 ★ Toprope

Climb the wide crack from the front of the formation. (Bring #4 Camalots for the anchor).

FA: *Chuck Lohn et al. 1990s*

Gear: toprope

No anchor   *50ft*

5. Eagle Spirit 5.10c ★★ Toprope

Jump from the boulder opposite of the climb to get onto the route, then follow a featured face along the diagonal finger crack to the top.

FA: *Chuck Lohn et al. 1990s*

5.11 Varaiaton Start: Boulder up the overhang from the ground to get established on top of the stance.

Gear: toprope

No anchor   *50ft*

6. Great White Buffalo 5.10d/A2 ★

Roof crack leads to a chimney higher up.

FA: *Chuck Lohn et al. 1990s*

Gear: wide gear

No anchor   *50ft*

Black water streaks

Wintergarden/Merlin Crack Area Approach:

1. From the parking area hike north on a well marked trail for 300-yards.
2. Walk west and downhill on a faint trail for approx. 100 yards.
3. Cross the creek and continue west uphill on the black water-streaked slabs.
4. Hike 10 minutes northwest towards the next canyon.
5. Follow this canyon west for 25 minutes towards **Wintergarden Wall.**
6. For **Merlin Area**, continue north towards the next canyon. Cross the gully with trees and boulder, then continue heading uphill towards the next canyon.

Wintergarden Wall

WINTERGARDEN WALL

Wintergarden Wall is reached from parking at the Post Oak Falls. The climbing area is located northwest of the parking and requires a lengthy approach.

The majority of the climbs are moderate crack climbs from 5.6–5.9 and there are three bolted climbs 5.10–5.11. There are 15 routes for this area ranging in height from 60–70 feet. The crag faces southwest which makes for a good winter destination in the afternoon and a morning climbing area in the summer months.

Approach: From the Post Oak Falls parking area walk north on the left trail for 300 yards. After that, pick up a faint trail that heads left (west) taking you downhill to the creek that feeds into Post Oak Lake.

Cross the creek and look for a slab with black water streaks on the west side of the hill. Head uphill on the black water streaked slabs for about 100 yards. Once on top of the slabs start walking to the right (north) and angling to the west for 10–15 minutes following cairns on a backcounrty trail (this is a grassy animal trail).

When you reach the canyon with large boulders down below in the creek, start heading to the west staying about mid-height on the south side of the canyon as you follow the trail west (do not drop down into the canyon by the creek).

Staying mid-height on the south side of the canyon, follow the trailheading west for about

20–25 minutes until the end of the canyon is reached. Wintergarden Wall will be visible to the right (northwest) as you drop down towards the end of the canyon. Cross the boulders down low making your way to the base Wintergarden Wall (see approach overview photo).

Approach time: 45–60 minutes

WEST WALL

West Wall is down and to the left of the Main Wall and is accessed by scrambling below the Main Wall's west side. Downclimb ledges, making your way to the ground by a tree. West Wall has a chimney just opposite of the climbing side. Some routes start off by stemming the chimney.

This wall has 4 routes 5.7–5.8. These routes are crack climbs that top out on the boulders north and west of Wintergarden Main Wall. There are no anchors on top. To descend West Wall, scramble down the boulders north and to the east to reach the Main Wall and the other routes.

1. Soul of the Heartland 5.8 R ★

Crack climb. Start by stemming the chimney for approximately 25 feet. Step over onto the wall with face climbing before reaching a finger/handcrack that angles up and to the left up higher. Continue on easier climbing to the top.

FA: *Chuck Lohn et al. 1990s*

Gear: .5 to hand-size cams

No anchor   *75ft*

WINTERGARDEN WALL (EAST)

Just left of the Main Wall with a chimney at the walls base. This 40-foot east-facing high wall has 2 routes.

5. Dragon Back 5.6

Start on the south end making your way up a crack which weaves its way to a large block forming a ledge up higher. A short section of face climbing leads to the top.

FA: *Chuck Lohn et al. 1990s*

Gear: .5 to hand-size cams

No anchor   40ft

6. Z System 5.8 ★

Located to the right of *Dragon Back*. Start down low in a short section of chimney climbing to gain the wall with a crack that forms the letter "Z." Follow this finger-size crack to the same ledge as *Dragon Back* with few face climbing moves to the top.

FA: *Chuck Lohn et al. 1990s*

Gear: .5 to hand-size cams

No anchor   40ft

"We choose to believe that the granite is alive. If life is movement, then rock—with its atoms flying around like stars in cosmos—is alive."

~Yvon Chouinard

2. Iconolast 5.8 R ★

Located to the right of *Soul of the Heartland*. Start by stemming up the chimney for 15 feet and then stepping across to a prominent stance making your way up to 2 small ledges opposite of each other. Continue up the crack that angles up and left leading to the top.

FA: *Chuck Lohn et al. 1990s*

Gear: .5 to hand-size cams

No anchor   65ft

3. Trickster Coyote 5.7 R

Located right of *Iconolast*. Climb up a small overhang and a black water streak with a crack.

FA: *Chuck Lohn et al. 1990s*

Gear: .5 to hand-size cams

No anchor   65ft

4. Changeling 5.7 R

Located 5 feet to the right of *Trickster Coyote*. This climb starts by a tree with branches touching the lower part of the climb. Move up starting on stacked rocks to a black water streak with a hand crack. Follow the hand crack to the top.

FA: *Chuck Lohn et al. 1990s*

Gear: .5 to hand-size cams

No anchor   65ft

start down low

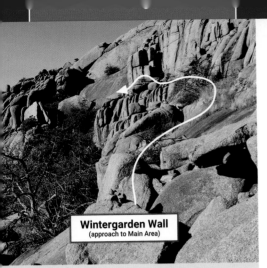

Wintergarden Wall
(approach to Main Area)

WINTERGARDEN MAIN WALL

This is the main area for the Wintergarden climbing. There are 9 routes listed from 5.6–5.11.

7. Bitchin' Piranha 5.10d ★★

Bolt-protected face climb starting on the slab to the right of *Z System*. Climb an easy slab for 30 feet to a sloping ledge. Follow the line of bolts with good edges on a short but steep face making your way to a ledge at the top.

FA: *Chuck Lohn et al. 1990s*
Gear: quickdraws & .5 to #2 for the anchor
No anchor   60ft

8. Falcon Nebula 5.10b ★★

Located 15 feet to the right of *Bitchin' Piranha*. Climb up an easy slab to a sloping ledge with two bolts on a short wall above.

FA: *Chuck Lohn et al. 1990s*
Gear: quickdraws, cams to #2 Camalot
No anchor   60ft

9. Falcon's Arbor 5.7 ★★

Crack climb just to the right of *Falcon Nebula* ending at the same ledge. Climb the corner to the right of *Falcon Nebula* leading to a tree with a finger crack above it that angles up and to the left ending at a ledge.

FA: *Chuck Lohn et al. 1990s*
Gear: cams to #2 Camalot
No anchor   60ft

10. Quality Crack 5.8 ★★

Located to the right of *Falcon's Arbor* on a yellow lichen-colored wall with a vertical hand crack.

FA: *Chuck Lohn et al. 1990s*
Gear: cams to #2.5 Camalot
No anchor   35ft

11. Grunge 5.6 R

To the right and around the corner from *Quality Crack*, is a large chockstone in a chimney to the left. *Grunge* starts a few feet to the right of this block. Climb up a gray-colored crack with loose sections of rock.

FA: *Chuck Lohn et al. 1990s*
Gear: fingers to hand-size cams
No anchor   50ft

12. Ben Sails the Severn 5.9 R

Just to the right of *Grunge*. Face climb up to a seam. Continue in a finger to hand-size crack leading to easier climbing at the top.

FA: *Chuck Lohn et al. 1990s*
Gear: .5 to hand-size cams
No anchor   50ft

Merlin Area

Merlin Crack Area Approach:
Cross the creek and follow the gully uphill towards the next canyon and **Merlin Crack Area.**

Winter Garden Wall Approach:
Hike west for 20-25 min. staying in the middle of this canyon—towards **Wintergarden Wall.**

13. Solar Flexes 5.9 ★

Located 5 feet to the right of *Ben Sails the Severn.* A block at the routes base marks the start. Climb fingers to fist crack leading to easier face climbing up higher.

FA: Chuck Lohn et al. 1990s

Gear: .5 to hand-size cams

No anchor   *50ft*

14. Hotrod Corner 5.11a ★★★

The hardest route at Wintergarden Wall. Located 5 feet to the right of *Solar Flexes.* Climb up the thin seam proteced by 3 bolts leading to a 2-bolt anchor.

FA: Chuck Lohn et al. 1990s

Gear: quickdraws

2-bolt anchor   *50ft*

15. Thor Crack 5.6

Climbs the easy crack to the right of *Hotrod Corner.* Climb up the corner with a short wide section up higher. Shares the anchor with *Hotrod Corner.*

FA: Chuck Lohn et al. 1990s

Gear: cams to #3 Camalot

2-bolt anchor   *50ft*

Merlin Crack
Area

MERLIN CRACK AREA

To reach Merlin Crack area see photo for Wintergarden Wall approach.

When you reach the canyon that takes you towards Wintergarden Wall, drop down into the canyon heading north (going west leads towards Wintergarden Wall).

Walk down the slabs heading north. Cross the creek, passing trees and boulders then head back up a gully on an animal trail which weaves its way between boulders.

Make your way to the top of the next canyon. Drop down the slabs and skirt the middle of the south side of this canyon. At this point look for a large roof that is close to a slab with a large boulder at its base.

1. Archie 5.6

Short crack climb just left of *Nimue.* Stay in the left crack to the top. Not pictured.

FA: Preston Pettirgrew 2015

Gear: cams to #2 Camalot

No anchor   *25ft*

2. Nimue 5.8+

Located left of *Merlin.* Corner crack climb. (no photo)

FA: Anthony Johnson 2015

Gear: TCUs and larger cams for the top

No anchor   *35ft*

Chase Webb climbing Merlin 5.13. | Photo by Anthony Johnson

WICHITA RUSH WALL A.K.A. SORCERER'S WALL

Directly across the canyon from *Merlin* is an obvious east-facing wall with a steep face leading to a thin crack. This wall has 4 climbs from 5.8–5.12b. Walk off to the right.

1. Gauntlet Runner 5.8 ★
Crack climb left of *Straphanger*.
FA: *Marucs Garcia, Jimmy Forester 1999*
Gear: cams to #2 Camalot
No anchor   60ft

2. Straphanger 5.10b ★★
Crack climb just to the left of *Wichita Rush Direct*. Start on *Gauntlet Runner* and then traversing into *Straphanger* halfway up *Gauntlet Runner* leading to the top.
FA: *Marucs Garcia, Jimmy Forester 1999*
Gear: cams to #2 Camalot
No anchor   70ft

3. Wichita Rush 5.11 ★★
A traversing climb starting on *Gauntlet Runner*. Climb *Gauntlet Runner* then traverse over to *Straphanger*, then traversing into *Wichita Rush* from about mid-height on *Straphanger*.
FA: *Marucs Garcia, Jimmy Forester 1999*
Gear: cams to #2 Camalot
No anchor   70ft

4. Wichita Rush Direct 5.12b Toprope ★★
Starting from a ledge, climb the steep face for 20 feet leading to a fingers-to-hand crack ending on top of the pillar. Currently a toprope climb.
FA: *Marucs Garcia, Jimmy Forester 1999*
Gear: toprope
No anchor   70ft

3. Merlin 5.13 ★★★
20-foot fist crack. This roof crack sits low to the ground next to a boulder and faces to the north. Climb a short slab to gain the roof. Climb out the roof on hands to fist, getting wider as you move towards the lip and up the vertical crack to the top.
FA: *Marcus Garcia*
Gear: cams to #5 Camalot
No anchor   25ft

4. The Wizard's Apprentice 5.10+
Roof crack located to the right of *Merlin*. No photo.
FA: *Anthony Johnson 2015*
Gear: TCUs and larger cams for the top
No anchor   35ft

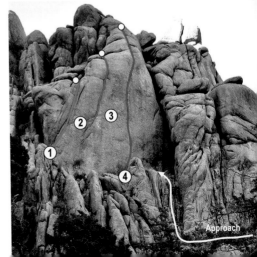

Elk Slabs

CRANK BOULDER

Crank Boulder is about a 15 minute walk from the parking area and offers some short climbs about 40 feet in length that are on a west-facing boulder. There are few lead climbs, this area is best for setting up topropes.

Approach: Follow the trail northeast from Post Oak Falls parking area. Make your way down to the stream bed. As you continue along the creek heading northeast. Crank Boulder is on your right side and is marked by the prominent water streaks on the face.

1. Nowhere 5.10+ ★★★ Toprope

This is the first climb on the wall, on the leftmost water streak. Climb the crack, which turns into face climbing towards the top.

FA: *Steve Gillam 1980s*
Gear: toprope
No anchor   40ft

2. Bodacious 5.9 R ★★

Hand crack located about 10 feet to the right of *Nowhere*.

FA: *Bill Ward, Jack Wurster 1986*
Gear: wires, small cams to #2 Camalot
No anchor   40ft

3. Give the Glory to God 5.11 ★★★ Toprope

Located a few feet right of *Bodacious*. Climb the face past the wavy flakes to easier climbing above.

FA: *Jon Frank 1986*
Gear: toprope
No anchor   40ft

4. The Water Faucet 5.7 ★

Climb the wide crack/gully to the right of *Give the Glory to God*.

FA: *Laura Vaughn, Bill Ward 1986*
Gear: wires, cams to #3 Camalot
No anchor   40ft

5. Strappado 5.8+ ★★

Climbs the hand crack to the right of *The Water Faucet*. Definition: a form of torture in which the victim is lifted off the ground by a rope attached to the wrists, which have been tied behind the back, and then is dropped partway to the ground with a jerk.

FA: *Jon Frank, Bill Ward, Jack Wurster 1986*
Gear: wires, cams to #3 Camalot
No anchor   40ft

Crank Boulder

Elk Slabs

① ②

Trisha Keuper Ray on Post Oak Falls. | Photo by Ryan Ray

Waterfall Wall

WATERFALL WALL

From Crank Boulder continue following the creek northeast. Waterfall Wall is on the right side of Post Oak Falls. Waterfall Wall faces north.

Approach time: (from Crank Boulder): 8–10 minutes.

On the right, as you look towards Post Oak Falls, is a black wall with two routes. Summer season this area is usually dry. In the winter months the falls can be frozen allowing for ice climbing up the falls. It is really special to catch this place in such conditions! Post Oak Falls Route WI 4 RX has been led, but can easily be toproped. The area remains shaded from the sun, which makes it a perfect spot to break out the ice tools during cold winter days.

1. Look Ma No Chalk 5.9 ★★ Toprope

Face climb to the left of the dihedral. Climb the face to a short roof followed by a crack, then finish on face climbing to the top.

FA: Jon Frank, Bill Ward, Jack Wurster 1986

Gear: toprope

No anchor   50ft

2. Pipe Wrench 5.10a ★★

Face and crack climb to the right of *Look Ma No Chalk.*

FA: Bill Ward, Jack Wurster 1986

Gear: small cams

No anchor   50ft

ELK MOUNTAIN A.K.A. ELK SLABS

The birthplace of Oklahoma climbing. This huge monolith can be seen from a great distance. The climbing routes at this historical area are well worth the hike. Most of the climbing is on low-angle rock with the exception of a few routes like *The Eliminator, Big Leap,* and *Buns Up.* A single set of cams and quickdraws should suffice for most routes.

After reviewing the original route information from older guidebooks, some of the routes have been restored to their original descriptions in both the topo and text. I have used some of the original route descriptions from *Southern Exposure* on these forgotten climbs. It is worth noting that they were written in such a way that re-describing these old gems would be an insult to the climbs.

Directions: To reach the Elk Mountain climbing area turn off Hwy 49 onto Indiahoma Road towards the Refuge Headquarters. Continue on Indiahoma Road to Treasure Lake turning right on Post Oak Lake Road (when you reach the Youth Camp turn north). Drive to the end of the road to the parking area. Elk Slabs can be seen from here. The distance from Hwy 49 to the parking area is about 5.5 miles.

From the trailhead, walk past the Phillip Mitchell Memorial plaque, heading northeast on the well-marked trail. Hike towards Crank Boulder then continue on the trail towards Waterfall Wall, heading northeast. Continue hiking over the ridge above Waterfall Wall following the trail east, it will turn to the north towards Elk Slabs. The descent from the routes on Elk Slabs can be made from the 2-bolt anchor station at the end of *Water Streak,* which requires two ropes, or by walking down the gully on the west side of the slab.

Approach time: 30 minutes

1. Dominator A2 ★

Thin aid seam to the immediate left of *The Eliminator*. Bring small gear and a standard aid rack. There is one bolt on this route.

FA: *Unknown 1990s*

Gear: aid rack

No anchor   40ft

2. The Eliminator 5.10c ★★★

Originally named Boulder Crack and rated 5.9 in *Southern Exposure*. Slightly overhanging crack climb. This climb starts on a huge boulder 100 feet to the left of *Water Streak*. Hand jam and layback your way up the crack turning the lip to a 2-bolt anchor. This route is short but feels longer due to its strenuous nature.

FA: *Greg Schooley 1976*

Gear: cams to #3 Camalot

2-bolt anchor   40ft

Elk Mountain   Elk Mountain
Parking

* *Southern exposure.*

3. JR 5.9 X ★★

Face climb starting up and to the left of *Buttress Route*. This was a free solo by Jimmy Ratzlaff.

FA: *Jimmy Ratzlaff 1980s*

Gear: free-solo

No anchor   150ft

4. Buttress Route 5.9 RX ★★

This route takes the black buttress 30 feet right of *The Eliminator*. This climb has two long pitches which are largely unprotected, but the hard moves are near the ground.

Pitch 1: Climb a steep, black buttress just left of the arching crack where the tree branches touch the wall. Climb through the branches, go up 30 feet then traverse right to a 2-bolt anchor in the black water streak.

Pitch 2: Work your way up the 5.7 slab to the left of the water streak. Exit left in the gully after 150 feet.*

FA: *Duane Raleigh 1970s*

Gear: cams to #3 Camalot

2-bolt anchor   220ft

5. Left Roof Exit 5.8 RX

Climb over the roof 25 feet to the left of *Buns Up* just before the roof curves up.*

FA: *Jimmy Ratzlaff, Jon Frank 1979*

Gear: free solo

No anchor   75ft

6. Water Streak 5.7 RX ★★★★

Face climb up the water streak in the middle of the slab. Although mostly unprotected this route has great friction climbing and is the best line on the wall.

Pitch 1: From a large ledge with a tree, start up the corner to a horizontal crack. The last gear before the 2-bolt belay can be found here. Step over the lip and continue up to the 2-bolt belay.

Pitch 2: From the belay continue up the slab on a runout face to a 2-bolt anchor just below a large roof. There are no bolts on the second pitch, but the climbing is more secure than the first pitch.

Pitch 3: Continue under the roof traversing left to easier climbing and set up a belay. *

FA: Kurt Shier & party
Gear: cams to #3 Camalot
2-bolt anchor   *220ft*

7. Buns Up 5.8+ RX ★★★★

Wide overhanging crack above the second pitch of *Water Streak*. This climb is usually added to *Water Streak* for a third pitch. Climb up the strenuous, overhanging corner and "belly flop" over the lip. This route is short but steep. You can set up the belay just over the lip, and then continue climbing low-angle rock up and to the left.

FA: Unknown
Gear: cams to #4, #4.5 Camalot
No anchor   *20ft*

8. Arching Crack 5.7+ RX ★★

Located to the right of *Water Streak*'s start.

An unusual style climb where you finish on the ground. This route follows the small arching crack in the middle of the slab. The route is hardest when done right to left.*

FA: Duane Raleigh 1970s
Gear: free-solo
No anchor   *50ft*

9. Take Off 5.8 X ★★

This route intersects *Face Route* and starts down and left of it. Climb up 30 feet, staying just to the left of the crack with grass growing out of it; continue up the face ending at the start of *Big Leap*.

FA: Jimmy Ratzlaff 1980s
Gear: free-solo
No anchor   *200ft*

10. Face Route 5.7 X ★★

Two pitches of unprotected face climbing. This route goes up the slab in between *Water Streak* and *Great Expectations*.

Pitch 1: Climb up the slab 150 feet then traverse left to a bolt belay on *Water Streak*.

Pitch 2: Traverse right onto the face and continue 120 feet to a small ledge with a large boulder.

Pitch 3: From the ledge, climb up the roof then traverse left and finish the same as *Water Streak*, or do one of the roof routes.*

FA: Duane Raleigh 1970s
Gear: cams to #3 Camalot
2-bolt anchor   *220ft*

Chris Grieg enjoying the fine granite crack on The Eliminator 5.10c. | Photo by Molly Hennesy

Climbers on Elk Slabs, first climbed in the 1950s. | Photo by Tony Mayse

11. Big Leap 5.10a RX ★★

Short face climb to the right of *Buns Up*. Climb up the face on sharp pockets to the slab above. Tri-cams can be used to protect the start. More of a boulder problem than a route except for the slab below. After making your way onto the slab continue up and right to easier climbing and the belay. The original route name has been renamed by the first ascentionist.

FA: *Duane Raleigh 1979*
Gear: small Tricams
No anchor   60ft

12. Great Expectations 5.6 ★★★★

The most popular route on Elk Slab and possibly the first rock climb in Oklahoma. The route follows the low-angle crack on the right side of the slab. The route starts from the tree at the route's base. Face climb to the crack. Continue up the crack for 80 feet, stepping right on a short face-traverse to the ledge with a tree.

FA: *Unknown 1940s*
Gear: cams to #3 Camalot
2-bolt anchor   120ft

13. Right Dihedral 5.6 ★★★

Dihedral to the right of *Great Expectations*. Climb up the dihedral ending the climb on the belay ledge of *Great Expectations*.

FA: *1950s*
Gear: cams to #3 Camalot
2-bolt anchor   120ft

14. Aid Corner 5.9 ★

Crack climb on the far right side of Elk Slabs. First climbed as an aid route.

FA: *Karl Bird, Steve Gillam 1981*
Gear: cams to #3 Camalot
No anchor   60ft

15. Middle Buttress Face 5.7 RX ★★

Previous guidebooks called this *Nike Route*; More than likely *Middle Buttress Face* was soloed and not given a name and then due to misinterpretation it became *Nike Route*.

Nike Route does go up from the same start but as the climbing gets steep and the rock more polished, climbers have opted to continue up and go to the top of the buttress which has a 2-bolt anchor added sometime in the early 90s. The *Nike Route* goes out to the right on the steeper side at the end of the horizontal crack. There is an obvious contrast to where the climbing gets less secure–this is the *Nike Route*.

FA: *1970s*
Gear: small cams, stoppers
2-bolt anchor   100ft

16. Nike Route 5.9 RX ★★★

Face climb to the right of *The Dihedral*. Climb up the face towards the right side of the horizontal crack then up and belay at the tree (small cam works nicely here). Continue right to the steeper side of the buttress belaying at the tree.

FA: *Duane Raleigh 1979 (free solo)*
Gear: small cams, stoppers
No anchor   100ft

17. Tree Route 5.5 ★★

Great route for beginner climbers. This route starts to the right of *Nike Route* and follows the gully up to a 2-bolt anchor.

FA: *Unknown*
Gear: cams to #4 Camalot
2-bolt anchor   165ft

18. Easy Face 5.5 X

Climbs the easy friction slab to the right of *Tree Route*. Make your way over to the anchor on top of *Middle Buttress Face*.

FA: *Unknown*
Gear: free solo
No anchor   130ft

Photo by Tony Mayse

"To have a great adventure, and survive, requires good judgment. Good judgment comes from experience. Experience, of course, is the result of poor judgment."

~Geoff Tabin

THE TREASURE COVE

The Treasure Cove is a unique area in the Charon Gardens Wilderness. Most of the routes are bolt-protected with a few cracks and some crack sections on the face routes creating good mixed climbs. Some of the climbs were bolted ground-up style, often times hanging off hooks to place bolts in keeping with the tradition of the climbing in Oklahoma. Chuck Lohn and Steve Hunt developed this area in the early 1990s on their weekend forays from Texas. At that time Chuck had a guide service named *Hangdog Mountaineering*.

The climbing varies from good solid rock to some sections that may be fragile and exfoliating. Moon Rock Wall is the exception for this area, as the rock is bullet-hard and flawless. All climbing areas take getting use to, this one is no exception. Learn how to climb carefully in areas where you encounter suspect rock.

The Treasure Cove has moderate-graded climbs; however, this is not a beginner area. You need experience for some of the more runout routes like *Quiche Lorraine*. This route has no gear opportunities for the first 50 feet. Read the topos and study the routes. The area does not have an easy approach nor is it a sport-climbing-type setting. It is more like an alpine adventure similar to the experience you get climbing on the Pear and Apple or Secret Agent Dome or in the Wonderland of Rocks, Joshua Tree, California. These long approaches reward you with solitude. The steep slab approach and the scrambling around boulders contribute to the intrigue of the Treasure Cove.

Please be advised that this area has had one fatality, in early 1992. There is a place requiring a traverse under large boulders with big drop-offs to access some areas in The Treasure Cove. A chain has since been installed, but is not maintained, so use caution.

The Treasure Cove is not a dog-friendly climbing area. There are big drop-offs and the rugged terrain make this area a dangerous place for pets.

The Treasure Cove is divided into the following areas: Moon Rock, Pyromania Area, Dog Wall, Refuge Rocks and the Snake Pit.

The areas face both east and west giving the climber an opportunity to escape the summer's sun or enjoy it depending on the time of year.

Most of the climbs are bolt-protected with anchors at the top. A single set of cams to a #3 Camalot with extras in the finger-size range along with quickdraws, should suffice for the majority of the climbs.

Area Reference:

East Facing Walls: on your left as you look up canyon.

Pyromania Wall, Dog Wall, Snake Pit and Refuge Rocks and gully descent.

West Facing Walls and reference points: *Fear of the Left* route. Moon Rock and the Chain Traverse.

Treasure Cove Trail View
(view looking north)

Labels in image: Dog Wall, Pyromania Wall, Moon Rock Wall, Approach, Elk Slabs

Approach from Sunset Parking:

From Sunset parking take the same approach as Pear and Apple (see overview map). Continue hiking past Pear and Apple heading south. The trail splits off just past the wood sign; go left, heading east. You will pass a canyon on your left (north), this is Secret Agent Dome and the backside of the Pear and Apple formation.

Continue east past two more canyons, the Treasure Cove is the second canyon on your left. (See Charon Gardens overview map on page 130.)

Approach time: 30 minutes

Approach from Post Oak Falls:

From the parking area hike north on the Charon Gardens trail towards Pear and Apple. Before reaching Pear and Apple take the trail east (right) at the trail sign. Heading east past the sign, you will pass a canyon on your left (north), this is the approach to Secret Agent Dome and the backside of Pear and Apple. Continue east to the second canyon on your left (north), this is The Treasure Cove.

(See Charon Gardens overview map on page 92.)

Approach time: 30 minutes

Climbers on Moonraker 5.10c | Photo by Tony Mayse

On the east side there is a long slab climb which arches above the canyon gully. This climb is an easy slab route named *Fear of the Left*, a play off of a route at Lost Dome named *Fear of the Right*. This climb tops out at the base of Moon Rock and is a good starting point.

Descent from the climbs:

Two 60-meter ropes are required for the longer rappel stations; some anchors like the one on top of Refuge Rocks do not have chains, only bolts with hangers. Walk off the top heading north then back to the canyon floor via the gully. It is not uncommon to get confused finding the downclimb once on top. Learn this area as there are steep drop-offs if you choose unwisely. Be safe.

"Embracing struggle for it's own sake is an important step on your path."

~Steve House, Training For the New Alpinism

MOON ROCK WALL

Moon Rock Wall is visible from the trail as you look up into Treasure Cove Canyon. Moon Rock Wall faces west and sits on the right side of the canyon. There are four routes on this wall; one route is a crack climb the others are bolt protected. There is also a route on the summit of Moon Rock Wall; this route is found on the northeast corner about 15 yards from the anchors. It is easy to spot, look for the 6"-wide vertical offwidth crack.

Descent: The top of Moon Rock Wall has a 2-bolt anchor rappel station.

1. Pull My Finger 5.9 RX

On the far left side of Moon Rock is an arching crack that curves its way up to the top. More of a seam than a crack, it can easily be toproped off the bolted anchor station with a directional cam.

FA: Chuck Lohn et al. 1990s
Gear: thin
2-bolt anchor   80ft

2. Moonraker 5.10c ★★★

Five feet to the right of *Pull My Finger*. Bolted face climb. Walk up the slab and clip the first bolt out to the right to avoid the runout bottom moves. Good climbing and well-protected.

FA: Chuck Lohn et al. 1990s
Gear: quickdraws
2-bolt anchor   80ft

3. Tranquility Base 5.10 RX ★★★★

Five feet to the right of *Moonraker*. Bolted face climb with three bolts. Climb solid rock up a steep section of flakes and edges for 20 feet to the first bolt. As you climb higher the holds get thinner. The crux is high on the route. Chuck Lohn compares this climb to *Dr. Coolhead* in The Narrows.

FA: Chuck Lohn et al. 1990s
Gear: quickdraws
2-bolt anchor   80ft

4. Apollo 5.11b R ★★★★

Five feet to the right of *Tranquility Base*. This is the hardest climb on Moon Rock Wall. Excellent line and a must-do for the grade. Climb up the arête protected by a line of bolts.

FA: Chuck Lohn et al. 1990s
Gear: quickdraws
2-bolt anchor   80ft

5. Houston We Have a Problem 5.11 ★★★

From the top of Moon Rock Wall walk 15 feet to the large boulder north of the belay station of Moon Rock Wall. This route climbs the 6" wide crack to the top of a large boulder.

FA: Tony Mayse & Joe Romero 2016
Gear: cams to #6 Camalot
No anchor   50ft

LOWER SLAB ROUTE AREA

This is the first route on your right (east) as you make your way into the The Treasure Cove area.

1. Fear of the Left 5.7

Bolted slab climb that leads to the base of Moon Rock Wall.

FA: Chuck Lohn et al. 1990s
Gear: quickdraws, #1, #2 cams for the belay
No anchor   150ft

Moon Rock
Wall

Climbers on Moon Rock Wall | Photo by Tony Mayse

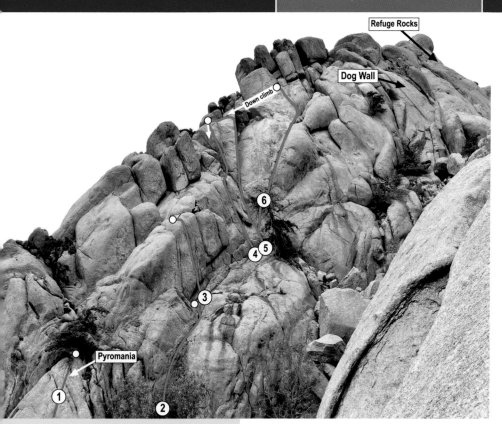

PYROMANIA AREA

This area is marked by an east-facing red-colored wall and is the first area on your left as you make your way into the Treasure Cove. Look for a short crack with a couple bolts behind a tree; this is *Pyromania*. The majority of the climbs are moderate routes with *Pyromania* being the most difficult for this area.

1. Pyromania 5.10c ★★

Crack climb with a couple bolts on a slightly bulging face. Start off on finger locks leading to a bolt-protected face and wider crack, climbing up higher before reaching the tree. Belay here.

FA: *Chuck Lohn et al. 1990s*

Gear: TCUs and cams to #2.5 Camalot

No anchor   *70ft*

2. Catwalk 5.6 ★

Slab climb to the right of *Pyromania*. A good climb to get you to the upper section of *Pyromania* Wall.

FA: *Chuck Lohn et al. 1990s*

Gear: TCUs and cams to #2.5 Camalot

No anchor   *70ft*

3. Nasty Habits 5.9 ★★

Crack climb up and to the left of *Catwalk*. Make your way to the top of *Pint-Sized Goddess* rappel station.

Back up the single-bolt anchor.

FA: *Chuck Lohn et al. 1990s*

Gear: TCUs and cams to #2.5 Camalot

No anchor   *50ft*

4. Pint-Sized Goddess 5.8 RX ★

Crack/face climb to the right of *Nasty Habits*. Gear can be found in the dihedral, leading to runout face climbing protected by one bolt up higher.

FA: *Chuck Lohn et al. 1990s*

Gear: TCUs and cams to #2.5 Camalot

Single-bolt anchor   *70ft*

5. Sunday Stroll 5.6 ★

An easy one to the right of *Pint-Sized Goddess*. Climbs the left dihedral to the anchor station of *Pint-Sized Goddess*.

FA: *Chuck Lohn et al. 1990s*

Gear: TCUs and cams to #2.5 Camalot

No anchor   *50ft*

6. Salty Dog 5.8 ★★

Climb the obvious dihedral to the right of *Sunday Stroll*. Crack climbing leads to easy face/slab up to a ledge. Traverse left to the same anchor station of *Pint-Sized Goddess*.

FA: *Chuck Lohn et al. 1990s*

Gear: TCUs and cams to #2.5 Camalot

No anchor   *75ft*

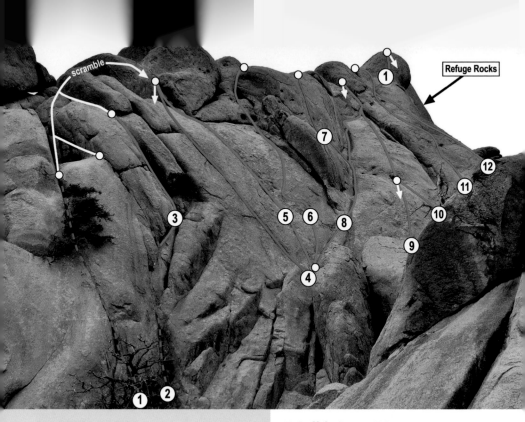

DOG WALL LEFT

One of the more striking areas of the Treasure Cove. This wall features a beautiful, clean, smooth face and some obvious thin cracks ending at trees on the lower part of the wall. The wall is east-facing, getting morning sun.

Approach: Located on the same side, and right of, the Pyromania Area, approximately 100 yards uphill.

Descent: Dog Wall Left has two rappel stations, both requiring double-rope rappels. Dog Wall Right has one rappel station at the top requiring two ropes (though a 70-meter rope can be used to reach the midway anchors). See topo for anchor stations. Bring two ropes for all rappels if you are unsure of the rappel station location.

1. Bullet Proof A2

Aid route on the lower left side of Dog Wall. Tapering crack ending at a tree.

FA: *Chuck Lohn et al. 1990s*

Gear: cams and aid rack

No anchor   *60ft*

2. Epilogue A2

Aid climb the corner to the right of *Bullet Proof* then nail out to the left.

FA: *Chuck Lohn et al. 1990s*

Gear: cams and aid rack

No anchor   *60ft*

3. Buffalo Stance 5.8

Same start as *Epilogue*, continue right and up, angling left in the dihedral opposite *Epilogue* aid crack.

FA: *Chuck Lohn et al. 1990s*

Gear: cams and aid rack

No anchor   *60ft*

4. Poodle Power 5.10c R ★★★

Located up and to the right of *Buffalo Stance*. Face climbing protected by two bolts, continuing in a diagonal finger crack, ending at a 2-bolt rap station. The face climbing through the opening moves has flakey rock but once you get past this the rock turns more solid. Great climbing with sustained moves.

FA: *Chuck Lohn et al. 1990s*

Gear: stoppers, small cams up #2 Camalot, quickdraws

2-bolt anchor   *150ft*

5. Poodle Bait 5.6 ★★

Easy crack climb to the right of *Poodle Power*. Climb the crack then exit onto the face with slab climbing to the top.

FA: *Chuck Lohn et al. 1990s*

Gear: stopper, small cams to #2 Camalot

2-bolt anchor   *150ft*

6. Fifi in a Blender 5.9 RX

Located to the right of *Poodle Bait*. Meandering face climb with 2 bolts leads to gear opportunities higher up on the route.

FA: Chuck Lohn et al. 1990s

Gear: stoppers, small cams, quickdraws

2-bolt anchor   *150ft*

7. Space Dogs 5.10 R ★★★

Start on *Quiche Lorraine* then climb left for a short section of crack climbing leading to a steep headwall. Climb out to the right on a bolt-protected face ending at a 2-bolt rap station. Nice exposure up a headwall.

FA: Chuck Lohn et al. 1990s

Gear: cams to #2 Camalot, quickdraws

2-bolt anchor   *150ft*

DOG WALL RIGHT

8. Quiche Loraine 5.7 ★★ RX

Moderate face/crack climb and the first route on Dog Wall Right. Climb right of the water streak. The face climbing up to the intersection of *Space Dogs* is unprotected. You can find hand-size cams in the *Space Dogs* crack before continuing up higher.

FA: Chuck Lohn et al. 1990s

Gear: small cams to #2 Camalot

2-bolt anchor   *150ft*

Joe Romero climbing the steep finger crack Poodle Power 5.10c on Treasure Cove's Dog Wall. | Photo by Tony Mayse

9. Jolly Rover 5.8 RX

Classic face climb for the Treasure Cove area. Found in the middle of Dog Wall Right with a large hueco.

FA: *Chuck Lohn et al. 1990s*

Gear: stoppers, small cams, quickdraws

2-bolt anchor   150ft

10. Doggie Diversions 5.9 Toprope

Toprope climb to the right of *Jolly Rover*.

FA: *Chuck Lohn et al. 1990s*

Gear: toprope

2-bolt anchor   80ft

11. Metamorphic Asshole 5.9 R

Mixed route with one bolt. Starting between the large boulder to the right of *Doggie Diversions* and ending at the anchors on top of Refuge Rocks Wall.

FA: *Chuck Lohn et al. 1990s*

Gear: stoppesr, small cams, quickdraws

2-bolt anchor   150ft

12. Phillip Mitchell Memorial Route 5.8 R ★★

This is a mixed route that climbs from the Snake Pit up the slabs leading to Refuge Rocks. From the Snake Pit climb up to a horn on the face. Continue up the slabs towards the top of Refuge Rocks. This climb is dedicated to Phillip Mitchell who tragically died in 1992 while attempting to traverse below the large boulders. Chains have now been installed.

FA: *Chuck Lohn et al. 1990s*

Gear: cams to #2 Camalot, quickdraws

2-bolt anchor   150ft

SNAKE PIT WALL

Approach: Located in the upper left (west side) of the the Treasure Cove. After passing through the chain-traverse boulders, scramble to the left to reach Snake Pit Wall. *Phillip Mitchell Memorial Route* is the only route which climbs to the top of Refuge Rocks Wall from the base of Snake Pit Wall ending at a belay/rappel station.

Descent: All routes on the Snake Pit Wall have rappel stations.

13. Viper 5.9 R ★

Start from a ledge up and to the right of *Phillip Mitchell Memorial*. Face climb up to a bolt then continue up moderate climbing to the anchor/rap station below Refuge Rocks Wall.

FA: *Chuck Lohn et al. 1990s*

Gear: stoppers, small cams, quickdraws

2-bolt anchor   80ft

14. Sidewinder 5.11b RX ★★

Mixed climb to the right of *Viper*. A short section of crack climbing leads to a bolt-protected face ending at a rap station.

FA: *Chuck Lohn et al. 1990s*

Gear: stoppers, small cams to #3 Camalot, quickdraws

2-bolt anchor   50ft

15. Copperhead 5.10 ★

Bolted face climb to the right of *Sidewinder*.

FA: *Chuck Lohn et al. 1990s*

Gear: stoppers, small cams, quickdraws

2-bolt anchor   50ft

16. Diamondback 5.9 ★

Face climb to the right of *Copperhead*. Climb to the first bolt of *Copperhead* then move right and up protected by two bolts leading to the shared rap station.

FA: *Chuck Lohn et al. 1990s*

Gear: stoppers, small cams, quickdraws

2-bolt anchor   50ft

17. Snakebite 5.9 ★★

Mixed climb to the right of *Copperhead* and *Diamondback*. Climb to the first bolt of *Copperhead*, traverse right and up to the bolt of *Diamondback*. Continue climbing right and up to the rap station below Refuge Rocks Wall.

FA: *Chuck Lohn et al. 1990s*

Gear: stoppers, small cams, quickdraws

2-bolt anchor   60ft

Joe Romero attempting Houston We Have a Problem 5.11. | Photo by Tony Mayse

Treasure Cove Chain Traverse. Installed in the early 90s shortly after the tragic accident of Phillip Mitchell. Use caution when negotiating this area. | Photo by Tony Mayse

REFUGE ROCKS WALL

Approach: The Refuge Rocks is the last area in the Treasure Cove. It is located on the upper-left side of the canyon. After passing through the chain traverse, make your way over to the ramp up and left of the large boulders. Refuge Rocks has a good concentration of harder climbs and excellent exposure. Sitting high up in the canyon it has the feel of being in an exotic climbing destination. (Routes are numbered 1–6)

Descent: Refuge Rocks has a bolted belay at the top of the formation as well as two midway anchors. (see topo). From the top of Refuge Rocks one long 165-foot rappel reaches the base of the Snake Pit or two 80-foot rappels via the midway acnhors. There is also a walk-off down the gully to the north (see topo).

1. The Gemstone 5.10d R ★★

Climb *Phillip Mitchell Memorial* route then continue up the face protected by 2 bolts leading to a 2-bolt anchor. This pitch can also be used as a continuation from one of the lower climbs ending at the ledge below *Gemstone*.

FA: *Chuck Lohn et al. 1990s*

Gear: quickdraws

2-bolt anchor   80ft

2. Adolph Smithler 5.11a R ★★

A mixed climb located on the left end of the ledge. Bouldery start on solid rock leads to a bolt then finger crack for 20 feet and another bolt protecting the slab climbing to the top.

FA: *Chuck Lohn et al. 1990s*

Gear: quickdraws, finger-size cams

2-bolt anchor   80ft

Joe Romero on the approach to Refuge Rocks. | Photo by Tony Mayse

3. Never Trust a Bolt-Steppin' Preacher 5.11b/c R ★★★

Ten feet to the right of *Adolph Smithler*. Climb 15 feet to the first bolt. Continue up steeper face climbing past 2 more bolts. This route is sustained from the first bolt to the top. Excellent!

FA: *Chuck Lohn et al. 1990s*

Gear: quickdraws

2-bolt anchor   *80ft*

4. Dauchau Doris 5.9 R ★★

Climb *Home a Lohn* to a ledge, then continue in the corner crack with featured rock on the face out right, making your way up to a bolted belay up top.

FA: *Chuck Lohn et al. 1990s*

Gear: cams to #4–#5 Camalot, quickdraws

2-bolt anchor   *80ft*

5. Home a Lohn 5.10b RX ★★★

Ten feet to the right of *Never Trust a Bolt-Steppin' Preacher*. Climb 15 feet to the first bolt on broken edges and steep rock. Two bolts protect the face climbing up to the ledge. From here continue up and to the right on the headwall, with better rock quality, protected by three bolts. Nice exposure on this route.

FA: *Chuck Lohn et al. 1990s*

Gear: quickdraws

2-bolt anchor   *80ft*

6. Super Sam Buries the Hatchet 5.10b Toprope

Toprope route to the right of *Home a Lohn*.

FA: *Chuck Lohn et al. 1990s*

Gear: toprope

2-bolt anchor   *80ft*

Joe Romero exploring new route possibilities in the Treasure Cove. | Photo by Tony Mayse

Secret Agent Dome

SECRET AGENT DOME

A very obscure formation, for those seeking high adventure and a bit of solitude. Located directly behind Pear and Apple. Established in the early 1980s with ground-up style bolting on lead. There are six routes at this location.. The routes are rated 5.7–5.10, and they have little to no protection except for the crack climb *Missed it by that Much*. Reminiscent of the runout rock climbs found in Tuolumne Meadows, California. Bring hand-size cams to #3 Camalot for the top as there are no anchors. The Secret Agent Dome faces to the south and southwest and makes for a great winter destination in the afternoon or early morning climbing in the summer months.

Approach from Post Oak Falls parking: Hike north from the parking area on the Charon Gardens Trail. Before reaching Pear and Apple formation take the trail east (see approach below).

Approach from Sunset parking: Hike the trail continuing south from Pear and Apple. Follow the trail, then head east as it splits about 100 yards past Pear and Apple. Hike east for 200 yards. The canyon directly behind Pear and Apple has a large boulder with a quartz band/dike running across the upper part of the formation, this is Secret Agent Dome. Scramble up from the west side of the canyon then make your way over to the base. Getting to the base of the large ledge below the routes requires some 4th class climbing and scrambling. The descent from the top of these climbs requires 4th class downclimbing (consider roping up).

(See Charon Gardens overview map on page 130.)

Approach time: 40–50 minutes.

1. Secret Agent Man 5.9 X ★★★★

Start just above the pool of water with a tree. Climb up the obvious dike for 60 feet to a horizontal crack where your first and only protection can be found. From here continue up on positive holds following the dike to where it turns horizontal, continue up the steep slab for 40 more feet to the belay ledge. The best climb on Secret Agent Dome.

FA: *Mark Herndon, Duane Raleigh 1982*
Gear: cams from fingers to #3 Camalot
No anchor   120ft

2. Matt Helm 5.9 X ★★★★

Just a few feet right of *Secret Agent Man* is a blank face that follows a line in between the two obvious horizontal seams 60 feet up the route. These seams take micro-cams. From here continue up on runout face climbing sharing the belay ledge of *Secret Agent Man*.

FA: *Keith Egan, Duane Raleigh 1982*
Gear: micro-cams
No anchor   100ft

3. Vincent Black Shadow 5.9 X ★★

Starting on the ledge above and to the right of *Secret Agent Man*. This is the first route on the left end of the ledge beginning from the stacked boulders below the face. Climb 50 feet to a bolt, then continue on steep face climbing making your way to the belay ledge up top. Committing.

FA: *Jack Hill, Duane Raleigh 1983*
Gear: quickdraw
No anchor   100ft

4. Get Smart 5.10a X ★★★

This route climbs sustained face climbing between *Vincent Black Shadow* and *Agent 99*. (Currently a toprope climb).

FA: Tony Mayse 2016

Gear: no gear

No anchor   100ft

5. Agent 99 5.9 X ★★

Fifteen feet to the right of *Vincent Black Shadow* is another stack of boulders with an arching flake which leads to a single bolt just above a small ledge. Climb up, following the flake making your way to a stance and continue up 10 feet on friction moves to a bolt. From here the climbing is sustained friction for 35 feet making your way to the shared belay ledge up top.

FA: Jack Hill, Duane Raleigh 1983

Gear: quickdraw, cams to #3 Camalot for the belay

No anchor   100ft

"A good scare is worth more to a man than good advice."

~Ed Howe, American Journalist & Author

~Quotable Climber by Jonathan Waterman

6. Missed it by that Much 5.7+ ★★★★

Located below the belay ledge of Secret Agent Dome. Climb the left-leaning crack with a cruxy start. Climb up on hand jams and finger locks to a ledge ending at the base of Secret Agent Dome.

FA: Tony Mayse (free solo), Joe Romero, Chris Corbett 2016

Gear: cams to #2 Camalot

No anchor   40ft

Tony Mayse enjoying stellar weather on Agent 99 5.9 X. | Photo by Chris Corbett

Tony Mayse climbing the spectacularly featured Secret Agent Man 5.9 X. | Photo by Chris Corbett

Charon Gardens Overview Map from Sunset Parking Area

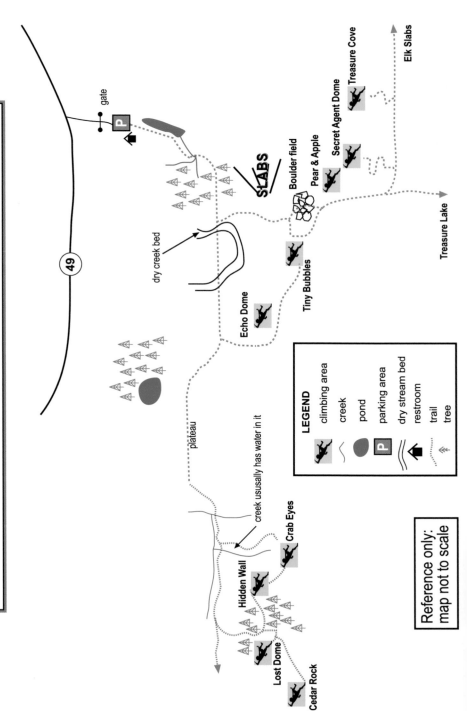

gate

49

SLABS

dry creek bed

Echo Dome

Tiny Bubbles

Boulder field

Pear & Apple

Secret Agent Dome

Treasure Cove

Elk Slabs

Treasure Lake

plateau

creek ususally has water in it

Crab Eyes

Hidden Wall

Lost Dome

Cedar Rock

LEGEND

climbing area
creek
pond
parking area
dry stream bed
restroom
trail
tree

Reference only:
map not to scale

Exit for Charon Gardens Climbing Areas:

Tiny Bubbles/Pear & Apple/Secret Agent Dome/Echo Dome/
Crab Eyes/Hidden Wall/Lost Dome/Cedar Rock

(view from first parking pullout on the right)

Charon Gardens Wilderness Area Trailhead

SUNSET PARKING AREA

Crab Eyes, Lost Dome, Hidden Wall, Echo Dome, Tiny Bubbles, Pear & Apple, Secret Agent Dome, and the Treasure Cove all can be reached from this parking area.

From the refuge entrance cattle guard (see overview map on page 41), drive 13.5 miles to reach the Sunset parking exit.

The entrance gate opens at 9:00 am and closes at sunset. For alpine starts you can park outside the gate in the designated parking area.

From the parking area walk west past the restrooms to pick up the well-marked trail which leads through the forest. Each area listed has approach descriptions.

Approximate approach times:

Tiny Bubbles: 20 minutes

Pear & Apple: 25 minutes

Secret Agent Dome: 30–40 minutes

The Treasure Cove: 30–40 minutes

Echo Dome: 20 minutes

Crab Eyes: 45–50 minutes

Hidden Wall: 35–40 minutes

Lost Dome: 35–40 minutes

Cedar Rock: 45 minutes

Photo by Mikael Males

Please be mindful of the wildlife in the Charon Gardens Wilderness Area. Rattlesnakes are very hard to spot and could pose a serious threat if provoked. Buffalo are a common sight and should be given plenty of room as they have been known to be aggressive, especially when they are caring for their calves.

Pear & Apple

Secret Agent Dome

Science Friction

Pear & Apple Overview
(trail view looking east)

PEAR & APPLE

There are seven routes listed for this area. The formation resembles a Pear and Apple facing west. The approach to the base of Pear and Apple starts left of the formation then ascends the trough which meanders up to the upper ledges. To descend the routes rappel from the 2-bolt anchors at the top of the formation (bring two ropes) or walk off to the north, then down the slabs to the base of the climbs.

Approach from Sunset parking area: From the parking area hike west to pick up the trailhead. Continue west on a well-traveled trail making your way to a dry streambed and trail sign. Hike south towards the boulderfield. Cross the boulderfield and look to your left (east). Pear and Apple can be seen sitting up high above the trail.

(See Charon Gardens overview map on page 130.)

Approach time: 20–25 minutes

Approach from Post Oak Falls parking area: Hike north from the parking area on the Charon Gardens Trail.

(See Charon Gardens overview map on page 130.)

Approach time: 20–25 minutes

1. Too Steep for Sheep 5.10b ★★★
Located approximately 30 yards to the left of Pear and Apple formation is a face climb with a few bolts. The route was named after Chuck Lohn's best friend affectionately called the "Sheep Man."
FA: Chuck Lohn 1990s
Gear: quickdraws
2-bolt anchor   *40ft*

2. Unknown Pear and Apple 5.8 RX ★★
Located just left of *Too Steep for Sheep* is a face climb with one bolt.
FA: Unknown
Gear: quickdraws
2-bolt anchor   *40ft*

3. Pear and Apple 5.9+ ★★★
Crack that turns face climb ending between the Pear and Apple. This route starts off at the tree located at the base of the formation, (or a variation start that climbs a short crack avoiding the wide start below). From here climb up the corner crack traversing right and up on friction moves to a 2-bolt belay station.
FA: Unknown
Gear: cams to #4 Camalot
2-bolt anchor   *130ft*

4. A Free Pear and Apple 5.11a R ★★

Same start as *Pear and Apple* route. Climb up the corner moving left and up on thin face moves protected by a pin. Formerly an aid line rated A2 until it went "free."

FA: *Rick McCusic, Stewart Stafford 1986*
Gear: TCUs, cams to #4 Camalot, small stoppers
No anchor   *120ft*

5. Superpseudomasochisticexpeealodo-chous 5.10 R ★★★

Face climb to the right of *Pear and Apple*. From the tree, climb up the slab and follow 4 bolts to the 2-bolt anchor. This climb has some loose flakes.

FA: *Chuck Lohn 1992*
Gear: quickdraws
2-bolt anchor   *140ft*

6. A Farewell to Arms 5.10 Toprope

Face climb just to the right of *Superpseudomasochisticexpeealodochous*. There is one bolt lower on the route. It is not known if it was an unfinished project so it became a toprope climb.

FA: *Unknown 1990s*
Gear: toprope
2-bolt anchor   *140ft*

7. Science Friction 5.9 RX ★★★

Face climb on the slab 50 yards down and to the left of the *Pear and Apple* route. Climb up the slab on good friction to a bolt; continue up the face on runout climbing to a 2-bolt anchor.

FA: *Unknown*
Gear: quickdraws
2-bolt anchor   *60ft*

TINY BUBBLES

This is a good area for learning how to rock climb. There are six routes from 5.6–5.10 which can easily be toproped. The area is located across the trail and west of Pear and Apple formation.

Approach: Take the trail heading south towards Pear & Apple from Sunset parking area.

To avoid the boulderfield and "boulder hopping" section of the hike, take the upper trail on the right (west-side) which is a friendly approach for small children and pets. Once past the boulderfield, look up to the west, there is a large outcrop with water streaks that faces east. Tiny Bubbles is 100 yards to the west of this outcrop. Tiny Bubbles is not visible from the trail though it is just a short walk uphill from the trail. The wall faces to the south and is a good winter destination or early in the morning in the summer.

Approach time: 20 minutes

1. Tiny Little Crack 5.5 ★★ Toprope
Located just down and to the left of Tiny Bubbles formation. Climb up a slab with the obvious crack in the center of the face.
FA: Unknown
Gear: toprope
No anchor   45ft

2. Tiny Big Crack 5.5 ★ Toprope
First route on the left. Climb the left leaning crack.
FA: Unknown
Gear: toprope
2-bolt anchor   45ft

3. Puke Shoes 5.10b ★ Toprope
Climb the steep bulge right of Tiny Big Crack. Apparently, my good friend Brian Jung had a bit too much libation the night before resulting in accidentally mistaking soapy water for drinking in the late hours...
FA: Brian Jung 1990s
Gear: toprope
2-bolt anchor   45ft

4. Tiny Left Crack 5.7 ★ Toprope
Starts with face climbing then leads to a short crack before topping out.
FA: Unknown
Gear: toprope
2-bolt anchor   45ft

5. Tiny Center Face 5.8+ ★★ Toprope
Fun face climb up the center of Tiny Bubbles.
FA: Unknown
Gear: toprope
2-bolt anchor   45ft

6. Tiny Right Face 5.7 ★ Toprope
Face climb on the right side of Tiny Bubbles.
FA: Unknown
Gear: toprope
2-bolt anchor   45ft

Tiny Bubbles

5 bolts behind slab (not visible)

ECHO DOME

Echo Dome is located in the Charon Gardens Wilderness and is reached by parking at the Sunset parking area. The area has moderate bolt-protected routes and a few crack climbs. The rock has a lot of exfoliating flakes that are solid enough for climbing as long as you pull down on them—not out. With a west-facing wall, it's a good winter spot or morning climbing area in the summer months. Large balconies and a spectacular view make this an ideal setting for climbing. Most routes are about 80-feet long; a 60-meter rope works for the rappels and topropes. All routes have anchor stations at the top. There are six routes listed here from 5.8–5.10.

Approach: From Sunset parking area hike west on the main trail. Walk west crossing two dry stream beds. The trail will open up and then turn south, continue walking south. Cairns will mark the trail leading south towards Echo Dome. (See Charon Gardens overview map on page 130.)

Approach time: 20 minutes

1. Lady Bugs and Gentlemen 5.9+ ★★★

This route is the leftmost bolted route on the wall. It follows a line of 7 bolts up the face with nice moves. The start of the route has a few 5.10 friction moves but the rest of the climb is 5.9.

FA: Aaron Gibson, Jason Magness 1990s
Gear: quickdraws
2-bolt anchor   *80ft*

2. Crack Pipe 5.9 ★★

The crack to the right of *Lady Bugs and Gentlemen*. Climb a 5.7 wide crack that turns thin at the top before ending. From here step right with face moves up to a bolt. Climb past the bolt to a large flake below the anchors.

FA: Aaron Gibson, Jason Magness 1990s
Gear: cams to #3 Camalot, quickdraws
2-bolt anchor   *80ft*

3. Frosted Flakes 5.9 ★★★

This route follows the line of 8 bolts to the right of *Crack Pipe*. Climb up the face over a couple of bulges with good moves and positive edges. A fun climb.

FA: Texas Mountaineers 1990s
Gear: quickdraws
2-bolt anchor   *80ft*

4. Finger Lickin' Good A.K.A. Sherman's Sister 5.10- R ★★

Climb *Little Sherman Creature Crack* continuing in the thin finger crack above the horizontal crack. Move up the crack on finger locks stepping left as the crack ends to the last bolt on *Frosted Flakes*. From here climb to the anchors on *Frosted Flakes*.

FA: Tony Mayse, Chris Corbett 2002
Gear TCUs, cams to #3 Camalot, small stoppers
2-bolt anchor   *80ft*

5. Little Sherman Creature Crack 5.8 ★★★★

Crack climb to the right of *Frosted Flakes*. Climb on good hand jams to a horizontal crack, step right on exciting moves, continue in the hand crack above.

FA: Jason Magness, Aaron Gibson 1990s
Gear: cams to #3 Camalot
2-bolt anchor   *80ft*

6. Worm Hole 5.8 ★★★

Bolted line to the right of *Little Sherman Creature Crack*. Climb up the face past 3 bolts up to a fourth bolt under an arching flake. From here step over the arch and move up the face and follow the line of bolts to the left of a thin flake to a 2-bolt anchor.

FA: Aaron Gibson, Jason Magness 1990s
Gear: quickdraws
2-bolt anchor   *80ft*

Echo Dome

CRAB EYES

Crab Eyes has some of the hardest crack climbs in the refuge. It's definitely the place to go to work on your crack climbing skills or test them. To find the area look for the two huge boulders perched on top of a rock formation resembling crab's eyes. This formation can be seen from the plateau on the hike in. The east side of Crab Eyes has the majority of the crack climbs. The west-facing wall has a couple cracks but mainly hard, bolted lines like *Moby Dick* and *Yellow Beard*. These routes are not sport routes; they were bolted with runouts.

Approach: From Sunset parking area follow the trail west past the restrooms to pick up the trailhead. Stay on the trail for about 0.25 miles crossing the first seasonal creek; continue for 200 yards past the second seasonal creek. Continue for about 0.25 miles eventually making your way up to the plateau. Crab Eyes formation can be seen from the top of the plateau. Follow the trail making your way down from the plateau continuing to head west. When you have made your way down, continue on the trail, which parallels a seasonal creek for about 0.5 mile,

then head south following the trail along the creek. Follow the trail heading uphill through rock outcroppings leading through an oftentimes brush-covered trail. You will eventually see the Crab Eyes formation to your right (west). This is the east face. (See Charon Gardens overview map on page 130.)

Approach time: 45–50 minutes

1. Alaskan King Crab 5.9 R ★★★

Start on *Moby Dick* staying to the right in the hand crack avoiding the bolts on the face out left. At a small ledge/stance traverse right then up to an obvious headwall. Well protected except for the short headwall section. (See the topo for West Crab Eyes for another view of this route).

FA: Matt King 2004

Gear: cams to #3 Camalot

No anchor   *75ft*

Crab Eyes

Clayton Reagan climbing The Claw 5.10+. | Photo by Tony Mayse

2. Crab Salad 5.8 R ★★★★
Located on the south end of Crab Eyes.

Pitch 1: Start up the easy (5.6) bombay chimney, step right to a shelf just below a short slab, belay here (cams to #2 Camalot for the belay).

Pitch 2: Continue up to a short section of crack climbing left of the belay to a horizontal crack (cams to #3 Camalot and a long runner here). Traverse right for 15 feet, then step up on good holds and big flakes with nice exposure and runout (5.7) face climbing to the top.

FA | Terry Andrews, Julie Emery, Matt King 2004
Gear: cams to #3 Camalot
No anchor   100ft

3. The Arête 5.6 X
Face with marginal pro until higher up on the route.
FA: Duane Raleigh et al. 1980s
Gear: same gear as for *Crab Salad*
No anchor   70ft

4. Where the Buffalo Roam 5.12 R ★★★
Located just to the left of *I Want to be in the Guide Book*. Climb the face up to the short dihedral, traverse right in the horizontal crack protected by a fixed piton. Continue on easier climbing ending at a shelf and belay spot.
FA: Duane Raleigh, Stuart Stafford 1986
Gear: TCUs to 1", stoppers
No anchor   60ft

5. I Want to be in the Guide Book 5.9 ★
Located a few feet to the right of *Where the Buffalo Roam*. Offwidth climb. Worm your way into the wide crack ending on a large ledge.
FA: Jon Frank, Mark Herndon 1984
Gear: cams to #6 Camalot
No anchor   60ft

6. Three Hour Craniotomy 5.10a RX
Face climb left of *Fun Ride*. Climb a short section below a roof to a stance. Move up and right on crimps. Gear can be found down low but marginal placements leading to the top.
Questionable rock lower on the route.
FA: 1990s
Gear: TCUs to 1"
No anchor   60ft

7. Catch Another Ride 5.12c ★★ Toprope
Located on the face a few feet left of *Karl Bird Crack*. Follow the blankest section of rock avoiding the flakes out left (see topo).
FA: Marcus Garcia 1990s
Gear: toprope
No anchor   60ft

Artwork by Elisha Gallegos

Tony Mayse climbing the classic thin finger crack Ra 5.11d on Crab Eyes. | Photo by Andrew Burr

8. Fun Ride 5.12a RX ★★★

Same start as *Karl Bird Crack*, then climb the horizontal crack left to a stance, move up and right to a solid flake, followed by hard pulls to a horizontal crack finishing on a short headwall. There is fragile rock left of this line, so if you find yourself on loose, broken rock you're probably off-route. An independent line from *Catch Another Ride*. Rehearsed on toprope then led. Sustained climbing on a steep face.

FA Unknown

Gear: TCUs to .5

No anchor   60ft

9. Karl Bird Crack 5.8+ ★★

Located 10 feet left of *The Claw*, this is the fist crack that angles right. The crack leans to the right for the first 15 feet. Continue up the corner to easier climbing.

FA: Karl Bird 1981

Gear: cams to #3.5 Camalot

No anchor   60ft

10. The Claw 5.10+ ★★★★

This is a deceptively steep, "full value" crack climb. A few moderate moves lead to a ledge; the ledge offers little rest before moving over the bulge. From here move up and left to gain the crack that leads to 30 feet of offwidth climbing. Continue in the crack to a stance below two boulders stacked on top of each other.

FA: Terry Andrews, Tom Cosgrove 1985

Gear: TCUs & cams to #4 Camalot

No anchor   70ft

10a. The Claw (Variation Start) 5.10+ ★★★★

Located 10 feet to the left of *The Claw*. Climb up the wide crack just in front the large flat boulder a few feet away from the wall. Climb up 12 feet then follow the horizontal hand crack (5.10) to the right gaining the finger crack of *The Claw*. Continue on *The Claw*.

FA: Tony Mayse, Joe Romero 2015

Gear: cams to #2 Camalot

No anchor   70ft

10b. The Claw (Variation Finish) 5.10+ ★★★

Climb *The Claw* for 50 feet. Continue out right onto the face avoiding the exit moves over the boulder. Airy moves protected by small cams.

FA: Unknown

Gear: finger-size cams to #2 Camalot

No anchor   70ft

11. Ra 5.11d ★★★★

Ra climbs the finger crack to the right of *The Claw*. From the start of *The Claw* climb (5.6) to a horizontal crack for 20 feet, tread right 10 feet to gain the finger crack. Continue up on face climbing and finger locks to the top. Solid gear and pumpy placements. One of the best trad routes anywhere!

FA: Terry Andrews (toprope)

FA: Duane Raleigh, Jon Frank (lead) 1988

Gear TCUs, cams to #1, small stoppers

No anchor   70ft

11a. Ra Direct Start 5.12a ★★

Climb the vertical face starting 10 feet right of *Ra's* start. Undercling and smears lead to thin holds climbing past horizontal seams making your way up to the bottom of *Ra's* finger crack.

FA: *Unknown*

Gear: small cams

No anchor   70ft

12. Power Series 5.10+ ★★★

This route is about 15 feet to the right of *Ra*. Look for a short blank face with few holds at the bottom of the route and a horizontal crack 12 feet above. A boulder problem start on polished rock leads to a horizontal crack. Move up over a bulge to a finger crack. From here continue up to a wide flaring crack that turns to hand size for 25 feet before topping out. Bring a variety of gear, it will take it all.

FA: *Jon Frank, Duane Raleigh 1982*

Gear: stoppers, cams to #3.5 Camalots

No anchor   70ft

12a. Power Series Direct Start 5.11 ★★★★

Boulder problem start off the slab with a thin sidepull and tricky footwork.

Climbing this route with Russell Hooper one day, he was so casual about the beta... "Just put your foot right there."

FA: *Russell Hooper early 90s*

Gear: same gear as *Power Series*

No anchor   70ft

Elisha Gallegos crushing Power Series 5.10+ | Photo by Andrew Burr

13. After Lunch 5.8 ★★★

One of the easier climbs at Crab Eyes. Located 20 feet right of *Power Series*. Climb up the dihedral on good jams and good pro, ending on top of a ramp and belay spot.

FA: *Terry Andrews 1985*

Gear: cams to #3 Camalot (1" to 2" for the belay)

No anchor   80ft

13a. After Lunch Top Out 5.9 RX ★★★

A committing and exciting finish gaining you the top of Crab Eyes eye! Climb *After Lunch*. Continue climbing over the large boulder precariously perched high above the Crab Eyes formation. Once on top there are no anchors, have your belayer lower you to the other side (south) of the boulder to set up the belay.

FA: *Terry Andrews 1990s*

Gear: cams to #3 Camalot (1" to 2" for the belay)

No anchor   80ft

14. Preserve the Bush 5.10b ★

Located 15 feet right of *After Lunch*. The route follows the diagonal crack as it turns vertical up to a small bush. Short route with a few interesting moves. Bring extra cams from 1" to 2" for the belay.

FA: *Luc Gruenther*, Terry Andrews 2004*

Gear: cams to #2 Camalot

No anchor   40ft

* Major Luc Gruenther is an American hero and former fighter pilot who was killed in a training accident. To learn more about this extraordinary man go to www.mlglf.org

CRAB EYES (WEST FACE)

1. Mesopotamia 5.11b R ★

Located downhill through the trees approximately 50 feet left of *Wild Planet*. Hard face moves next to a tree. Climb the short face up to a bolt, continue up the face to a large ledge, and belay here. Walk off to the right. No Photo.

FA: *Steve Gillam, Duane Raleigh 1982*

Gear: a quickdraw

No anchor   50ft

2. Wild Planet 5.9+ RX ★★★

Scantily protected face climb 50 feet left of *Women on Mopeds*. Before dropping downhill through the trees look to your right. *Wild Planet* is easily overlooked.

FA: *Duane Raleigh, Steve Gillam 1982*
Gear: cams to #2 Camalot
No anchor   65ft

3. Tarzan Traverse 5.9 ★★

Located 20 feet to the left of *Corndog*. Climb up a large flake, traverse right and continue up a vertical crack leading to a horizontal hand crack up higher.

FA: *Chris Marks, Rob Leinau 2005*
Gear: cams to #3 Camalot
No anchor   65ft

4. Corndog 5.11b/c R ★★

Located 30 feet to the left of *Women on Mopeds*. Start up the face to a prominent flake about 10 feet up; make your way to a 4" horizontal crack. Move up to an undercling flake. Climb over the roof to gain the diagonal finger crack. Continue up the finger crack then climb right on face holds to a ledge. Continue up the slab (5.6) to a horizontal crack for the belay, cams to #2 Camalot for the anchor.

FA: *Terry Andrews 2003*
Gear: cams to #4 Camalot, small wires
No anchor   60ft

5. Slab Route 5.5 ★★

Left of *Women on Mopeds* is low-angle rock with a nice slab that leads to ramp slabs just below Crab Eyes summit.

FA: *Unknown 1980s*
Gear: cams to #2 Camalot
No anchor   65ft

6. Wide Crack 5.6 ★

Climbs the wide corner to the left of *Women on Mopeds* start.

FA: *Unknown 1980s*
Gear: cams to #4 Camalot
No anchor   45ft

7. Women on Mopeds 5.10a ★★★

The classic hand crack on Crab Eyes! Scramble up the corner 15 feet to a ledge, step right and up (awkward) to get to the crack. From here climb fingers-to-hand size crack with good jams, 30 feet to an alcove (belay here). Traverse left under the overhang or continue up with *Babes on Harleys*.

FA: *Jon Frank, Mark Herndon, Duane Raleigh 1982*
Gear: #1 to #3 Camalot (#2–#3 for belay)
No anchor   50ft

7a. Women on Mopeds (Variation Start) 5.10- ★★★

Same start as *Rowins Andrews*, then step left and climb the face just below a small ledge leading to the starting finger crack of *Women on Mopeds*.

FA: *Tony Mayse, Joe Romero 2015*
Gear: finger-size cams
No anchor   35ft

8. Babes on Harleys 5.10+ ★★★

A wide-crack continuation to *Women on Mopeds*. Climb the offwidth crack above the alcove belay of *Women on Mopeds*. From the belay ledge step over the overhang to gain the offwidth, continue in the wide crack to the top. Burly.

FA: *Terry Andrews, Eric Arntzen 1993*
Gear: #3 to #5 Camalot (#2–#3 for belay)
No anchor   50ft

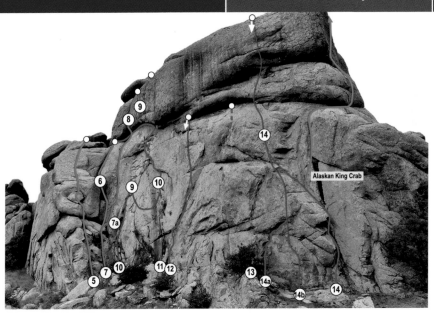

Alaskan King Crab

9. Rowins Andrews A2+ ★★

Aid route 10 feet right of *Women on Mopeds*. Climb a loose arching corner to a bolt 20 feet up, continue up past three rivets. Move right to a short vertical crack that leads to horizontal cracks above. Move up and over the horizontal cracks to gain the arching roof. Continue left 15 feet to a bulge with a rivet-ladder exit. This is a clean aid route; leave your pins at home.

FA: *Chris Rowins, Terry Andrews 1981*
Gear: TCUs, cams to #4 Camalot, offsets, stoppers
No anchor   80ft

10. Are You a God? 5.12c X ★★★

Thin, steep face climb to the right of *Rowins Andrews*. A key hold broke off this route shortly after the first ascent. On the first ascent in 1986, Duane Raleigh and Stuart Stanford hiked into Crab Eyes on a hot summer day carrying an ice chest full of water and Gatorade. The chest was carried "safari style" in between the two of them with a broom handle. The temps were so hot that they both soaked their hands in the ice to cool their skin in between attempts. Several falls were taken on the first ascent. The name of this climb came from the original *Ghost Busters* movie... When the ghost, Gozer, asked Ghostbuster Ray Stantz, "Are You a God?"

In 1982 an aid route named *Iron Love* (A4) climbed up fragile flakes intersecting with *Are You a God?* A quarter-inch bolt was placed on that ascent (since broken off). This bolt was used on the ascent of *Are You a God?* with a two-rope system.

FA: *Duane Raleigh, Stuart Stafford 1986*
Gear: quickdraws and cams to #3 Camalot.
No anchor   70ft

11. Iron Love A4 X ★★

Aid route starting 15 feet to the right of *Are You a God?*
FA: *Duane Raleigh 1982*
Gear: aid rack
No anchor   70ft

12. Yellow Beard 5.12c RX ★★★★

Formerly and aid climb named *Blade Runner*. Face climb up a yellow-colored wall, located about 5 feet to the right of *Iron Love*. Climb a short (5.10) face below a horizontal crack 10 feet to the first bolt. From here pull over the horizontal crack and traverse right and up 15 feet (5.9) on flakes to the second bolt. Move up to the third bolt continuing up steep and thin face climbing, ending at a 2-bolt anchor. Committing.

FA: *Russell Hooper, Tony Wilson 1991*
Gear: quickdraws
2-bolt anchor   60ft

13. Yellow Jacket A3 RX ★★

This is an aid climb just left of *Moby Dick Direct*. There is an old 1/4" bolt high on the route. Follow the arching seam to a horizontal crack up higher.
FA: *Duane Raleigh 1982*
Gear: hooks, beaks, and balls!
No anchor   55ft

Duane Raleigh on his test-piece route Are You a God? 5.12c X, circa 1980s. | Photo from the Doug Robinson collection

14. Moby Dick 5.12b ★★★★

This route follows a bolted line through a series of bulges up the face located 20 yards to the right of *Yellow Beard*. Climb the corner crack (5.8) up to the second bolt; continue on good edges and steep rock (5.11) up to the fourth bolt. The horizontal crack below the bulge and last bolt takes a variety of gear, Climb over the bulge protected by a bolt making your way to a 2-bolt anchor. Bouldery crux.

FA: Russell Hooper, Andrews 1991
Gear: cams to #2 Camalot, quickdraws
2-bolt anchor   *80ft*

14a. Moby Dick (Crack Start) 5.13a ★★

Climb the arching crack 6 feet left of *Moby Dick Direct*. Follow the arching crack to the first bolt. Climb over the bulge exiting right onto the slab leading to the second bolt. Continue on *Moby Dick*.

FA: Marcus Garcia 1990s
Gear: cams to #1 Camalot, quickdraws
2-bolt anchor   *80ft*

14b. Moby Dick Direct 5.13a ★★★

Direct start to *Moby Dick*. Climb the boulder problem face starting with a holdless undercling. Move up then slightly to the left to a bolt. Climb over the bulge exiting right onto the slab leading to the second bolt. Continue on *Moby Dick*.

FA: Terry Andrews 1990s
Gear: TCUs, quickdraws
2-bolt anchor   *80ft*

> *"The Rock Warrior knows that his time on earth is short, so he will make the most out of it."*
>
> ~Arno Ilgner | The Rock Warriors Way

Tony Mayse climbing Moby Dick 5.12b. | Photo by Andrew Burr

Tony Wilson on his route *Yellow Beard* 5.12c RX on the west side of Crab Eyes. | Photo by Harrison Shull

HIDDEN WALL

Hidden Wall is located a short distance from Lost Dome. The easiest way to reach Hidden Wall is to get to Lost Dome's south face and look back to your east, the formation can be seen with a prominent dihedral that snakes its way up a multicolored wall. Walk the trail in the direction of the wall then scramble up the boulder field to reach the base of the climbs.

The wall gets afternoon sun. Good spot for early summer mornings or later in the day during winter.

Approach time: 35–40 minutes

1. El Primo 5.9+ ★★★★
Located 30 feet to the left of *Serpentine*. Scramble up the large blocked steps to a ledge and belay spot. This route follows the horizontal crack for 30 feet then turns to a short vertical finger/hand crack before topping out on a nice ledge with a crack just made for the belay.

FA: *Unknown 1980s*

Gear: 0.5 to #2 Camalot
No anchor   65ft

2. Serpentine 5.11d ★★★★
This improbable looking line follows the prominent dihedral protected by three bolts and a fixed pin. From the ledge with a tree make your way up to another ledge, step left, then make your way up the corner to an overhang with a bolt. From the first bolt, the wall gets steep and bereft of any obvious holds. The best route on the cliff!

FA: *Duane Raleigh, Stewart Stafford 1986*

Gear: TCUs, cams to #2 Camalot, quickdraws
2-bolt anchor   60ft

3. Hidden Corner 5.9 ★★
Twenty feet right of *Serpentine*. Climb the corner crack with good gear for 40 feet, from here stoppers protect the face moves with a 15 foot runout to the belay ledge. Bring extra #1,#2 cams for the anchor.

FA: *Rick McCusic, Stewart Stafford 1986*

Gear: cams to #3 Camalot, stoppers
No anchor   60ft

4. Moves Among Serpents 5.10b X ★★
Face protected by gear just to the right of *Hidden Corner*. Start about 5 feet to the right of *Hidden Corner*. Steep climbing on featured rock. Good protection at the bottom horizontal crack, continue up with marginal placements until higher up on the route. Bring extra #1 and #2 cams for the anchor.

FA: *Jimmy Forester 2006*

Gear: 0.5 to #2 Camalot
No anchor   60ft

5. Unknown 5.12+ RX ★★
Located far to the right of *Moves Among Serpents*. Starting at ground level climb up an easy slab to the base of a bulge with a horizontal crack. Pull up over the overhanging bulge to a cruxy stemming section and small gear placement which protects this sustained section. The rock to the right of the starting bulge is exfoliating, stay left. Bring extra #1, #2 cams for the anchor.

FA: *Marcus Garcia 2002*

Gear: small wires, TCUs, cams to #2 Camalot
No anchor   60ft

Hidden Wall

Stanley Vrba climbing the overhanging Serpentine 5.11d. | Photo by Andrew Burr

Cedar Rock

6. Scary Terry 5.10c ★★

Located in the corridor behind Hidden Wall. From the climb *Forgotten* walk north behind Hidden Wall. *Scary Terry* is the obvious diagonal finger crack on the west-facing wall (no topo).

FA: *Terry Andrews 2005*

Gear: small cams

No anchor   60ft

7. Forgotten 5.10b ★★★

Finger crack located on a small, west-facing outcrop 50 yards south of *Serpentine*. Climb up easy rock to the start of the finger crack. Continue up the diagonal crack to the top.

FA: *Chris Marks 2006*

Gear: small cams to #1 Camalot

No anchor   50ft

> "A few hours of mountain climbing
>
> turn a villain and a saint
>
> into two rather equal creatures.
>
> Exhaustion is the shortest way
>
> to equality and fraternity."
>
> ~Friedrich Nietzche

LOST DOME

Lost Dome is located in the Charon Gardens Wilderness Area. It is about a 35–40 minute walk from the Sunset parking. Lost Dome is just to the west and downhill from Crab Eyes. (See overview map on page 130.) There are 27 routes at the Lost Dome formation ranging from 5.6–5.13. The route heights vary from 60 feet to the classic 140 foot *Lost My Religion*.

Lost Dome is divided into three areas: Lost Dome (West Face), Lost Dome (East Wall) and Lost Dome (South Face). Two 60-meter ropes are recommended; a 70-meter rope reaches the bottom of the cliff from the top anchors, however use caution.

Approach time: 35–40 minutes

LOST DOME (EAST WALL)

Located 100 yards uphill from the South Face. The routes start in the shade of large cedar trees with a flat base. There are four routes on this wall rated 5.6–5.11. This is a late-afternoon summer climbing area or morning destination in the winter months.

Molly Hennesy on the crux of Come Get Your Love 5.10b. | Photo by Preston Pettigrew

1. Pimpin' Ain't Easy 5.11 ★★★

Located 10 feet to the left of *Come Get Your Love* and just to the right of a large cedar tree. Climb up and over 2 bulges leading to a shelf and easier climbing. The easier climbing ends at the bottom of a short overhanging headwall. Climb up the overhanging section on diagonal rails, continuing up steep rock to a horizontal crack which intersects with *Papa was a Rollin' Stone*, ending on a large ledge. The route has been led with a fixed static line pending bolt application. (A future mixed route.)

FA: Tony, Buster, Five Mayse   Dec. 24, 2016

Gear: toprope

No anchor   65ft

2. Papa was a Rollin' Stone 5.9 ★★★

Climb up to the first 4 bolts on *Come Get Your Love* then continue out to the left in a horizontal crack on hand jams. At the crack's end, make your way to a large ledge above.

FA: Tony, Buster & Five Mayse   Dec. 24, 2016

Gear: fingers to #3 Camalot

No anchor   65ft

3. Come Get Your Love 5.10b ★★★

Located 10 yards to the right of *Pimpin' Ain't Easy*. Climb up the face on solid rock and good edges past 4 bolts. The fifth bolt sits below a short, vertical wall leading to the anchors. Climb past this bolt through a tricky section for 10 feet. (Stepping out to the right below the fifth bolt avoids the crux, reducing the grade to 5.9.)

FA: Peter Holcombe, Aaron Gibson 1995

Gear: quickdraws

2-bolt anchor   60ft

4. 5.6 Corner ★

Corner crack climb to the right of *Come Get Your Love*. Climb the corner which leads up to the left sharing the anchors of *Come Get Your Love*.

FA: Unknown 1990s

Gear: cams to #3 Camalot

2-bolt anchor   60ft

Lost Dome

Tony Mayse climbing Drop Dead 5.11b. Established in the 80s, this remains a sought-after crack climb in Charon Gardens. | Photo by Andrew Burr

LOST DOME (SOUTH FACE)

The majority of Lost Dome's climbs are located on a south-facing red and yellow, lichen-covered wall. The first climbs established here were in the late 1970s and through the 1980s. Classic crack routes are *Fear of the Right*, *For a Rocker*, *Larry's Folly*, *Drop Dead*, and *Steep Show* to name a few. The hard, slick face climb *Slime of the Century* was also climbed in ground-up style without bolts. Later, bolts were added with permission from the first ascentionist.

In the early 1990s, some of the hardest bolted face climbs in the Wichita's were established, with routes like *Rap Bolters from Hell*, *Lost My Religion*, *Made in the Shade*, and the venerable *Tied to the Whipping Post*. Some easier bolted lines like *Crack-a-Lolo* were established ground-up and *Come Get Your Love* (bolted on rappel), were climbed in the mid 90s.

5. Show Stopper 5.12b Toprope ★★

A strenuous overhanging crack climb located 5 feet to the left of *Steep Show*. Powerful moves from the start and continuing up a steep lieback crack, lead to face moves then the upper crack of *Steep Show*.

FA: Tony Mayse, Stanley Vrba 2011
Gear: toprope
No anchor   70ft

6. Steep Show 5.11d ★★★★

Located a few feet to the right of *Show Stopper*. Hand to fist-crack that starts from a large ledge. Climb up easy rock (3rd class) to a stance. From here climb right to an overhanging hand crack. Climb up the crack to a fist-size section, and then move up and left to easier climbing to the top. (Currently a fixed sling is at the top for the belay, inspect the webbing.)

FA: Duane Raleigh 1986
Gear: 0.5 to #2 Camalot
No anchor   70ft

7. Drop Dead 5.11b R ★★★

Starts from the same ledge as *Steep Show*, 10 feet left of *Slime of the Century*. From the ledge move up on lie back moves to a vertical crack. Face climb on steep rock 20 feet to a small ledge. Climb left and up to a hand crack and another stance, continue on thin edges and a flaring crack up to the anchors.

FA: Duane Raleigh 1986
Gear: TCUs to #2 Camalot, stoppers
2-bolt anchor   60ft

7a. Drop Dead Continuation 5.11c/d ★

Continue past the anchor, moving out to the right (5.11c) protected by the anchor bolt. From a good stance continue climbing on moderate ground to the sling belay of *Steep Show*.

FA: *Tony Mayse, Mike Hankins 2007*

Gear: cams to #2 Camalot

2-bolt anchor   30ft

8. Slime of the Century 5.11c ★★★★

Bolted line 20 feet left of *Rap Bolters from Hell*. Climb 12 feet up the smooth face (start is usually wet) to a bolt, step right and up to a short hand crack. Work your way to an overhang and continue on a steep bolt protected face to a 2-bolt anchor.

FA: *Duane Raleigh 1986*

Gear: quickdraws, (1) #0.75 cam

2-bolt anchor   70ft

9. Rap Bolters from Hell 5.12a R ★★★★

Bolted line left of *Tied to the Whipping Post*. Climb up 15 feet to the first bolt; move up and to the left 12 feet on steep rock to the second bolt. From here, follow sustained (5.12) climbing protected by 4 bolts and a fixed pin. A prized redpoint!

FA: *Terry Andrews 1991*

Gear: quickdraws

2-bolt anchor   70ft

Tony Mayse climbing Tied to the Whipping Post 5.13a. Photo by Stanley Vrba

The late Jimmy Forester on Rap Bolters from Hell 5.12a. | Photo by Ryan Ray

In October 2015 Climbing Magazine listed Rap Bolters from Hell as one of "America's 100 Best Sport Climbing Routes." This route is as "backcountry" as is gets for the Sooner State. A two mile hike through the beautiful and wildlife-filled (bison anyone?) Charon Gardens Wilderness Area will make you think you're in Vedauwoo, and this beautiful crimp-filled face has the fun and techy climbing of Smith Rock with the "crowds" of, well, Oklahoma.

~Climbing Magazine October 2015

10. Tied to the Whipping Post 5.13a ★★★★

Climbs the bolted line up a water streak. Climb 15 feet to the first bolt, step right and move up over a short roof to the second bolt, from here continue up the bolt-protected face on water smoothed holds. This is the hardest route on Lost Dome and the first (5.13) in the refuge.

FA: *Tony Wilson, Russell Hooper 1991*

Gear: quickdraws

2-bolt anchor   70ft

In October 2015 Climbing Magazine listed Tied to the Whipping Post as "America's 100 Best Sport Climbing Routes." Located on the Lost Dome with Rap Bolters from Hell, this "old school" 5.13 line climbs a gray water streak on perfect red granite covered with green lichen in a beautiful setting far enough from the car that it's almost guaranteed you'll be alone. What else could you want?

~Climbing Magazine October 2015

Molly Hennesy climbing Larry's Folly 5.8+ at Lost Dome. | Photo by Preston Pettigrew

11. Lost My Religion 5.12a/b R ★★★★
A mixed climb starting 12 feet down and to the right of *Tied to the Whipping Post*. Climb a (5.9) slab for 20 feet to the first bolt. Continue up and to the right to a bolt below a short overhang. Continue up to a stance and a bolt. From here climb the crack, protected by a pin and gear, making your way to a final slab protected by two bolts. Use two ropes to rappel from the top anchors.

FA: Russell Hooper 1991
Gear: quickdraws, cams to #2 Camalot
2-bolt anchor　　　　　　　　　140ft

12. Larry's Folly A.K.A. Fuson's Folly 5.8+ ★★
Twenty feet right of *Lost My Religion* is a small ledge with a wide diagonal crack above. Climb the crack to a fixed pin, move past the pin, continue in a crack that turns into a chimney, exit onto the slab and belay station. Named after Larry Fuson who took a big fall while on the first-ascent attempt of this climb with his partner Ramsey Telley. Towards the top of the climb, as it enters the chimney, Larry fell, almost hitting the ground. Larry never made it back to Lost Dome to complete the climb, as such the route was named after him and the big whip!

FA: Marc Johnston, Larry Fuson 1981
Gear: cams to #3 Camalot
2-bolt anchor　　　　　　　　　140ft

13. The Dutchman 5.9+ RX ★★★
This route climbs the unprotected slab to the right of *Larry's Folly*. The lower slab has featured rock with no protection until higher up and just below the horizontal crack. Climb onto the headwall and a bolt. Continue up the face, protected by a small TCU, to easier climbing. Bring a couple #2 cams for the anchor then rappel off Lost Dome's top anchors.

FA: Tony Wilson, Russell Hooper 1990s
Gear: small cams #2 Camalot
No anchor　　　　　　　　　　　75ft

14. Crack-a-LoLo 5.10c R ★★★
This is the first route on Lost Dome's south face; the route is located just right of the tree before you walk up to the rock steps towards the sunny face of Lost Dome. Boulder up 15 feet (5.11) to a shelf with a good stance. Continue to a short crack, then climb on good edges past three bolts moving onto to a low-angle slab that leads to a 2-bolt anchor. To avoid the boulder start, some climbers opt for the easy start in the corner to the left and then step back right. The base of this climb is a great summer hang with its shaded trees.

FA: Tony Mayse, Lori & Alex Boren, Carl Murray 1993
Gear: quickdraws, #1.5 cam
2-bolt anchor　　　　　　　　　70ft

Stanley Vrba climbing Larry's Folly 5.8+ | Photo by Andrew Burr

Angry Inch Boulder Problem

This angry little problem is located about 100 yards south of Lost Dome. East facing with a flat base. Look for an obvious overhanging boulder with rails leading to crimps and a slab top out.

Angry Inch 5.13 ★★★★

Sit start, toe hook and lock down on a rail leading to crimps and a long reach out to the left making your way to the top.
FA: Sean Dosset

Angry Inch

John Tarkington cranking down on the Angry Inch 5.13. | Photo by Sierra Tarkington

climb UP

BY CLIMBERS. FOR CLIMBERS.

NORMAN (405) 310-4648
CLIMBUPGYM.COM

PROFESSIONAL INSTRUCTION

EXPANSIVE BOULDERING

YOGA STUDIO & KIDS PROGRAMS

2 UNIQUE LOCATIONS!

OUR PARTNERS

15. For a Rocker 5.8+ ★★

Around the corner 20 feet right from *Crack-a-LoLo*. Undercling moves get you started on the smooth face, move left and up and then continue to a stance below the hand crack. Climb the crack exiting left to the anchors on *Crack-a-LoLo*.

FA: Terry Andrews, Carl Murray 1978
Gear: cams to #3.5 Camalot
2-bolt anchor   70ft

16. Made in the Shade 5.12 RX ★★★

Hard face climb a few feet to the right of *For a Rocker*. Boulder up 15 feet to a stance, move up 10 feet to the first bolt, continue up thin holds and steeper climbing to the second bolt making your way over the bulge to a slab leading to the belay anchors of *Crack-a-LoLo*.

FA: Terry Andrews, Carl Murray 1990
Gear: quickdraws
2-bolt anchor   70ft

17. Gong Show 5.7

Located to the right of *Made in the Shade* is a large flake that "gongs" when you hit it. Climb the Gong flake; continue in the crack which leads to a large ledge up top.

FA: Terry Andrews 2004
Gear: cams to #3 Camalot
No anchor   50ft

18. Blades of Steel 5.10d R ★

Short face climb located by a tree 15 yards to the right of *Made in the Shade*. Climb up the face 10 feet to a bolt, move up on thin smears to a stance just left of the crack (at one time protected by fixed copperheads). Continue up the face past two bolts making your way to a two bolt anchor with rap hangers.

FA: Steve Gillam, Mike Hankins 1988
Gear: quickdraws
2-bolt anchor   40ft

19. Hand Crack 5.7+ ★★

In between *Blades of Steel* and *Fear of the Right* is a short hand crack that never gets climbed. Climb the crack and continue on *Fear of the Right*.

FA: 1980s
Gear: cams to #3 Camalot
No anchor   75ft

20. Fear of the Right 5.10 R ★★

Start on the same ledge as *Last Rites* but move up and left to a stance below a bolt. Continue up the face and climb the dihedral left of *Last Rites*. Rappel from the anchors on *Baptists on the Rampage*.

FA: Marc Johnson, Steve Harwell, Keith Egan 1982
Gear: cams to #3 Camalot
No anchor   75ft

21. Last Rites 5.9+ ★★

Located a few feet to the right of *Fear of the Right*. Climb up the corner to the roof, then move right following the dihedral; continue to the anchors on *Baptists on the Rampage*. Tricky start.

FA: Keith Egan, Steve Harwell, Marc Johnston 1981
Gear: quickdraws
2-bolt anchor   80ft

22. Baptists on the Rampage 5.11a R ★★

Located to the right of *Last Rites*. Climb steep rock to a bolt; move right and up face climbing past four bolts to a 2-bolt anchor. Sustained face climbing.

FA: Steve Gillam, Mike Hankins 1988
Gear: quickdraws
2-bolt anchor   90ft

23. Sugar Momma 5.10b ★★

Located 15 feet to the right of *Baptists on the Rampage*. Climb up a corner just to the right of a short slab, making your way to a small roof with a loose chockstone. Climb up and over the roof and continue up a corner crack which leads to an offwidth size crack ending at the anchors of *Baptists on the Rampage*.

FA: Daniel Schuerch, Elisha Gallegos 2016
Gear: wires to large cams
2-bolt anchor   80ft

24. Dance Hall Girls A3 ★★

Aid climb approximately 30 feet to the right of *Baptists on the Rampage*. Rarely climbed.

FA: Steve Gillam, Mike Hankins 1988
Gear: standard aid rack
No anchor   60ft

LOST DOME WEST FACE

Approach: From Lost Dome (East Wall) walk to the south for approximately 100 yards, then turn right making your way through a narrow corridor and scramble down the large boulders towards the base of Lost Dome's west face. There are three routes on this seldom climbed wall and all are worth doing. These forgotten routes were established in the early 1980s. Bring hand-size cams for the belay on top as there are no anchors. Walk off to the north and downclimb the northwest corner to get back to the base. (See overview map on page 41.)

1. O.U. Mountaineer's Route 5.9 ★★

Established by one of the early pioneers of this area, Marc Johnson. Crack climb on the far left side of the wall. Climb the right angling-crack until it intersects with a vertical hand crack leading to the top. Thread through the boulders up top to set up the belay.

FA: Marc Johnson et al. 1981
Gear: cams to #3 Camalot
No anchor   75ft

CEDAR ROCK

Cedar Rock is a formation south and west of Lost Dome. It is easily reached by first hiking to Lost Dome and then uphill to *Come and get Your Love* and then along the wall to the top westernmost part of the wall. It is at this rise that you get a great view of the main face of Lost Dome and the South face of Cedar Rock. Hike down into a boulder-socked gully and find the path of least resistance through the rocks until reaching the opposite side of the gully where you will find a faint trail leading to crag. The most prominent line is a crack route on the right side of the formation which forms a precarious looking pillar at the top. There are 6 routes from 5.6–5.12.

Approach time from Lost Dome: 5 minutes

1. Patch 5.6 ★

This is the short crack on the left side of the wall that gets you to the top of the formation.

FA: Aaron Gibson 2006

Gear: medium to wide cams

No anchor   50ft

2. Obscene Phone Calls 5.8+ R ★★★

Located in between *O.U. Mountaineers* and *Jack Slap*. Face climb up knobs and good edges left of *Jack Slap*. This route intersects with, and continues up, the vertical hand crack of *O.U. Mountaineers Route*. Another excellent climb by Marc Johnson.

FA: Marc Johnson et al. 1981

Gear: finger size cams to #2 Camalot

No anchor   75ft

3. Jack Slap 5.10b ★★★★

Mixed climb with bolts to the right of *Obscene Phone Calls*. Climb the easy ramp to a bolt, continue up on knobs and steep face climbing protected by bolts to a belay in between boulders up top. Walk off to the north then scramble back down to the base. Outstanding.

FA: Jack Hill et al 1984

Gear: cams to #2 Camalot

No anchor   75ft

> *"This route is sustained but submits to good footwork."* ~Bob Kamps

2. O-Face 5.10d ★★★

This route combines technical face climbing with a couple of small roofs. Gear is required before the first bolt. After clipping the first bolt pull onto the face and climb up underneath a small roof. Here you can place a solid small/med cam. Pull through the roof and clip the second bolt. After clipping the second bolt pull through another bulge section and make a few face moves to reach the top.

FA: Aaron Gibson 2006

Gear: quickdraws, small cams (aliens) & cams to #1 Camalot

2-bolt anchor   40ft

Lost Dome
West Face

Aaron Gibson hand-drilling a bolt on the first ascent of O-Face 5.10d. | Photo from Gibson Collection

Cedar Rock

3. Kubrick Corner 5.10c ★★ Toprope
Begin at the base of *O-Face* and climb up and right following the angling feature to what appears to be a shallow dihedral. A short but technical climb.

FA: *Aaron Gibson*

Gear: toprope

No anchor   40ft

4. Crack of Fate A.K.A. Pillar of Fate 5.8 - ★★★
This is the most obvious line on Cedar Rock. A crack splits the right side and forms a precariously perched pillar formation at the top. The climb starts on the lower right side hidden in the trees. Climb a well-featured face to a dihedral/mini-roof. Step up and left, a tricky sequence leads to a bomber crack leading to the top.

FA: *Aaron Gibson et al.*

Gear: cams to #3 Camalot

No anchor   60ft

5. Steady Like Stedman 5.11a ★★ Toprope
Begins just downhill and right of *Crack of Fate*. Climb a balancy face up and right until reaching a crack system that takes you to the top of the formation.

FA: *Aaron Gibson 2006*

Gear: toprope

No anchor   60ft

6. Steady Like Stedman Direct Toprope 5.12? ★★
Begins downhill from *Crack of Fate* in the cave-like overhang area. Climb the steep overhang directly up to the beginning of the crack system, turn the lip and head directly up.

FA: *Open Project*

Gear: toprope

No anchor   60ft

Pick up trail in front of sign

Big Whiskey Area Parking
(road view looking east)

BIG WHISKEY PEAK

Big Whiskey Peak has four routes on a west-facing cliff with a long approach. This is a good place if you are looking for a bit of solitude and a few hard climbs.

Approach: Located on the far west end of the refuge on Hwy 49. From the cattle guard at the entrance to the refuge zero out your odometer; the pullout for Big Whiskey Peak will be 16.6 miles (see overview map on page 41). Park at the very last pullout on your left (south), if you have gone over the cattle guard you have gone too far. After parking your vehicle at the pullout, walk towards the refuge sign heading east on Hwy 49 for 20 yards, then turn right (south), walking through the clearing then eventually picking up a trail taking you through trees. Continue walking south and follow the boundary-line fence which will be to your right (west). Continue south keeping the fence in sight. Once you get out of the trees there will be three rolling hills in an open field. Continue heading south then turning southeast and crossing a few small creeks along the way. The fence will at some point turn back to the west (do not follow it), continue heading southeast. A west-facing yellow lichen-covered cliff should be visible to your south and east from the last rolling hill in the open field. The hike takes about an hour—at least it did for me and my wife with three dogs on our first time hiking to Big Whiskey Peak.

(See the overview photo.)

Approach time: 45-60 minutes

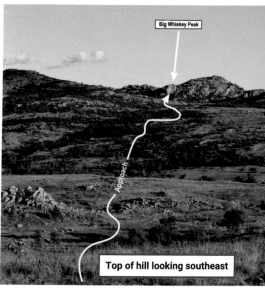

Big Whiskey Peak

Approach

Top of hill looking southeast

1. The Elk Horn Special 5.12d ★★★★

Leftmost bolted line and the hardest route on Big Whiskey Peak. The anchor for *The Elk Horn Special* is actually behind the ramp and is a separate anchor. Bolted in the 90s by Tony Wilson. Several attempts were made over a 10-year period until Russell Hooper finally sent it! Check out the video of Russell Hooper making the first ascent.

FA: Russell Hooper early 2000s

Gear: quickdraws

2-bolt anchor 60ft

Russell Hooper
Video

2. Here Comes a Horseman 5.11c ★★★

Bolted line just to the right of *The Elk Horn Special*.
Climb a steep face ending at a 2-bolt anchor.

FA: *Tony Wilson, Russell Hooper 1990s*

Gear: quickdraws

2-bolt anchor   60ft

3. The Unforgiven 5.11b/c ★★★

Finger crack located in the middle of the formation.
Climb up the seam to an undercling flake leading
to a corner. Continue up the corner with good
protection ending on a ramp. Easy climbing to the
top.

FA: *Tony Wilson, Russell Hooper 1990s*

Gear: small cams to #1 Camalot

No anchor   60ft

4. 5.9 Crack ★

Located on the upper right corner of Big Whiskey
Peak. Climb the dihedral flake with good protection.

FA: *Unknown*

Gear: cams to #2 Camalot

No anchor   50ft

*"There is nothing else than now. There is neither
yesterday, certainly, nor is there any tomorrow. How
old must you be before you know that? There is only
now, and if now is only two days, then two days is
your life and everything in it will be in proportion.
This is how you live a life in two days. And if you stop
complaining and asking for what you will never get,
you will have a good life."*

~Ernest Hemingway | For Whom the Bell Tolls

THE PARTNERSHIP
By Tony Wilson

Being a rock climber in Oklahoma in the late 70s and early 80s was no small feat. While there were a handful of hardcore regulars who furiously gobbled up the mostly virgin faces of the Wichita Mountain Wildlife Refuge and Quartz Mountain, they were more like a secret society than the vanguard of a new sport. At least, that's how I remember it.

I had been fascinated with rock climbing ever since seeing climbers at the Garden of the Gods in Colorado while on a family vacation in the late 60s. However, I had not managed to learn how to do anything about it up until college when a friend, Don Moseley, and I began roaming the Wichitas, climbing up anything we could muster the courage to tackle. Since we had no gear or training our success was limited. Our best effort was to climb *Great Expectations* of Elk Mountain slabs with no more than my orange converse basketball shoes and his gigantic waffle-stomper boots. I still recall scooting on our butts with our backs to the wall of the overhang until we could downclimb the gully on the west. Since it was the late 70s, I'm sure the two technical climbers hanging at the belay below us were likely secret society members, who may still be telling stories about the fools they witnessed that day. I often wonder who they were and if I've climbed with them since.

After this I moved to North Carolina for graduate school and didn't pursue any more climbing till returning to Oklahoma in the early 80s. Don had left to be an NFL trainer so I hooked up with his brother, Bruce, and we took a climbing course offered by Doug Robinson through Backwoods outdoor store. After learning the basics, I bought a rope, some EB shoes, and a swami belt and began teaching myself with the help of Royal Robbins' book, *Basic Rock Craft*.

I remember we somehow found Quartz Mountain and spent the weekend camped on the back side throwing ourselves at the green slabs, finally topping out the last day, and then seeing people on the real rock climbing side. We were so embarrassed at our ineptitude that we downclimbed and scurried away.

I kept coming back, though, now with my new girlfriend, Pam, who 30 years later is still tolerating my climbing obsession. Our first date was rock climbing and with her I started leading climbs like *Bourbon Street*, *Crazy Alice*, and the fearsome *S Wall*. I was finally a real climber.

Soon after, I decided to go to Red Rocks, Nevada for some of the big climbs I'd read about. I'd met a guy through the Moseley brothers from Amarillo who was climbing some at Quartz. He said he'd go with me but wanted to bring along his partner. I said sure but warned, "be sure he can keep up with us." That guy was Russell Hooper.

When we got to Red Rocks we of course picked out *Dream of the Wild Turkeys* as the climb for us. On the first pitch my Texas friend discovered he didn't like heights so we lowered him down and Russ and I forged on, only to grind to a halt one pitch higher. We moved over to the *Solar Slab* (5.6), which was more our speed, and 1,000 or so feet later, we topped out. Even though we had an epic descent in the dark with no headlamps, the die was cast. Russ and I were officially partners and remained so for the next 26 years.

The Legend of the Wichitas: Russell Hooper. Always with a smile after punching laps on the incomparable *Tied to the Whipping Post* 5.13a, circa 2009

Back home in Oklahoma, we climbed every chance we could, gradually working our way up through the grades till we became worthy, at least in our own eyes, to start mixing with the secret society clan. At some point I climbed enough with Duane Raleigh, who stood atop the clan hierarchy, to learn how to put up new routes. After partnering with him on *Space Balls*, and a few others, I began watching out for routes of my own. Duane moved to Colorado, and Russ, who always favored established routes, at first avoided working on new routes. He'd say, "Too much work, I just want to climb." Forced to forage for routes solo I wondered around Charon Gardens and by chance found Lost Dome. Looking up the wall, I saw a fresh line of bolts that Terry Andrews, another original clansman, had placed just the week before on the route he called Tap Dancers from Hell but later changed to *Rap Bolters from Hell*. It looked like a great climb but my eyes shifted to the right

Tony Wilson climbing *Yellow Beard* 5.12c RX, 1990s

onto the beautiful rock that became *Tied to the Whipping Post*. I was back the next weekend with bolts and quickly punched in the line and began working it with Pam belaying. It quickly became obvious it was above my pay grade and I set in for the long haul.

It didn't take long before Russ joined me and we were at Lost Dome every chance we could. Russ worked *Whipping Post* but agreed it was going to take time so he moved over to the right and put up *Lost My Religion* while I continued to dial in the moves on *Whipping Post*.

Russ got *Lost My Religion* first then we switched and I soon did the same. It took several more months before either of us could lead *Whipping Post*. I was focused on just getting strong enough to pull the crux move, which involves a long reach to the crescent. Russ was a small guy and was shut down by the move not because of strength but due to the long reach. Eventually I got the move and made the chains. In the meantime, Russ shifted gears and figured out a crux sequence that I've never seen anyone else use. For him it was the key, and he soon got the lead. Thinking back, it was a grand experience that brought out the best in us.

After that our appetite for new climbs soared. We had started tower climbing in Utah, which required aid skills which we quickly embraced. Russ also began climbing a lot at the old Rock Quarry north of Snyder, Oklahoma. He was focused on the some of the hardest routes there, which were mostly out of my reach unless I lost about 20 pounds.

Not willing to give up any more calories, hard aid climbing became my focus. In order to train for new routes in Utah, I searched out places in the refuge to practice. *Crab Eyes* was already home to cutting-edge aid routes put up by Duane in years past. *Blade Runner* on the west face looked like the plum. On a solo trip up *Blade Runner* it dawned on me that this might be free-climbable. When I told Russ I'd tried it and put in bolts there was no hesitation; we both began working the route. We named it *Yellow Beard* since I was currently on a Monty Python movie binge and it fit the colors of the wall. This time Russ got the first lead with me getting the second. We were ecstatic to have such high-quality climbs on the two major formations in Charon Gardens.

After that we searched out the backcountry for more of the same but didn't find anything comparable. It was on a weekend backcountry trip that Pam and I stumbled onto the formation we named Big Whiskey. It seemed like a mirage when we found it. Since we had climbing gear with us, I quickly went to work and got the bolts in and began working the routes. I didn't get anything led that weekend but over the next few weekends Russ and I spent all our time there. Since I had found the cliff and done the bolting work, Russ graciously allowed me to work on the first ascents. *The Unforgiven* was the first and then *Comes a Horseman*. He quickly did the same. However, *The Elkhorn Special* became a beast for us both. In the crux I couldn't let go to clip the bolt. Russ had the same problem. We eventually focused on other climbs and would come back periodically but never succeeded. Years went by and Russ had continued climbing hard, in spite of dealing with various cancer treatments, while I had become focused on my new daughter, Adalia, and going back to graduate school. At some point Russ and I were climbing at Quartz when I said, "You know, if we had any kind of gumption we would go straight to Big Whiskey and see if you could put *Elkhorn* to bed." We were at the base in a couple of hours and, incredibly, Aaron Gibson was there with his video camera. You can watch Russ's amazing ascent on YouTube. In an inspired effort, he climbed past the crux bolt and then clipped it from above. When he hit the anchors, *The Elkhorn Special* was his. I still get excited when I remember what it felt like to belay him that day.

These memories are just a fraction of the 26 years we shared together. I think they provide a window into how some of those Oklahoma classics came to be. Our partnership was a treasure. Only now that he is gone do I fully realize the uniqueness we shared together. I was lucky to know and climb with him. Every time I start up a route I hear him saying "Don't Suck!" and it makes me bear down to try and climb up to his standards. I hope those who are beginning their climbing career are half as fortunate in the partners they find.

Jimmy Ratzlaff climbing the thin edges on Silent Scream 5.10b RX, while being belayed by Jon Frank circa the early 1980s. | Photo from the Jimmy Ratzlaff Collection.

INTRODUCTION TO QUARTZ MOUNTAIN

The climbing at Quartz Mountain offers some of the best granite you will find anywhere on earth, with flawless stretches of clean rock. Climbing at Quartz is an adventure; this is not a sport climbing area, with bolts every few feet, most bolts at Quartz have been placed on lead from the ground-up. This has resulted in many runout sections between bolts. The majority of the old ¼-inch bolts have been replaced with new ⅜-inch or ½-inch bolts. The crux moves are usually protected, with the run out sections having easier climbing.

Routes at Quartz Mountain will not submit to a casual state of mind; you better have your "lead head" on when stepping out on the sharp end. Not all of the routes are runout. Some climbs like *El Tesoro, Romper Room, Accidents Will Happen* and *Super Slide* have had bolts installed with the first ascentionist's permission. Before retro-bolting, these climbs were solo climbs with no protection. The Super Slide Area was bolted in early 2000 prior to Old Baldy being purchased by the climbing community. This area gives climbers new to Quartz Mountain a protected introduction to the climbing.

A standard set of stoppers and cams up to #3 Camalot, slings, and a few quickdraws for the occasional bolt should suffice for protection needed on the majority of the climbs at Old Baldy. A 60-meter rope is the standard; however, a 70-meter rope is preferred.

Please do not set up toprope climbs on the rappel links, use your own slings and carabiners.

Quartz, with its south-facing walls, is a great winter destination. You can climb in the summer if you get up early to beat the heat, then as the day warms up head to Lake Altus for some swimming.

These are the climbing areas; S Wall, Head Wall, Sea of Screams, South America Wall, Grunt Chamber, Watch Me Wall, Stray Cats Wall, Quartz Backside, and Quartz Mountain Bouldering.

Duane Raleigh, Bill Thomas, Jimmy Ratzlaff, Jon Frank, Mark Herndon, Chris Rowins, Terry Andrews, Greg Schooley and many others are responsible for establishing the majority of the routes at Quartz Mountain in a style that is still revered to this day. The climbing at Quartz is runout for the most part, however, the climbs were not established to make a statement of boldness. They were done with the intellectual cunning and savvy that comes from experience. The routes were climbed by individuals that put their time into the climbing here. The newcomer to Quartz Mountain rock climbing must also learn this style in order to develop the skill set needed. Experience is only gained through hard work and effort. The desire to learn and improve makes all this possible.

> *"It's like a Tuolumne dome that got lost and ended up in a wheat field in Oklahoma."*
>
> ~Doug Robinson

Photo by Andrew Burr

Tony Mayse on the "sketchy" slab of Master Race 5.12a RX. | Photo by Andrew Burr

GETTING TO QUARTZ MOUNTAIN

• **From Oklahoma City**: Drive west on Interstate 40 for about 100 miles, take the Foss Altus exit. Turn south on Hwy 44. You will pass through the towns of Burns Flat, Sentinel, and Lone Wolf. Stay on Hwy 44, which winds it's way around Lake Altus. When you reach the sign that says Quartz Mountain Resort turn right (north) on Hwy 44A. Drive 1.5 miles to the fork in the road; turn left (west) at the fork which heads towards the town of Granite. Follow this winding road for about 2.4 miles. Turn right (north) on the first paved road. Stay on the paved road for one mile; turning right on a dirt road (you should be able to see a farm house on the left side of the road just slightly northwest of the dirt road). Follow the dirt road that leads to the parking area below the south face of Quartz. The drive from Oklahoma City is about 2½ hours.

• **From Dallas, Texas**: Drive north on Hwy 287 to Vernon. Exit on Hwy 283 to Altus. From Altus drive 15 miles north passing through the town of Blair. From Blair take Hwy 283 to Hwy 44. At the sign that says Quartz Mountain Resort turn left (north) on Hwy 44A. Drive 1.5 miles to a fork in the road. Turn left (west) following a winding road for 2.4 miles. Turn right (north) on the first paved road. Follow the paved road for one mile. Turn right (east) on the dirt road; follow the dirt road to the parking area below the south face of Quartz

Emergency Numbers
Call 911 then ask for Greer County Sheriff. This will put you in contact with the local law enforcement.

QUARTZ MOUNTAIN/OLD BALDY RULES & REGULATIONS

Old Baldy climbing area has the same rules as the neighboring state park. The area is routinely patrolled by the local Greer County Sheriff. Certain rules do apply while visiting and climbing here.

Day use only area.

No camping.

No fires.

Pets must be leashed and attended at all times. (Please do not tie your dog up and go rock climbing).

No hunting.

No drones.

No mountain bike riding.

No bolting without the approval from the bolting committee.

See www.wichitamountains.org for more information.

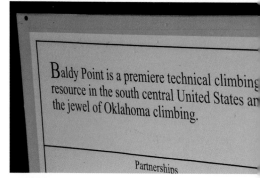

Baldy Point is a premiere technical climbing resource in the south central United States and the jewel of Oklahoma climbing.

Partnerships

Photos by Andrew Burr

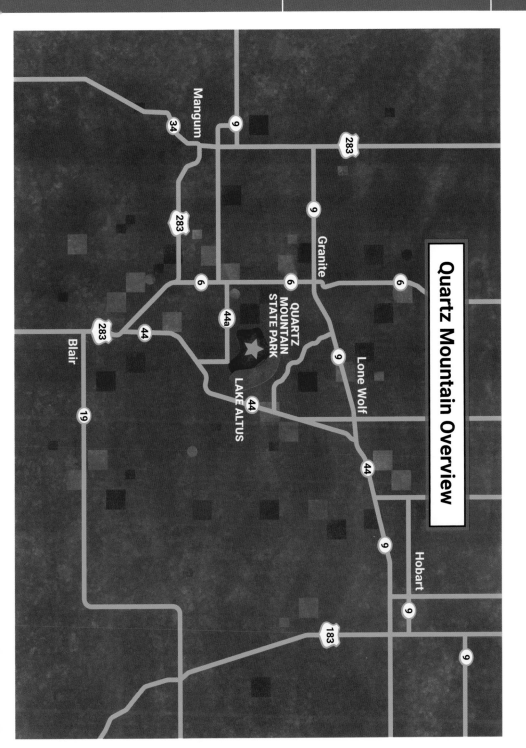

Quartz Mountain Overview

Quartz Mountain Area Map

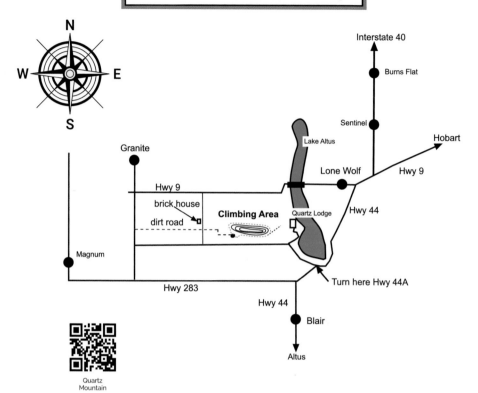

Climbing Area

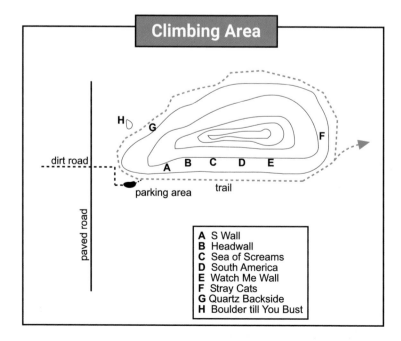

A S Wall
B Headwall
C Sea of Screams
D South America
E Watch Me Wall
F Stray Cats
G Quartz Backside
H Boulder till You Bust

Fall Gathering 2016

CAMPING

The Quartz Mountain State Park campground is two miles east of Quartz. There are rest rooms, showers, electrical hook-ups and a seasonal convenience store. Old Baldy allows camping during the "Fall Gathering" usually held the first weekend of November and the "Spring Fling" which is usually the first weekend in April every year.

QUARTZ MOUNTAIN RESORT ARTS & CONFERENCE CENTER

 Located just a few miles east from the climbing area. The lodge has a nice restaurant, bar and all the amenities for deluxe evenings as well lodging: www.quartzmountainresort.com.

Reservations Toll Free (877) 999-5567

Local number (580) 563-3028

QUARTZ MOUNTAIN PLACES TO EAT

Quartz Mountain State Lodge

Mountain retreat offering rustic-chic lodging, event space, a performance hall & outdoor recreation.
(580) 563-2424 | www.quartzmountainresort.com

Sunny's Express

Located 5-10 minutes from Old Baldy. This convenience store has food, fuel and beer.
Hours 4:30am-11:00pm Monday-Sunday
301 E.1st Street, Granite, OK 73547

Luigi's Restaurant

Located in the town of Blair, about 15 minutes south from Quartz Mtn. The food is excellent, service great and way affordable. Drive into Blair past the only blinking traffic light. Luigi's is on your left (east).

118 Main Street, Blair, OK 73526 (580) 563-9380. Closed on Mondays.

MY FRIENDS TED AND MARGARET JOHNSON

By Tony Mayse

Several years ago I had the opportunity to meet Ted and Margaret Johnson at Quartz Mountain on one of my many climbing weekends. I thanked Ted for allowing us to climb on his land and tried to think of a way to show my appreciation. Ted and Margaret allowed the climbing community to enjoy this wonderful place out of their gracious nature and fondness for rock climbers. When I got home from spending the weekend climbing at Quartz I called Ted and invited him and Margaret to lunch at the State Lodge. The following weekend, we met Ted and Margaret at the lodge. This was the start of my friendship with Ted Johnson. I would call him on weekends to let him know we would be coming to Quartz and I stayed in touch with him regularly.

One weekend I called to say hello, Margaret said that Ted was in the Comanche Memorial Hospital in Lawton and was being released the next day. Ted was having some health problems and had spent a few days in the hospital. After I got off the phone with Margaret I called the hospital and spoke with Ted. He said that he was doing fine and was ready to go home. I offered him a ride home from the hospital, but he graciously declined. The next day I learned of Ted's passing.

During my friendship with Ted, he granted permission for a climber's annual get-together. It was during one of our Fall Gatherings several years after Ted's passing we noticed "For Sale" signs at Quartz. We notified our good friend Marion Hutchison with the Wichita Mountains Climber's Coalition. Marion quickly contacted Susie Spradlin, Ted's stepdaughter in California. Susie had no idea that climbers were interested in purchasing Quartz. Marion contacted the Access Fund and it was left up to the climbing community to raise most of the money for the purchase. Needless to say, it seemed that anyone who had ever stepped foot on Quartz called in to donate money. Bob & Bonnie Kamps and Doug Robinson out of California contributed as well as many, many others. Less than a year later we were at the Quartz Mountain Dedication Ceremony.

On May 5, 2001, the Access Fund, who had purchased the Baldy Point land (mostly referred to as "Old Baldy") from the Ted Johnson family, officially donated Quartz Mountain to Quartz Mountain Nature Park. Several climbers, Access Fund board members, state park officials and a former senator of the state of Oklahoma attended a very emotional dedication ceremony. My Dad even flew in from Massachusetts.

In the time that I began climbing at Quartz many things have changed, but one thing that hasn't is the climbing. The history here is wonderful, and I have been so lucky to have been able to spend the last 26 years climbing here. My hopes are that future generations of climbers treat this area as a valued asset and strive towards keeping Old Baldy pristine and not letting the area fall into disrepair. It's up to us folks!

QUARTZ... PROTECTING A RESOURCE, PRESERVING A TRADITION

By Marion Hutchison

For more than 40-years, climbers from across the Midwest have been venturing to Baldy Point for the opportunity to experience some of the finest granite face climbing in this region of the country. And thanks to the dedication and efforts of our local climbing community, we've all been able to sleep a little easier for the past twenty years knowing that Baldy Point will forever be available to anyone wishing to test their skills on its classic lines. But, while Baldy's climbing resources have been protected, what about the traditions and values of this special place that we so reverently and affectionately call "Quartz"?

More than any other climbing area in the Wichita Mountain range, Quartz symbolizes the adventurous spirit and honored traditions of Oklahoma climbing. Of the nearly one hundred routes found at Quartz today, nearly all were established in traditional style during the Wichita's "golden age" of climbing in the late 1970s and early 1980s. That style had as its core value the understanding that all routes were to be established from the ground-up, and that all protection, including fixed anchors, were to be placed on lead.

That ground-up style was a respected, historical tradition that was rooted in the foundations of classic mountaineering. Throughout the world, it had become the fundamental value on which all climbing was based. For a while the goal of climbing was to reach the top, the value of climbing was in the challenge of getting there. Anything that diminished that experience took away from the adventure. Fixed anchors, to some degree, fell under that category. Even though they were often necessary on many first ascents, excessive use often eliminated the adventure of a climb by assuring the outcome and eliminating the risk. As a result, another historical climbing value adopted in the Wichitas was the belief that fixed anchors were to be used in very limited numbers and only when nothing else would work.

A third core value that was adopted in Oklahoma was the strict free-climbing ethic that had emerged from places like Eldorado Canyon, the Shawangunks, and Tuolumne Meadows in the early 1970s. Seeking to push the challenge and adventure of climbing even further, climbers in those areas had adopted tough standards which made even the slightest use of aid while climbing unethical.

Combined together, these ideals made up the basis for the traditional values that served as the foundation of climbing at Quartz in the late 1970s and early 1980s. Climbs were considered to have been done in good style if they were established from the ground-up, with all protection, including fixed anchors, placed on lead. In addition, on free ascents, no toprope previewing or rehearsing was permitted, and the use of any type of aid was prohibited, even while placing fixed anchors. Bolts were to be placed only as a last resort, and when they were necessary, only the bare minimum were to be used.

As a result, most of the face routes at Quartz that ascended the steep, featureless granite were equipped with just a few bolts. Those fixed anchors were located, if stances allowed, so that the most difficult moves were protected. In between the crux sections, long runouts on easy to moderate terrain were common. And while there were a few routes which were considered desperate and poorly protected, all of the routes at Quartz were valued and respected because of what they stood for.

For you see, there was a greater purpose in the traditions of Quartz and the style of those routes. The goal was to prepare yourself, physically and mentally for greater challenges yet to come. The way to get there was clear. Learn technique, develop strength, push your limits, control your fear, and build confidence. And the routes at Quartz did just that.

Those valuable lines remain today, as originally established. Over the years the local climbing community has chosen to preserve the character of those routes and the tradition of Quartz. By doing so, we honor not only the past, but also the future. Because the climbs at Quartz have more to offer than just a casual weekend outing on some fine granite. Their true value lies in giving climbers the inspiration to seek greater adventures, and in providing them with the experience and confidence to attempt those climbs in good style.

There's an incredible world of climbing out there beyond the local crag and neighborhood gym. Big walls in Yosemite, desert towers in the west, large alpine faces in the Rockies and the Alps, and enormous granite peaks in Alaska and Patagonia. For many of us, being a climber means aspiring to those kinds of experiences.

But in order to survive and succeed in that arena, you've got to develop traditional climbing skills outdoors on real rock. And not just your physical abilities, but your mental fortitude as well. You'll need to learn to control your fear, and know how to climb confidently in difficult and uncertain situations.

Because in the bigger world of climbing, there aren't bolts every ten feet to guarantee your safety, or arrows to show you where to go. You'll often be placed in threatening situations where you must trust your abilities and be comfortable leading with only minimal protection.

That's why so many of us support maintaining the traditionally established lines at Quartz. We respect those routes and honor the style, not because of the fact that we've done them, but because of the lessons they taught us and the doorway they opened.

The climbs at Quartz are not relics of the past, they're learning opportunities for those now and in the future who want more from climbing than a secure weekend outing or a gymnastic clip-up. By preserving those routes and the tradition of Quartz, we maintain its value as both a physical and mental training ground. In doing so, we keep the doorway open.

And so it is, that Quartz is much more than just a wonderful climbing crag. It's also a passage for those in our local climbing community aspiring to grander adventures on the great walls and peaks across this country and around the world. As such, we owe it to ourselves and to those who will follow to not only protect the resource, but to also preserve the tradition.

Photo by Andrew Burr

MIKE HANKINS
By Tony Mayse

Climbers sometimes refer to fellow climbers as being strong or powerful, or by some other adjective describing their abilities. These descriptions are often used when that climber has climbed a hard route or boulder problem. However, herein lies the quintessential caveat, the line drawn in the sand so to speak. Climbing is not just about power, or even good technique. What truly separates most climbers from the rest, is when the rope is removed. Bob Kamps once mentioned that when that happens he turns to mush!

Mike Hankins climbing alone on the Quartz classic Amazon Woman 5.10b RX. | Photo by Alan Ellis

It wasn't too long after I first started rock climbing at Quartz Mountain, Mike Hankins name came up. The stories about Mike were, for me at the time, other-worldly. Mike had a reputation for climbing hard routes sans rope. Being young and new to rock climbing I was mystified that these climbs, which I could barely—or not even—do with a rope, were being climbed by Mike without one. I heard stories of Mike running laps on *Last of the Good Guys*, and ropeless adventures on *Baptism*, *Amazon Woman*, and most routes at Quartz Mountain.

Several years into climbing I finally ran into Mike while at Quartz Mountain. I had just climbed *South Pacific* and there was Mike sitting on top of the South America Wall belay station. He had a nice smile, but with a pun on his tongue when he spoke. I liked him immediately; we briefly chatted about climbing. Mike hadn't climbed in several years after a bad fall while working as a carpenter. He had shoulder surgery which did not allow him to do the heavy manual labor of lifting boards that is the norm for carpentry-type work. Mike went back to school earning a degree as a network administrator. Mike was well respected at work and took his job seriously. He would always razz me about computer software, saying I was a pirate! He had a sense of humor, but often times looked serious. Mike is not a little guy; he has a presence with his 6' 1" frame and broad shoulders.

A couple months after first meeting the Legend of Quartz, we met again at OKC Rocks climbing gym where Kurt Smith was giving a slide show. We made plans to meet for some Quartz climbing! I was stoked to finally get to climb with Mike. That next weekend rolled around and there I was, at Old Baldy ready to climb with Mike Hankins, someone I had held in high regard for many years, I was stoked!

The first thing I noticed about Mike's climbing was that his balance on the rock was about as natural as walking is to most people. He just flowed with the stone. Never did he stop and place a foot then a hand and then a crimp as is the style at Old Baldy. Mike never did that. I watched him climb and you could never tell when the climbing got hard…he just flowed. Our styles were so different. Mike moved so naturally, it was a pleasure just to watch him. It was not something you can mimic, this was his own style and it was impressive. My thoughts that day were, this guy is bad to the bone!

We climbed a lot together over the next several years, spending time at Quartz and the wildlife refuge as well as out of state trips. The Quartz days were the most memorable for me. Our normal climbing day there would start off with some roped climbs then lead to "ropeless romps" around the entire place! It was such a casual affair, that it's really hard to explain, it just happened, probably because we were just having a blast! Mike was a master at ropeless climbing, and he could downclimb everything he could up climb. He made it look so easy that I decided to downclimb one of the easy 5.8s…first thing I realized was that going up is a totally separate line than going down. The movement was entirely different and much scarier. Soloing *Amazon Woman* for Mike was a cruise and down-soloing was equally as easy, it was a sight to see and not at all scary, it just looked like he was doing what came naturally, just like quietly flowing water, so calm and serene. Those days were a time in my life that I think about often. I miss climbing with Mike.

Mike had an unfortunate climbing accident while on a family trip in Colorado several years ago. He doesn't climb any longer. It's doubtful that Quartz will ever see someone as skilled romping around these walls with such finesse and seeminly effortless movement. Mike's days at Quartz add another chapter to the rich tradition of hard climbing on Old Baldy and the rich history which makes climbing in Oklahoma so special.

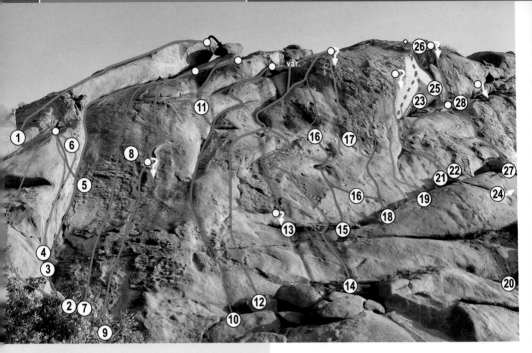

S WALL

This area is best found by looking up to the left side of the south face; a prominent feature resembling the letter "S" can be seen halfway up the wall. All of the routes in this area are descended from the Headwall anchors (use two 60 meter ropes) or by walking off the backside.

1. Snake's Head 5.5 X ★★

Located about 50 feet to the left of S Wall. Face climb up a feature resembling a snake's head After you reach the alcove, follow the crack to the left up to the huge slab. Follow this "runway" of granite reaching the anchors on top. From here take the leap to the boulder for the descent (at your own risk). There is no protection on this route although the climbing is not too difficult.

FA: Ken Rose & party 1970s

Gear: free solo

2-bolt anchor   150ft

2. LSAT 5.11b/c RX ★★

LSAT (Law School Admittance Test) is located on the slab 18 feet left of the S Wall. From the routes base, climb to a hueco and continue on unprotected climbing to an overlap with a bulge and a bolt. Climb past the bolt on thin moves making your way to the same belay as Moosehead.

FA: Unknown 1980s

Gear: quickdraw, .5 to #1 Camalot for the belay

No anchor   65ft

3. Snakeshead Dihedral 5.8 RX ★★★

Climb the dihedral to the left of S Wall.

Pitch 1: Climb easy knobs then a wide crack going out under the roof. Traverse right below the roof on smooth rock, then layback the corner to easier climbing.

Pitch 2: Continue up the corner on easy but unprotected climbing to the belay ledge. Bring medium size cams for the belay on top.

FA: Unknown

Gear: #2 to #5 Camalot

No anchor   190ft

4. Moosehead 5.11 R ★★★★

The classic hand crack of Quartz Mountain. Located on the wall above the dihedral to the left of S Wall. Climb up the low-angle slab on easy knobs for 25 feet, step onto the face with buckets at head level, and continue up on 5.11 face moves before entering the crack. Continue on 5.10 jams, traverse right then up to a bulge. Follow the crack to easier climbing to the top.

FA: Mike & David Panciera, Bernie Wire 1978

2nd Ascent: July 8, 1979 Jon Frank, Jimmy Ratzlaff

Gear: TCUs, cams to #2 Camalot

No anchor   60ft

5. Moosebite 5.10c ★★ Toprope

Located up the slab about 20 feet from the start of Moosehead. Climb the overhanging wall starting on the slab Snakeshead Dihedral.

FA: Duane Raleigh 1980s

Gear: #1, #2 Camalots for toprope

No anchor   40ft

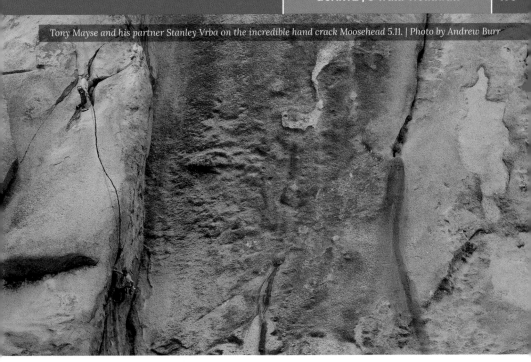
Tony Mayse and his partner Stanley Vrba on the incredible hand crack Moosehead 5.11. | Photo by Andrew Burr

6. Today is a Good Day to Die 5.11b RX ★★
Same start as *Moosehead.* Climb *Moosehead* to where the crack starts to go over the bulge. From here continue right in the thin crack making your way to a bolt which protects the face moves to the belay.
Established on aid by Mark Herndon and Jimmy Ratzlaff. March 11, 1981 at 5.9 A2. FA: Duane Raleigh 1987 (free)
Gear: wires, TCUs, HB offsets, cams to #2 Camalot
No anchor   65ft

7. Big Bite Direct 5.9 RX ★★★
Located a few feet left of S *Wall.* Climb up on moderate terrain to a bolt; clip the bolt and move up to a second bolt which is *Big Bite.* Continue on *Big Bite.* (See description for *Big Bite.*)
FA: Jimmy Ratzlaff, Sam Audrain Mar.14, 1981
Gear: quickdraws, cams to 1" for the belay
No anchor   190ft

8. Big Bite 5.10 X ★★★
Runout face climbing to the left of S *Wall.* This route is usually started from the belay in the "S." From the belay step left then up about 20 feet to a bolt, continue up on unprotected climbing 5.10 to the top. On an early ascent Mark Herndon took a fall at the top of the pitch resulting in "The *Big Bite;*" luckily he was not hurt very seriously.
FA: Duane Raleigh, Rick Thomas 1980
Gear: same as S *Wall*
No anchor   190ft

9. S Wall 5.9 RX ★★★★
The Quartz Mountain Classic. This route climbs through the prominent "S" feature to the right of the dihedral.
Pitch 1: Climb 60 feet up easy (5.6) climbing to the first and only bolt on the pitch. Continue up the face stepping into the "S."
Pitch 2: Climb 25 feet up past the "S" traversing right to the bolt above the belay. Clip the bolt and continue up the face on runout climbing; the difficulty never exceeds 5.8, but the long runout makes it feel much harder. Continue up to a wide ledge for the belay. Climb the easy slab up and right that leads to the headwall anchors. Classic!
FA: Bill Thomas, Duane Raleigh 1979
2nd Ascent: Jimmy Ratzlaff, Jon Frank July 8, 1979
Gear: quickdraws, #1.5–#2.5 cams for belay
No anchor   220ft

10. Baptism 5.10b/c RX ★★★
Climb the water streak/crack right of S *Wall.*
Pitch 1: From a small ledge below the water streak climb up on steep unprotected 5.10 face climbing to a low-angle slab, step over the bulge to a bolt. Continue up the face making your way up to the crack for 50 feet to a belay stance (#3, #4 cams for the belay).
Pitch 2: Continue following the crack up and to the right. Climb over the bulge to easier climbing leading to a belay. Quartz way of getting baptized.
FA: Duane Raleigh, Terry Andrews 1980
Gear: stoppers, TCUs, cams to #4
No anchor   190ft

11. Desire 5.10b X ★★
Runout face climbing above the first pitch of *Baptism*.

Pitch 1: Climb the first pitch of *Baptism*.

Pitch 2: From the belay step over the bulge to a runout slab up and right of S *Wall*, climbing past a black hole in the face just below the top-out ledge.

FA: *Duane Raleigh, Jon Frank 1980*
Gear: cams to #4 Camalot
No anchor   *190ft*

12. Geek Feet 5.8+ X ★
Originally named *The Conversion* and free soloed on March 11, 1986 by Jimmy Ratzlaff. The name was later changed. This route climbs the slab between *Baptism* and *Bourbon Street* eventually joining the upper part of *Bourbon Street* ending at the headwall anchor. There is no protection on this climb until it joins the upper section of *Bourbon Street*.

FA: *Jimmy Ratzlaff, March 11, 1986*
Gear: free solo
No anchor   *190ft*

HEADWALL
This wall is the most prominent face seen when driving up to Quartz. Located to the right of the *Bourbon Street* is a huge face with outstanding bolt-protected climbing. Most routes start from the ramp above and to the right of Bourbon Street Ledge with the exception of *Chicago Bound Direct*.

Jimmy Ratzlaff on the first ascent of Chicago Bound 5.11c RX. | Photo from the Jimmy Ratzlaff Collection

13. Bourbon Street 5.8 R ★★★★
The first bolted route at Quartz Mountain. Originally started from the shelf 30 feet below Bourbon Street Ledge. Climbers nowadays start by walking down the ramp below the headwall routes to a grassy belay ledge with a 2-bolt anchor below the routes start.

Pitch 1: From Bourbon Street Ledge climb up over the lip above the 2-bolt belay and continue up the water streak past two bolts, traversing right at the arching horizontal crack 25 feet to another bolt. Step over the bulge and climb up a short slab to a stance below the crack.

Pitch 2: Climb up the crack then follow the ramp to the dark triangle in the face to the right of the chimney leading exposed face climbing. Continue up to the headwall anchors. The original second pitch climbed the 5.8 chimney to the left. The route can be led in one pitch using runners down lower on the climb. A classic mixed route.

FA: *Bernie Wire, Greg Schooley 1978*
2nd Ascent: *Marion Hutchison, Terry Andrews 1978*
Gear: quickdraws, #1 to #4 Camalot
2-bolt anchor   *150ft*

14. Pot Hole Route A.KA. Bourbon Street Direct 5.8 X ★★★
Located 12 feet right of the start to *Bourbon Street*. Climb up the face on unprotected climbing for 60 feet to a bolt below the horizontal crack, climb over the bulge protected by a bolt, continue up to a stance below the chimney, and belay here. The second pitch is the same as *Bourbon Street*.

FA: *Duane Raleigh, Rick Thomas 1980*
Gear: quickdraws, #1 to #4 Camalot
2-bolt anchor   *150ft*

15. Chicago Bound Direct 5.10d X ★★★★

A direct start to *Chicago Bound*. From the rightmost end of *Bourbon Street Ledge* climb up 15 feet on thin edges to a bolt, continue on sustained 5.10 to another bolt. From here climb up and to the right of a large hueco and a bolt. Continue up *Chicago Bound* or *Watch Me I'm Wasted*. Dicey start.

FA: Jimmy Ratzlaff, Herndon, Raleigh, Frank, Audrain March 13, 1981

Gear: quickdraws

2-bolt anchor   70ft

16. Watch Me I'm Wasted 5.10b RX ★★★

Face climb 10 feet to the left of *Chicago Bound*. This route can be done by climbing *Chicago Bound Direct* or by clipping the first bolt of *Last of the Good Guys* then treading left and up past two more bolts to gain the bolt of *Watch Me I'm Wasted* which is directly underneath a bulge. Move up and right to a mantel move. Sustained climbing past the mantel with no protection opportunities. Continue on the upper section of *Bourbon Street*.

FA: Audrain, Frank, Herndon, Raleigh, and Ratzlaff March 12, 1981

Gear: quickdraws

2-bolt anchor   120ft

> *"All routes have been safely climbed with the existing protection. Falling from what were previously considered desperate places have been taken with little injury. Some routes still await this test. Use caution on all routes and don't trust anything but yourself when your neck is on the line."*
>
> *– Duane Raleigh, Southern Exposure*

17. Chicago Bound 5.11c RX ★★★★

Thin, sustained face climbing to the left of *Last of the Good Guys*. Climb up the face to the first bolt of *Last of the Good Guys*, traverse left and up about 15 feet to another bolt, continue on 5.10 face climbing to a large pothole with a bolt. From here continue right then up to a stance with a bolt. Step right a few feet, and continue up the face protected by two more bolts leading to the headwall anchors. This route meanders up the face; as a result a belay was taken in the pothole on the first ascent.

FA: Duane Raleigh, Jimmy Ratzlaff June 5, 1980

Gear: quickdraws

2-bolt anchor   140ft

This route is a true test piece and still a committing lead. It was established during a major heat wave. On the first ascent, Duane and Jimmy took turns belaying in the large pothole off of an aluminum bashy clipped to a white sling. They then continued up, though initial attempts while hand-drilling bolts on lead were repulsed. The last bolt was installed using a hook to hang off while on lead, the only time a hook was used was during the first ascent.

During the time of the first ascent, Jimmy was dating a girl who lived in Chicago...

18. Last of the Good Guys 5.10b/c R ★★★★

First route established on the headwall. Step over the chimney onto the face to the first bolt, continue on friction climbing past the second bolt. Climb up to a horn making your way to steeper climbing on the headwall protected by four bolts to the top. One of the best climbs at Quartz Mountain. A classic!

FA: Duane Raleigh, Bill Thomas 1979

Gear: quickdraws

2-bolt anchor   150ft

19. Angry Youth 5.11c/d ★★★

Thin face climb to the right of *Last of the Good Guys*. To get to the start of this route walk up the ramp to a ledge on the right side of the headwall. From the ledge climb up a slab moving left towards the headwall, clip a bolt, and step onto the face. Move up past the second bolt on thin edges and high-angle smearing, following the line of bolts through the almost featureless section to the right of *Last of the Good Guys*. From the slab at the top traverse left to headwall anchors. This route has sustained 5.11 climbing with a couple hard clips. Bolted by Mike Ritchey, but remained unclimbed until Russell Hooper & company showed up to get the send!

FA: Russell Hooper, Phil Bram, James Dixon 1991

Gear: quickdraws

2-bolt anchor   150ft

> *"Sometimes the best gear for a climb is a good excuse."* ~John Sherman

Tony Mayse on Master Race. | Photo by Andrew Burr

Tony Mayse and Stanley Vrba on the Head Wall classic Last of the Good Guys 5.10 b/c R. | Photo by Andrew Burr

20. Anorexia C3 ★★★★

Aid climb to the right of *Wild Child*. Climb the unprotected 5.9 face start of *Wild Child* then continue up the corner to a stance with two rivets under the overhang. From the second rivet, move up to gain the crack. Follow the seam leading to a thin crack traversing right eventually climbing up the steep face at the crack's end. Move up the face protected by rivets and fixed heads. Free climb over the slab making your way to a shelf on the top for the belay.

FA: Chris Rowins (aid solo) 1979
2nd Ascent: Mark Herndon

Gear: camhooks, hooks, wires, TCUs to #3 Camalot

No anchor   *150ft*

NOTE: *This route accepts clean gear, do not use pitons. Cam hooks work where pitons use to be the standard. On the first ascent the route was started from below the headwall (see topo). Now it is climbed from the ledge below the route. The bolts above the Anorexia crack were installed years after the first ascent for a free climb. Clipping the bolts reduces the grade to (A0) and is not considered the aid climb Anorexia.*

20a. Anorexia Free 5.13+ ★★★★

The free version has not been completed, this is an open project. There are seven bolts that protect the climbing. To gain the *Anorexia* crack, climb *Wild Child* then step down and to the right clipping the first bolt of *Anorexia*..

FA: Open project

Gear: #2 Camalot, quickdraws

No anchor   *130ft*

21. Dick Bump 5.9 RX ★★

Same 5.9 face start as *Wild Child*. Continue up the slab under *Anorexia* trending right. Follow the line of least resistance up the slab, eventually ending at the *Hobbit* belay ledge. Protection can be found in the vegetated crack below *Anorexia*.

(For clarity the line for *Dick Bump* was drawn left of *Wild Child*. Both routes start at the same point).

FA: Sam Audrain, Terry Andrews 1980

Gear: cams to #2 Camalot, long runners

No anchor   *70ft*

22. Wild Child 5.11d RX ★★★★

Climb the arête to the right of *Angry Youth*. Climb up the water streak 15 feet to the right of *Angry Youth* on unprotected 5.9 face climbing to a stance on the slab below a bulge. Climb up the arête 15 feet to a bolt then move up and left onto the face, making your way to a 2-bolt anchor. There is one bolt on this climb. On the first ascent the route was rated 5.10d, then sometime in the late 80s or early 90s a key hold broke off the start giving the climb its current rating of 5.11d. Hard and committing.

FA: Duane Raleigh, Bill Thomas 1986
Gear: quickdraws, cams, #2 Camalot
2-bolt anchor   *70ft*

23. Hook Roof A4 X ★

Located in the upper alcove below *Anorexia*. From the slab, hook moves lead to marginal flakes and a bolt 20 feet up. Once the lip of the roof is turned fixed copperheads protect the seam which leads to the upper part of *Anorexia*.

FA: Chris Rowins 1980
Gear: see description for *Anorexia*
No anchor   *70ft*

24. Scream Seam 5.11b RX ★★★

Short thin crack/face climb on natural gear. Below the ramp to the far right of Bourbon Street Ledge is a short face with a thin crack (the crack usually has some grass growing out of it). This is a challenging route and mental test piece.

FA: Duane Raleigh, Rick Thomas 1981
Gear: TCUs, stoppers
No anchor   *40ft*

25. Master Race 5.12 R ★★★★

Steep face climb under a large roof. This route starts 10 feet left of the second pitch belay ledge of *Hobbit*. Climb up 15 feet to a bolt (once protected by a knife blade). From here continue up and left onto a smooth face past two bolts underneath the roof, turn the corner at the roof's left end continuing onto the slab above. Demanding footwork and sequency moves along with some of the best exposure of any route at Quartz make this climb the appropriate one to be Quartz Mountain's first route rated 5.12.

FA: Duane Raleigh 1982
Gear: cams to #3 Camalot, quickdraws
No anchor   *70ft*

26. Master's Roof 5.12b R ★★★

Climbs the roof above *Master Race*. Climb to the third bolt of *Master Race*, then continue over the roof protected by a bolt just over the lip. Continue up the slab to a ledge up top. Hard.

FA: Duane Raleigh 1987
Gear: cams to #3 Camalot, quickdraws
No anchor   *70ft*

"On routes like the Baptism, Jet Stream, Desire, and the Big Bite (all 5.10), the difference between success and failure meant the difference being fed at the lodge that night or fed through a straw."

~Duane Raleigh | Climbing Magazine #68 1981

SEA OF SCREAMS

The routes in this area start to the right of the Headwall climbs.

27. Hobbit 5.7 ★★★★

One of the first and most popular climbs at Quartz.
Pitch 1: Starting in the hole below the crack. Climb up to a flake, continuing in the crack 60 feet to a ledge.
Pitch 2: Continue up the corner on lieback moves and hand jams to the top. The anchors are on a stacked boulder at the top.

FA: James Hollingsworth, Jay Lowell 1973
Gear: cams to #3 Camalot
2-bolt anchor   *150ft*

28. Cruzin' for a Bruzin' 5.11c ★★★★

Face climb with four bolts to the right of *Hobbit's* second pitch. Start with a 5.11c boulder problem past the first bolt. From here, climb sustained 5.11, past three bolts, to a ledge.

Originally climbed on aid with hooks, knifeblades, and copperheads at A3. Later it was free climbed with the fixed copperheads for protection until bolts replaced the old wires. Not a typical Quartz climb.

FA: Duane Raleigh, Mark Herndon (Aid) early 1980
FA: Duane Raleigh 1987
Gear: quickdraws
2-bolt anchor   *60ft*

29. Soft and Pretty 5.8+ R ★★★★

From the base of *Snow White*, climb up the corner crack. As the wall gets steeper move left and crank over the bulge. Continue on unprotected face climbing to the top. Belay at the *Hobbit* belay ledge.

FA: Duane Raleigh, Bill Thomas 1979
Gear: cams to #2 Camalot
No anchor   *70ft*

30. Little Women 5.9 X ★★

This route climbs the water streak between *Soft and Pretty* and *Snow White*. Climb up the face 10 feet left of *Snow White*, step over the bulge, continue up to the second bulge and black water streak making your way to the *Hobbit* belay ledge.

FA: Duane Raleigh, Bill Thomas 1980
Gear: cams to #3 Camalot
2-bolt anchor   *100ft*

31. Snow White 5.10b RX ★★★

Face climb 20 feet right of *Hobbit*.

Climb knobs for 15 feet to a horizontal crack protecting the move over the bulge then continue up 30 feet of unprotected face climbing to a bolt. Lieback the flake to the second bolt and continue climbing 30 feet in the water streak to a bolted belay. Rappel the route with a 60-meter rope.

FA: Duane Raleigh, Bill Thomas 1980
Gear: quickdraws, cams to #2 Camalot
2-bolt anchor   *100ft*

31a. Snow White (Variation Start) 5.10b X ★★★

Climb up to a horizontal crack below the bulge, high step onto the face then continue on edges to a stance. Traverse out to the right on a slick slab to the first bolt (see topo).

32. Jet Stream 5.10b X ★★★

Face climb in the water streak right of *Snow White*. A "cat's paw print" marks the start of the route. Climb up the streak to the first bolt above the "cat's paw," move up and over the bulge to runout climbing for 50 feet to the second bolt. From here continue up the water streak to a ledge with an anchor. Rappel down *Snow White* with a 60-meter rope.

FA: Duane Raleigh, Bill Thomas 1980
Gear: (2) quickdraws
2-bolt anchor   *120ft*

33. Taken By Force 5.9+ X ★★★

Face climb to the right of *Jet Stream*. Climb a short layback crack to a stance. Continue climbing up a steep face protected by a bolt making your way to a 2-bolt anchor up and right. Sustained 5.9 climbing.

FA: Hunt, Raleigh, Rowins 1980
Gear: cams to #1 Camalot
2-bolt anchor   *70ft*

34. Silent Scream 5.10d RX ★★★★

Face climb to the right of *Taken by Force*. The base of the wall has a 4-inch "ankle-eating crack." Climb up 15 feet on thin edges to a bolt, and then traverse left and up to another bolt. From here step left, then up to a low-angle slab for 30 feet to the anchor. This route ends on the same ledge as *Taken by Force*. (Formerly rated 5.10b, some key holds broken off in the mid-2000s.)

FA: Duane Raleigh, Bill Thomas 1980
Gear: (2) quickdraws
2-bolt anchor   *80ft*

"The first ascent was accidental and involved a case of bouldering where it was deemed safer to continue than attempt retreat."

— *Duane Raleigh, Southern Exposure*

35. No Screaming Allowed 5.10c RX ★★

From the second bolt of *Silent Scream*, crank directly over the bulge by the bolt. Continue on thin, unprotected face climbing making your way to the bolted belay.

FA: Tony Mayse, Mike Hankins 2005
Gear: (2) quickdraws
2-bolt anchor   *70ft*

36. Scream Dream 5.11 X ★★★

Start on top of the large boulder right and up from *Silent Scream*. Step left and move up to a bolt, then continue on runout face climbing making your way to a bolted belay. Superb!

FA: Jimmy Ratzlaff, Jon Frank, Duane Raleigh 1980
Gear: (1) quickdraw
2-bolt anchor   *60ft*

37. Cheap Skate 5.11 X ★★

Route just right of *Scream Dream*. Boulder up 20 feet to a bolt and continue to the anchors up and left.

FA: Bob Pearson, Duane Raleigh 1984
Gear: (1) quickdraw
2-bolt anchor   *60ft*

38. Cheap Tape 5.10c X ★★

A few feet right of *Cheap Skate*. Climb up 10 feet to a bolt then continue to the anchors up and left.

FA: Charlie Hays, Duane Raleigh, Jimmy Ratzlaff 1980
Gear: (1) quickdraw
2-bolt anchor   *60ft*

Super Slide, Accidents Will Happen, and *Who's got the Juice* were established ropeless. These climbs remained boltless until, in early 2000, the first ascentionist granted permission to add bolts, giving new climbers to Quartz a protected introduction to the climbing.

39. Monkey on a Football 5.5 ★★★

Easiest route at Quartz Mountain. *Monkey on a Football* used to be the standard scramble that was done in sneakers. Bolts were added later. This route climbs the face protected by two bolts to the left of *Accidents Will Happen*. The anchor accepts a variety of gear.

FA: Jay Lowell, Kurt Scheir (free solo) 1974
Gear: quickdraws
No anchor   *70ft*

40. Accidents Will Happen 5.9 ★★★

Face climb with three bolts to the left of *Super Slide*. This route has some crunchy rock lower on the route.

FA: Jimmy Ratzlaff (free solo) March 13, 1981
Gear: quickdraws
2-bolt anchor   *70ft*

Tony Mayse climbing Cruzin' for a Bruzin' 5.11c. An old aid line high up on Old Baldy. | Photo by Andrew Burr

41. Super Slide 5.10d ★★★

Face climb up the middle water streak protected by 3 bolts. Climb up the face on very thin smears for 12 feet to the first bolt. Continue on sustained friction moves past 2 bolts to a grassy-ledge with an anchor. Great friction climb.

FA: *Duane Raleigh (free solo) 1979*
Gear: quickdraws
2-bolt anchor   *70ft*

42. Who's Got the Juice? 5.7 ★★★

Face climb with three bolts to the right of *Super Slide*.

FA: *Unknown (free solo) 1979*
(Equipped by Marion Hutchison, Tony Mayse 2001)
Gear: quickdraws
2-bolt anchor   *70ft*

43. Cream 5.8 RX ★★

This route starts from the grassy ledge 120 feet to the right of *Silent Scream*. From the ledge climb the face to a wide crack, which ends at a ledge. From here continue up and right 30 feet to a bolt, follow the crack to the top and belay. This route will create some rope drag due to its wandering nature; you can set up a belay on the ledge before moving up the face to the bolt.

FA: *Bill Thomas, Duane Raleigh 1980*
Gear: cams to #4 Camalot
No anchor   *150ft*

43a. Typhoon 5.7 R ★

A short face climb starting on *Cream* and continuing on *Pauper* up higher. After exiting *Cream's* lower crack, climb straight up the face then traverse to the right entering *Pauper's* lower finger crack. Continue on *Pauper* to the top.

FA: *Jimmy Ratzlaff, Mark Herndon 1981*
Gear: same as Cream
No anchor   *40ft*

44. Pauper 5.10c/d RX ★★★

Climbs the long thin crack a few right of *Cream*. From the grassy ledge climb up 10 feet to a horn, continue up the face on unprotected climbing until you reach the crack. Follow the flaring crack up to a bulge (once protected by a copperhead). Continue over the bulge to easier climbing. To avoid the crux bulge, step right (5.10a, this was the original finish). *Southern Exposure* referred to this route as the "classic thin crack" on Baldy.

FA: *Duane Raleigh, Bill Thomas 1979*
Gear: TCUs, cams to #2 Camalot
No anchor   *120ft*

"Life is either a great adventure or nothing."

~Helen Keller

Marisa Cones with perfect weather for Who's Got the Juice? 5.7. | Photo by Molly Hennesy

SOUTH AMERICA WALL

The routes in this area start with South Pacific, which is located a few feet left of the feature that resembles the continent of South America; some people say it looks like a guitar or an elephant's head. The routes that finish on top of South America Wall have rappel anchors on the ledge; rappels from here require two ropes.

45. Charlie Manson Look-a-Like Contest 5.10d X ★★

Face climb located 15 feet to the left of *South Pacific*. Climb a short slab to the start of the route. A horizontal crack protects the starting moves which lead to runout face climbing below the one bolt. Climb past the bolt to the top of the large flake, belay, and continue on *South Pacific*. Committing.

FA: *Duane Raleigh, Doug Robinson 1986*
Gear: cams to #3 Camalot, (1) quickdraw
No anchor   *50ft*

46. South Pacific 5.7 ★★★★

Climb up a steep face on lieback moves to a short finger crack above the roof. Continue up the finger crack to a ledge, and traverse left on hand jams making your way around the corner. Follow the dihedral to the top exiting right, and then make your way to the bolted belay of *Amazon Woman*. The best 5.7 at Quartz!

FA: *Kenny Stearns, Jay Lowell 1973*
Gear: cams to #3 Camalot, stoppers
No anchor   *140ft*

46a. South Pacific Direct Start 5.9 RX ★★★

Climb the unprotected 5.9 face just left of the lieback crack, joining the finger crack up higher.

FA: *Unknown*
Gear: no gear
No anchor   *20ft*

46b. South Pacific Continuation 5.7 ★★

Climb up and left to a boulder with a short hand crack. Climb the hand crack for 20 feet, and set up the belay on top of the boulder.

FA: *Unknown*
Gear: cams to #2 Camalot
No anchor   *20ft*

47. South Africa 5.8 ★★

The wide crack to the right of *South Pacific*, finishing on the exit cracks that lead to the belay anchors on top of South America Wall.

FA: *Duane Raleigh, Lee Stewart 1979*
Gear: cams to #4 Camalot
2-bolt anchor   *120ft*

> "I continued with whatever 'qualified climbers' I could con into this rather uncompromising venture."
>
> ~Warren Harding, on the first ascent of El Capitan's Nose Route.

Quartz Mountain Porcupine

Mike Klein climbing the amazing Amazon Woman 5.10b R on South America Wall. | Photo by Andrew Burr

48. Amazon Woman 5.10b R ★★★★

Face climb protected by 4 bolts to the right of *South Pacific*. From the ramp below and to the right of South America Wall climb over an arching flake onto a face that leads to a bolt, move right then up the face protected by 3 bolts to a roof. Surmount the roof, climb left then up to a ledge with an anchor. One of the best 5.10s in the country!

FA: Duane Raleigh, John Sanders 1979
2nd Ascent: Terry Andrews, Marion Hutchison 1979
Gear: (4) quickdraws
2-bolt anchor   *150ft*

48a. Amazon Woman Direct Finish 5.11 X ★★

Direct finish at the top of *Amazon Woman* was established by Mike Hankins in 2006. Climb the unprotected bulge out right leading to the anchors.

FA: Mike Hankins 2006
Gear: no gear
2-bolt anchor   *30ft*

> *"The way you live your life is exactly the way you will climb." ~John Long*

49. LA Woman 5.11c RX ★★★★

Hard face climb to the right of *Amazon Woman*. From the second bolt of *Amazon Woman* step right and up to a bolt, then climb out to the right on a rib of rock and a precarious move to a stance. From here a disco-move step through to the left and up to a bolt protected "shield," climb a steep holdless slab section leading to easier but unprotected climbing for 40 feet to the top. A Quartz Classic!

FA: Audrain, Frank, and Raleigh, Ratzlaff March 10, 1981
Gear: (4) quickdraws
2-bolt anchor   *150ft*

49a. LA Direct Finish 5.11c RX ★★★★

Climb to the first bolt of *LA Woman* then climb straight up to a horizontal rail. Continue climbing to the bolt protected "shield" from here.

Direct: Mike Hankins, Tony Mayse 2005

50. Woman in Bondage 5.11b RX ★★★★

Face climb to the right of *LA Woman*. Climb to the first bolt of *LA Woman* then traverse right to a rib of rock and continue up to the water streak with a bolt. Step over the bulge, and climb the water streak to a shared belay ledge with an anchor.

FA: Duane Raleigh, Bill Thomas 1981
Gear: quickdraws
2-bolt anchor   *150ft*

51. Black Magic Woman 5.11 R ★★
Bolted climb on the right side of South America Wall starting below *Women in Bondage*. From a stance on the *Atlantic Route*, move up and to the left just below a bolt on the face. Climb featured rock to a second bolt and continue on *Women in Bondage*.

FA: *Tony Wilson, Russell Hooper 1990s*
Gear: cams to #2 Camalot, quickdraws
2-bolt anchor   80ft

52. Atlantic Route 5.7 ★★★
Crack climb on the right side of South America Wall. Follow the diagonal finger crack to the corner that leads to a chimney. Follow the chimney up and left over a short overhang ending on a ledge with a 2-bolt anchor.

FA: *Kenny Stearns, Jay Lowell 1973*
Gear: cams to #4 Camalot, stoppers
2-bolt anchor   140ft

53. Grand Morass 5.9 ★
Same start as the *Atlantic Route*. Climb the slab to the right of *Atlantic Route*. At the second crescent shaped flake (finger crack visible to your left) continue up the face above the flake making your way to a large arching flake. Climb over the arching flake; continue up the easy ramp to anchors on top of *Power Grip*. Continue on any route taking you to the top or rappel. The rappel requires two ropes.

FA: *Duane Raleigh, Chris Rowins 1982*
Gear: cams to #4 Camalot
2-bolt anchor   100ft

54. Glass 5.9 RX ★★
Located above and to the right from the top of *Atlantic Route*. Climb a short polished dihedral with thought-provoking moves. From the top of *Glass* continue climbing up and right making your way to a shared belay station of *Saturn* at the top of the cliff. This climb was also the scene of the first helicopter rescue off of Old Baldly. A bad fall resulting in a broken leg. "An *airy adventure up smooth rock*." −Southern Exposure.

FA: *Jon Frank, Jimmy Ratzlaff 1980*
Gear: small cams to #3 Camalot
2-bolt anchor   90ft

55. Atomic Dust Dance 5.10c RX ★★★★
A mixed route to the right of *Atlantic Route*. Climb a short slab to a large undercling flake. Traverse right and continue up the face protected by 3 bolts leading to a horizontal crack below the steep bolt-protected face of *Power Grip*. Continue up *Power Grip* to a bolted belay. Two ropes are required for the rappel.

FA: *Mike Ritchey, Jane Bull 1992*
2nd Ascent: Tony Mayse, Lori Boren 1992
Gear: cams to #3.5 or #4 Camalot, quickdraws
2-bolt anchor   150ft

56. Saturn 5.11 ★★★★
Face climb with 5 bolts above *Power Grip*. From the anchors above *Power Grip* climb up the face following the line of bolts to a ledge with a bolted belay. The rappel to the *Power Grip* belay is 80 feet. The second pitch of *Power Grip* was climbed without fixed protection in 1982, though the exact line was unclear. In the late 90s the face was bolted and named *Saturn*. An excellent pitch of sustained face climbing up a smooth face.

FA: *Unknown Late 1990s*
Gear: #1, #2 Camalot, quickdraws
2-bolt anchor   80ft

57. Power Grip 5.10c R ★★
A mixed climb located a few feet left of *Field of Opportunity*. From a grassy ledge climb an easy slab to an arching crack. Pull over the crack onto a ledge. From the ledge climb up to a bolt on the face and continue up to another ledge with an anchor. This is a good continuation to *Atomic Dust Dance*.

FA: *Duane Raleigh, Chris Rowins 1982*
Gear: cams to #4 Camalot, quickdraws
2-bolt anchor   120ft

52, 55, 54. "Atomic, Power Grip, Saturn Link-Up" 5.11 ★★★★
The longest route at Quartz Mountain: linking these three climbs offers 230 feet of sustained (5.10/5.11) face climbing. The anchors are set up to allow for rappelling the route (note: two ropes are required from the anchors on *Power Grip* to the ground).
Pitch 1: Climb *Atomic Dust Dance*, then move up and right to gain the bolt on *Power Grip* continuing to a bolted belay station.
Pitch 2: Climb *Saturn* protected by five bolts.

58. Field of Opportunity 5.8 ★★★★
Crack climb to the right of *Power Grip*.
Pitch 1: From the grassy ledge climb the dihedral stepping right as the crack ends. From here step over a bulge onto a polished slab with a bolt. Continue up past the second bolt and finish in a large hole for the belay.
Pitch 2: Climb the corner above the belay, continuing in the crack system that leads to the top.

FA: *Terry Andrews, Greg Schooley 1979*
Gear: cams to #3 Camalot, stoppers, quickdraws
No anchor   190ft

58a. Field of Opportunity Roof Finish 5.7+ ★★★
A steeper finish. Traverse left on the slab for 15 feet to a short roof crack. Jam to roof ending on a spacious ledge. This is the original finish but is rarely climbed.

FA: *Terry Andrews, Greg Schooley 1979*
Gear: cams to #3 Camalot
No anchor   30ft

59. Field Triple Direct 5.9 ★

Same start as *Field of Opportunity*. Climb up the dihedral of *Field of Opportunity* then continue up a thin dihedral making your way past a grassy ledge, over a bulge with a large hueco and another bulge, ending at the same anchors as *Saturn*. Rappel from here or walk off.

FA: *Duane Raleigh, Chris Rowins 1979*
Gear: cams to #4 Camalot
2-bolt anchor   100ft

60. Field Direct 5.7 ★★★

Face climb up a water streak to the right of *Field of Opportunity*. Climb up the water streak past three bolts, ending at a large hueco for the belay. Continue on *Field of Opportunity*.

FA: *Rick Thomas, Duane Raleigh 1980*
Gear: cams to #3 Camalot, quickdraws
No anchor   60ft

61. Macho Man 5.7 ★★

Crack climb to the right of *Field Direct*.
Pitch 1: Climb the left-leaning cracks up and right of *Field Direct* ending at the large hole on *Field of Opportunity*.
Pitch 2: Continue by following the second pitch of *Field of Opportunity*.

FA: *Greg Schooley 1979*
Gear: cams to #4 Camalot
No anchor   190ft

62. The Gauntlet 5.9 ★★

Begins 10 feet left of the start to *El Tesoro*. Climb 20 feet up and left on thin face holds to a slightly overhanging arch. Clip a bolt and follow a narrow band of rock, eventually intersecting the *Macho Man* dihedral. Climb the left-arching corner for 30 feet to an obvious bucket flake on the right wall. Turn the small overhang, move up and right to a bolt 15 feet above. Continue climbing on thin face holds to the *El Tesoro* belay anchors. Two ropes are required for the rappel.

FA: *Marion Hutchison, Sam Audrain, Rick McCusic 1985*
(Direct Start: Hutchison, Andrews, Dan Pickard 2002)
Gear: quickdraws, medium cams
2-bolt anchor   130ft

63. El Tesoro A.K.A Last of the Dead Guys 5.10a R ★★★★

Located about 15 feet to the right of *Macho Man*. Starts from a flat boulder. Climb up a steep section of rock to the first bolt. Continue up on good holds and easier climbing (5.8–5.9). From the last bolt the wall gets steeper and the holds get smaller; it's about 30 feet to the anchors. The original name of this route is *Last of the Dead Guys*. The first ascent was a free solo by Duane Raleigh. Permission from the first ascentionist was given to protect this route with modern hardware. (Two ropes are required for the rappel.)

FA: *Duane Raleigh 1979 free solo*
FA: *(bolted line) Tony Wilson, Marion Hutchison 2002*
Gear: quickdraws
2-bolt anchor   130ft

63a. El Tesoro/Three Bolt (variation) 5.10 ★★

This route climbs the first two bolts of *El Tesoro* then traverses up and to the right to another bolt ending at *Three Bolts* anchors. Continue up *Three Bolt* or rappel.

FA: *Unknown*
Gear: same as *Three Bolt*
2-bolt anchor   75ft

64. The Pretender 5.9 RX ★★★

Follows the dark water streak to the left of *Romper Room*. Climb the same start as *Three Bolt*, then step over the roof protected by a bolt, continue up the face to the second bolt. The climbing becomes less difficult up and past the third bolt leading to the anchors. Two ropes are required for the rappel.

FA: *Sam Audrain, Duane Raleigh 1979*
Gear: quickdraws
2-bolt anchor   130ft

65. Romper Room 5.7 ★★★

Climbs the faint water streak right of *The Pretender*. Climb the face left of the dihedral, protected by four bolts. From the fourth bolt step left and continue climbing the water steak of *The Pretender*. On the first ascent the route was a free solo romp. Permission was given by the first ascentionist to add fixed protection. Two ropes are required for the rappel from the belay on top.

FA: *Duane Raleigh, Bill Thomas 1980*
Gear: quickdraws
2-bolt anchor   130ft

"For me, the most relevant factor in my ability to perform well on the rock has to do with my love of climbing. After nearly thirty years of climbing, I still love to do it whenever possible!"

~Lynn Hill

66. Three Bolt 5.7 ★★★★

A Quartz Mountain classic. Follow the ramp right of *Macho Man* for approximately 100 feet. *Three Bolt* starts in the corner below the large horizontal crack.

Pitch 1: Layback the corner to the horizontal crack, traverse left moving past a bolt on the face, and continue to a 2-bolt belay around the corner.

Pitch 2: Step right and up into a short hand crack with good jams 25 feet to a short face ending on a ledge with an anchor. Two ropes are required for the rappel. On the first ascent Terry Andrews and Greg Schooley (who was studying physics in college at the time) had calculated that the bolts used were not strong enough to hold a fall so "Three Bolts" were installed at the belay. The anchors have since been replaced with two ⅜" bolts.

FA: *Greg Schooley, Terry Andrews 1979*
Gear: cams to #3 Camalot, quickdraws
2-bolt anchor   *150ft*

67. Thin Lizzy A.K.A. Goon Squad 5.10b X ★★

Located 30 feet to the right of *Romper Room*, climb the short water streak with no pro.

FA: *Jimmy Ratzlaff 1980*
Gear: free solo
No anchor   *30ft*

GRUNT CHAMBER

The Grunt Chamber is located 300 yards east from the parking area. The faint trail goes down into a gully then turns back towards the wall. This area is often hard to find after summer vegetation has taken over the trail. Look for an opening at the base of the wall with a boulder stuck at the foot of the entrance (see topo photo).

Scramble over the boulder and into a small room with three routes. This is a good place to work on your offwidth skills. Walk off to the west to descend all routes in the Grunt Chamber.

1. Born Again Hard 5.12c ★★

Bolted route on the left side of the entrance to the Grunt Chamber. Climb on smooth face holds past two bolts to the top. This climb is more of a highball boulder problem with bolts.

FA: *Unknown*
Gear: quickdraws
No anchor   *30ft*

Grunt Chamber

2. Kilo Crack 5.10 ★★

Crack climb that starts on the left side of the Grunt Chamber. Start in a finger crack on the back wall, continue making your way up to a hand crack that leads out left, to a short roof with slick feet. Finish around the corner to the top.

FA: *Greg Schooley, David Panciera 1978*
Gear: cams to #4 Camalot, stoppers
No anchor   *50ft*

3. Jimmy Dean 5.10c ★★

Offwidth climb on the right side of Grunt Chamber. Climb up a polished face to the start of the crack; continue up the corner crack to the offwidth squeeze ending at a ledge.

FA: *Duane Raleigh, Rick Thomas 1980*
Gear: TCUs, cams to #4 Camalot, stoppers
No anchor   *50ft*

> *"It's the only thing we've got.*
>
> *Let's protect it while we can."*
>
> ~*The Dead Kennedy's, Hellination*

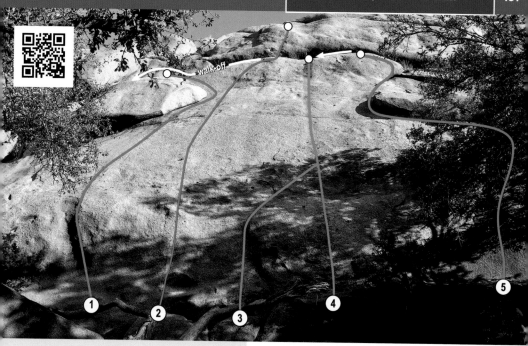

WATCH ME WALL

Watch Me Wall is down the trail 30 yards east of the Grunt Chamber. Scramble up large boulders to reach the base of the first five routes. The other routes are just to the east and are a short walk (30 yards) from *Earth Man*.

Descent: From the top follow the slabs down to your left (west) leading to the base and back to the trail. Routes starting with *Texas Cruise* descend to the right (east).

1. 5.8 Start RX ★

This is the first route on the Watch Me Wall. It is easy to locate; look for the obvious trough. Originally climbed as a free solo on the first ascent. Climb the trough, then up the slab going around the roof, it is possible to get protection here before continuing up and left to the top.

FA: *Duane Raleigh 1980 free solo*

Gear: cams to #2 Camalot

No anchor   100ft

2. Lady Luck 5.10b X ★★

Face climb with three bolts on the left side of the wall. Climb up the short steep 5.9 section with a bolt; continue up the slab 60 feet to a steep headwall protected by a second bolt. Climb over the bulge and horizontal crack making your way to another bolt, continue on easier climbing to the top. The last section of this route was added as a second pitch but can be done in one long pitch.

FA: *Rick Thomas, Sam Audrain 1980*

Gear: cams to #3 Camalot, quickdraws

No anchor   160ft

3. Gulf Pride 5.11b X ★

This route climbs the blank section of rock between *Lady Luck* and *Icabod Crank*. According to *Southern Exposure* it may be possible to protect this climb by stringing runners between *Lady Luck* and *Icabod Crank*.

FA: *Duane Raleigh 1980*

Gear: slings

No anchor   80ft

4. Icabod Crank 5.11a X ★★

Face climb to the right of *Gulf Pride* with one bolt. From the ledge climb up the face to a bolt, high step into a dish and continue on runout friction to the horizontal crack above (belay here). Traverse off to the left.

FA: *Duane Raleigh, Rick Thomas 1980*

Gear: cams to #3 Camalot, quickdraws

No anchor   80ft

5. 50 Lashes 5.9 X ★

Located 20 feet to the right of *Icabod Crank*. Starting at ground level, ascend the red rock below the ledge; it is possible to start off the ledge climbing through the tree branches. Climb up the slab to an unprotected roof, climb over the roof and continue up the slab to the ledge and belay. A fall from this route will result in the dreaded "50 Lashes" from the branches which touch the route.

FA: *Duane Raleigh, Rick Thomas 1980*

Gear: cams to #3 Camalot

No anchor   100ft

Texas Cruise →

"They say every man needs protection, They say that every man must fall. Yet I swear I see my reflection, Somewhere so high above this wall."

~Bob Dylan

6. Earth Man 5.12b ★★★

Face climb 10 yards right of *Fifty Lashes*. Climb a polished slab to the first bolt, and then continue up a steep section to the second bolt. The top of this route ends on a ledge. This route has had few ascents.

FA: *Chris Rowins (aid) 1979, Duane Raleigh (free) 1983*
Gear: quickdraws
No anchor   60ft

7. Texas Cruise 5.8 ★★

Located 30 yards to the right of *Earth Man*. Start in a hand crack with an obvious knob on the face to the right. Jam your way 25 feet up to a ledge. Belay on the ledge to avoid rope drag. Continue up the crack, pulling over a short roof, set up the belay past the roof.

FA: *Unknown*
Gear: cams to #3 Camalot, stoppers
No anchor   100ft

7a. Texas Booze A.K.A. Texas Cruise Turn Off 5.7 ★★

After climbing *Texas Cruise* for 50 feet, step right for 10 feet to a short slab that leads to a finger crack.

FA: *Jimmy Ratzlaff, Mark Herndon 1980*
Gear: cams to #3 Camalot, stoppers
No anchor   100ft

7b. Super Grim Raw Adrenalin Crank Pump Burn Out 5.7 ★★

Climb the water streak just right of the last section of *Texas Cruise*.

FA: *Jimmy Ratzlaff, Mark Herndon 1980*
Gear: cams to #3 Camalot, stoppers
No anchor   100ft

Have Gun Will Travel →

Earth Man

8. Hand Crack 5.8+ ★★

Hand crack 20 yards right of *Texas Cruise*. Climb a short face that starts next to a tree. Continue in a hand crack on good jams to a ledge (belay here).

FA: Bill Thomas, Duane Raleigh 1978
Gear: cams to #3.5, stoppers
No anchor   90ft

9. Large Dihedral 5.7 ★

Large Dihedral is located 100 feet to the right of *Hand Crack*. Unprotected climbing up the polished dihedral until higher up where gear opportunities are available. Belay on one of the many ledges up top. Walk off to the right and down the talus slope.

FA: Unknown 1980s
Gear: cams to #4 Camalot
No anchor   100ft

10. Jomby 5.8

Single-bolt climb to the right of *Large Dihedral*. Climb the slab to a bolt then traverse to the right continuing with *Cowboys and Cossacks*. This route is a variation start to *Cowboys and Cossacks*.

FA: Unknown 1990s
Gear: (1) quickdraw
No anchor   70ft

11. Cowboys and Cossacks 5.8+ ★★

This is the bolted line left of *Have Gun Will Travel*, ending at a belay ledge up top. Bolted in the early 90s by a visiting climber.

FA: Kansas George 1990s
Gear: quickdraws, #2, #3 cams for belay
No anchor   60ft

12. Have Gun Will Travel 5.8+ ★★★

Face climb with three bolts 20 feet to the right of *Cowboys and Cossacks*. This wall has a large flake resembling a horse's head. Scramble up slabs to the right then make your way down and left on a ramp to a good belay spot. Climb the face on easy friction past two bolts to a stance on a knob below the third bolt. Continue up the face past the third bolt and steeper climbing to a ledge. Great friction climb!

FA: Tony Mayse, Lori Boren 1991
Gear: quickdraws, #2, #3 cams for belay
No anchor   75ft

13. Rock Angel 5.10c RX ★★

To the right of *Have Gun Will Travel* is a steep face route with one bolt. Climb sustained unprotected climbing up 30 feet to a bolt. Continue up to the top.

FA: Unknown 1980s
Gear: quickdraws, #2 cams for belay
No anchor   60ft

14. Wave Length 5.9 ★★

Down and to the right of *Rock Angel*. Look for the obvious waves in the granite slabs. Bouldery moves over the waves protected by a bolt. Belay on the ledge up higher. Walk off to the right.

FA: Unknown 1990s
Gear: quickdraws, #2 cams for belay
No anchor   60ft

Have Gun Will Travel

STRAY CATS WALL

Stray Cats Wall is located on the east side of Quartz Mountain. Walk down the trail past all the routes on the south face until the trail starts to head north. The climber trail leads to the north. After passing the tall walls with water streaks on your left, Stray Cats Wall can be seen from the bottom of the trail as you look up the hill to your west. A splitter hand crack runs up the wall; this is the *Stray Cats* route. Stray Cats Wall is east-facing and a good afternoon spot when the sun is baking the south face. From the parking area Stray Cats Wall is about a 15-minute walk. To descend the routes walk off to the south, this gets you back to the base of the climbs.

1. Unfinished Route 5.13?

Located fifteen feet to the left of *Stray Cats*. Climb straight up on 5.11 moves before reaching the bolt. Variation start: Just left of *Stray Cats*, climb up the broken rock band past the horizontal cracks making your way to a fixed piton, from here move left and up over the bulge gaining the bolt. The route was started in 1981 by Duane Raleigh and has not been completed to date. Note: Previous guides called this route 5.11. The upper reaches of the climb will be harder.

FA: Open Project
Gear: (1) quickdraw
No anchor   50ft

2. Stray Cats 5.10d ★★★

This route climbs the hand crack up the Stray Cats Wall. Climb broken rock for 15 feet to a short roof, step over the roof on good edges to a stance below the hand crack. Step right and up on good jams and steep rock for 40 feet to a ledge.

On the first ascent Duane and the boys lugged up a tape deck to the base of the climb. *Stray Cat Blues* from the Rolling Stones was playing!

FA: Duane Raleigh 1982
Gear: stoppers, TCUs, cams to #2 Camalot
No anchor   55ft

3. Little Reality 5.10d ★★

Five-foot roof crack to the right of *Stray Cats*. Climb 20 feet up a steep corner to the roof; from here move out the roof to a hand jam over the lip. This move feels committing even with gear placed above you. Cut your feet loose and heel hook over the roof; continue on easier climbing to the top.

FA: Jon Frank, Terry Andrews 1980
Gear: stoppers, TCUs, cams to #2 Camalot
No anchor   40ft

4. Deception Corners 5.8 ★★

Located in the large dihedral with a grassy area in the middle. This climb starts to the left of Stray Cats Wall on gray streaked walls. First ascent was climbed in the rain. (no topo available)

FA: Terry Andrews, Greg Schooley 1979
Gear: gear to #3 Camalot
No anchor   100ft

I Want to Be Smooth

QUARTZ BACKSIDE

The routes in this area are located by walking north on the trail starting in the Main Boulder Field. There are a eight routes from 5.5–5.12. This area stays in the shade until late afternoon.

SMOOTH MOVE WALL

Located uphill and north from Devil's Slide. This wall faces west and has three climbs: *Aid Roof*, *Move Smooth*, and *Smooth Move*. Just downhill and slightly northwest is an overhanging outcropping with a mixed climb named *I Want to Be Smooth*.

1. I Want to be Smooth 5.12b ★★★

Steep face climb on a west-facing yellow-lichen-colored outcropping with a smooth slab at it's south side. This route is located 50 yards north and slightly downhill from Smooth Move Wall. Climb broken rock for six feet, then move up and left on solid rock following a thin, arching crack below an overhang. The overhanging section is protected by two bolts. The most difficult route on the Quartz Backside. Steep & pumpy!

Bolted by Tony Wilson & Russell Hooper in the 90s.

FA: Tony Mayse 2016

Gear: small cams, quickdraws

No anchor   50ft

2. Aid Roof A2 ★

Large aid roof around the corner and to the left (north) of *Smooth Move*. Climb up the easy slab (5.5) to the bottom of the roof. Aid up and to the right following a thin crack until it turns vertical leading to the belay. There are some fixed pins in the roof.

FA: Unknown 1980s

Gear: standard aid rack

No anchor   60ft

3. Move Smooth 5.11b ★★

This route has the same start as *Smooth Move* but traverses left on the blank face below the roof then follows the crack up to the shared belay ledge of *Smooth Move*.

FA: Duane Raleigh, Tony Wilson 1987

Gear: same as *Smooth Move*

No anchor   45ft

4. Smooth Move 5.10b ★★★

Located to the right of *Move Smooth*. Climb easy but broken rock for 20 feet. Climb the corner on thin smears protected by small wires and TCUs to a horizontal crack under a roof. Traverse left on tenuous moves to a stance at the left end of the roof (belay here). This route, although quite short, is well worth the approach if you want some adventure and a bit of exposure.

FA: Duane Raleigh 1983

Gear: small wires, TCUs, cams to #3 Camalot

No anchor   45ft

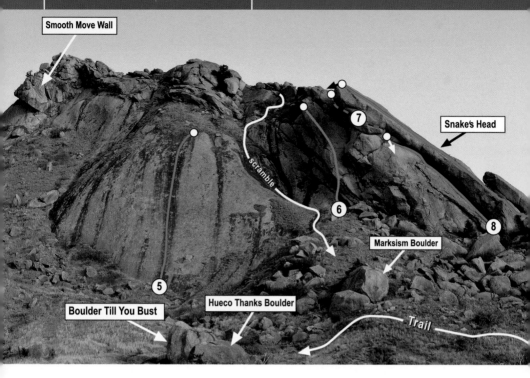

Smooth Move Wall

Snake's Head

scramble

Marksism Boulder

Boulder Till You Bust

Hueco Thanks Boulder

Trail

5. Devil's Slide 5.5 X

Face climb in the center of the large slab. This route climbs up loose flakes in the water streak with no protection. According to *Southern Exposure*, it may be possible to tie off the flakes for protection.

FA: *James Hollingsworth, Jay Lowell*

Gear: Unknown

No anchor   90ft

6. Bolted Now 5.11 ★★

Bolted Now was an aid climb named *Charlie Don't Surf*. The route now has three bolts protecting the short overhang which leads to a slab and easier climbing.

FA: *Russell Hooper, Tony Wilson early 1990s*

Gear: quickdraws

2-bolt anchor   50ft

7. Cardinal Fang A4 ★★

Cardinal Fang is an aid route which climbs the "fang" of *Snake's Head*.

FA: *Chris Rowins, Brent Choate 1981*

Gear: standard aid rack

No anchor   50ft

8. The Arm Pit 5.6 RX ★★

This route climbs the large dihedral starting down and to the right of *Bolted Now*. Climb up the slab past a large window. At the top of the slab a hand-size crack protects the moves arching to the left and up to the belay. No protection on the bottom of this climb. The climbing is very similar to the level of difficulty found on *Snake's Head*.

Rarely climbed but worth doing.

FA: *Art and party 1972*

Gear: cams to #2 Camalot

2-bolt anchor   100ft

"Climb the mountains and get their good tidings.
Nature's peace will flow into you as sunshine
flows into the trees. The winds will blow their own
freshness into you, and the storms their energy, while
cares drop away from you like the leaves of Autumn."
~John Muir

Photo by Tony Mayse

03 QUARTZ MOUNTAIN BOULDERING

QUARTZ MOUNTAIN BOULDERING

The history of Quartz Mountain bouldering dates back to the days when the first routes were being climbed at Old Baldy. The area seems to have an inexhaustible amount of boulders to climb. With several boulders just off the parking area it was hard for these big rocks not to get climbed and also mentioned in the first guidebook *Southern Exposure*, by Duane Raleigh and Bill Thomas.

One of the larger boulders located just a stone's throw from the parking area is the Gill Boulder, named after the father of bouldering John Gill. John Gill was one of the first to boulder exclusively on cutting-edge problems. To this day some of his problems are rarely repeated and almost incomprehensible even with current ratings far exceeding those of that era—problems such as the highball crystal-pinching boulder problem the *Thimble* (in South Dakota) onsight solo climbed in the spring of 1961. This was a feat of extraordinary skill and mental control, as it is rated 5.12, is 30 feet high, and offered a bad landing on a guardrail (since removed). John Gill was legendary and thus the Gill Boulder was named after him.

Molly Hennesy on the Gill Problem.

> "Bouldering isn't really a sport. It's a climbing activity with metaphysical, mystical and philosophical overtones."
> ~John Gill

The Gill Boulder has several classic problems such as *The Gill Problem*, *Finger Tip Trip*, *Black Scratch*, and *Right Edge* which are climbed regularly. The ever popular *Pizza Face* on the Practice Wall was the "easy" highball of the day. The Run and Jump Boulder has several problems that quickly gained popularity, especially, the namesake problem *Run and Jump*, originally done with a run and jump onto the slab. Later the shin knocking high step would become the way the problem is done. Even with sticky shoes the problem is still slick and sketchy! Heel Hook Boulder just around the corner was done with a "trick heel hook" and made the must-do list.

RUN AND JUMP PROBLEM IN THE LATE 1970s

In the Stray Cats area (also known now as Cedar Valley), *Munge Lunge* was the 5.11 problem of the day and is still uber popular. This area has many problems strewn out on the hillside below the Stray Cats Wall.

The Backside area also saw activity with the Mushroom Boulder being a favorite destination. Later Steve Gillam added *Boulder Till You Bust*—a toprope problem on a large boulder. The Backside has several problems located in a large open area, much different from that of the Main Bouldering Area where the boulders are much closer to each other. All three areas are unique and still have much potential for exploration.

The need for a bouldering guide has been long overdue. At the 2016 Fall Gathering and 20th Anniversary of the event, Preston Pettigrew with the help of Molly Hennesy produced *Small Rocks in a Wheatfield*, a handwritten paperback guide with nicely drawn maps and descriptions. As expected it was an instant hit.

The bouldering rating system is the same as the climbing routes. This system seems to be the most efficient for rating the many problems in this guide. The bouldering section is divided into three areas: Main Bouldering Area, Stray Cats/Cedar Valley Area and Quartz Backside.

Happy Bouldering.

Artwork by Elisha Gallegos

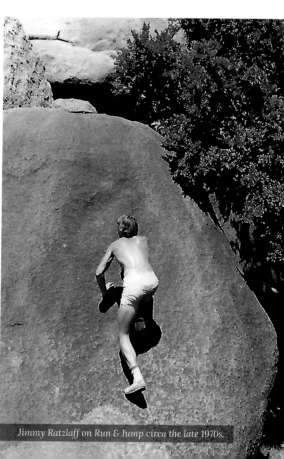

Jimmy Ratzlaff on Run & Jump circa the late 1970s.

Quartz Mountain Bouldering Map

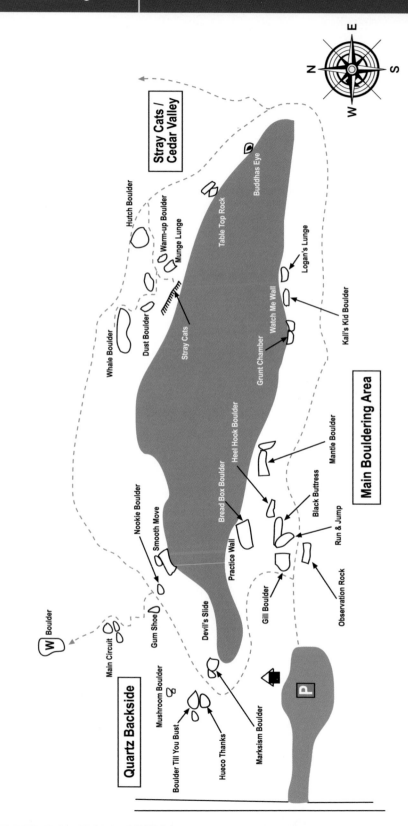

Stray Cats / Cedar Valley

Main Bouldering Area

Quartz Backside

Hutch Boulder
Warm-up Boulder
Munge Lunge
Dust Boulder
Whale Boulder
Stray Cats
Table Top Rock
Buddhas Eye
Logan's Lunge
Watch Me Wall
Kali's Kid Boulder
Grunt Chamber
Heel Hook Boulder
Mantle Boulder
Bread Box Boulder
Black Buttress
Run & Jump
Nookie Boulder
Smooth Move
Practice Wall
Gill Boulder
Observation Rock
Devil's Slide
Gum Shoe
Main Circuit
W Boulder
Mushroom Boulder
Boulder Till You Bust
Hueco Thanks
Marksism Boulder
P

Gill Direct

MAIN BOULDER FIELD

Main Boulder Field is located 50 yards from the parking area. From here the rest of the boulders are easily located. (See bouldering cverview map for reference.)

GILL BOULDER

From the parking area, Gill Boulder is about 100 feet down the trail and sits off to the left with 4 climbable sides. Seven problems are listed for this boulder.

1. The Gill Problem 5.12 ★★★★

The namesake to the Gill Boulder. Done with a run and jump to a sloping hold or step off the boulder out right to gain the sloping hold. From here continue up on positive holds to the top.

2. Tree Face A.K.A. Sugar's Problem 5.6 ★★★

Slab climb on the Gill's south face. This is also the downclimb to all of the other problems. Climb the polished slab right of the tree.

3. Trippin' 5.11 ★★★

Located to the right of *Tree Face/Sugar's Problem*. Jump for a hole with an edge in the middle of the east face. From here work your way up less-than-steep rock to the top.

4. Finger Tip Trip 5.9 ★★★★

Same start as *Trippin'*. Reach for a small pocket with a sharp edge, from here pull up over the bulge, making your way to the top. A Quartz Classic!

5. Overhanging Corner 5.10 ★★

Start right of *Finger Tip Trip* at ground level. Step up the broken corner, work your way up the arête to the top.

6. Black Scratch A.K.A. The North Face Problem 5.11 ★★★★

Thin holds on a steep face just right of *Overhanging Corner*. Step up on a good edge and crimps to get established in or below the scoop. Hard move to the top-out. Outstanding crimp problem.

7. Right Edge 5.10+ ★★★★

Climb the arête right of *Black Scratch* on smooth and polished rock. Sketchy start, though there's better holds up higher.

Stanley Vrba cranking on Black Scratch. | Photo by Tony Mayse

PRACTICE WALL

Walk the trail north for 50 feet past the Gill Boulder. Located next to the trees below the ledges that lead to the S Wall approach. *Rowin's Roof* in the furthest left problem, all other problems are to the right.

1. Rowin's Roof 5.12

Roof problem at the far left (west) end of the Practice Wall. Originally climbed with a bat-hook and bolt (5.10 A1). At the time, Duane, not wanting a bolt on such a short wall, removed the offending bolt and free soloed the route at 5.12. "A line of strength."

FA: *Chris Rowins 1980s (on aid)*
FFA: *Duane Raleigh 1980s (free)*

2. Practice Crack 5.7 ★★

To the right of *Rowin's Roof*. Climb a polished slab that leads to a crack. Cruxy top-out. Highball.

3. Pizza Face 5.7 ★★★★

To the right of *Practice Crack*. Climb a slab to an overhanging pocketed "pizza face." Classic highball.

BREAD BOX BOULDER
Large, rectangular boulder, right of the approach steps that lead to the S Wall. There are two committing lines on this boulder. Stepping out right is a committing prospect mimicking the style of climbing found at Old Baldy.

4. Bread Box Traverse A.K.A. LoLo Traverse 5.10 ★★★
Face climb traverse over a talus field starting on the boulder's left side. Highball.

5. Just a Thin Slice 5.9 ★★
Start in the middle of Bread Box Boulder on a flat rock down low. Climb a thin face up to the top. Highball.

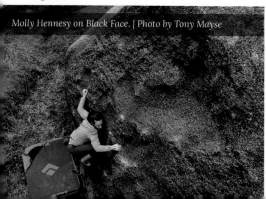

Molly Hennesy on Black Face. | Photo by Tony Mayse

Molly Hennesy on Black Scratch. | Photo by Tony Mayse

Surprisingly, for as large us this boulder is and its close proximity to the walk-up for the roped climbs, rarely will you see another climber tip-toeing up or across this intimidating rock. Shaped like a bread box and sitting high above the Main Boulder Field. There is probably a good reason that most climbers walk by. Mimicking the style of the roped climbs, this overlooked treat has it all—committing, heady, intimidating, thin friction, with micro-crimps to top it off!

Here Molly Hennesy uses great form and keeps a cool head on Just a Thin Slice. Spotter: Preston Pettigrew

Photo by Tony Mayse

Tony Mayse on the upper ledges classic boulder problem, Hooper's Arête. | Photo by Stanley Vrba

HOOPER'S ARÊTE

Striking arête up high. *The Hooper's Arête* sits high atop the Headwall balcony, guarding the passage to Quartz Mountain's mega-classic Headwall climbs. Make your way up to the upper ledges and just to the left of *Hobbit's* start.

1. Hooper's Arête 5.12- ★★★★

Step up on good feet and good hands. Steep start leads to pinch and crimp moves up the arête to top-out. Down climb the back.

RUN AND JUMP BOULDER

Run and Jump is located opposite Gill Boulder. It used to begin with a run, starting from Observation Rock, then a jump onto the very end of the boulder and continuing up the slab to the top. Nowadays done with a high-step on the smoothest part of the boulder just off the trail. Beware of the dreaded shin knocker if you blow it!

1. Corner Mantel 5.11 ★★

First problem on the leftmost corner. Located under a tree with branches touching the rock. Toe-in under the overhanging corner, heel hook out right, and mantel up. Hard start.

2. Knob Job 5.7 ★★★

Look for the obvious knob towards the top. Start out on the slab, with a good left foot, smearing out to the right, and working your way up to a knob.

3. Seam 5.9 ★★★

With a thin smear at the start, work your way up to the seam, trending left for the top.

Molly Hennesy warming up on the Run & Jump Boulder. | Photo by Tony Mayse

Preston Pettigrew on the steep side of Run & Jump Boulder, cranking out the last move of Hard Face 5.12. | Photo by Tony Mays

4. Run and Jump 5.10 ★★★★

The namesake problem for this boulder. Move out off the slab onto the grass right of the *Seam* problem. Step up with a high foot on a small crystal and stand up. Smooth-as-glass smearing to the top. Classic Quartz problem.

5. Hard Face 5.12- ★★★★

Around the corner on the east side of *Run and Jump.* Climb a polished face with small holds. Crank up on small holds with no feet, paddling your way up to get established. The sidepull way right on *Black Face* is off. Hard.

6. Black Face 5.10 ★★★★

A few feet right of *Hard Face.* Good knobs and dished-out footholds get you established in the scoop, continue with a reach to a knob.

BLACK BUTTRESS

A black slab located just around the corner and touching the Run and Jump Boulder. Probably the best boulder to work and hone your friction skills for the Quartz climbing.

1. Black Buttress 5.11 ★★★★

Super-slick arête with moves that feel like you could blow any second. Start on the slab underneath and to the left of the arête." Use a sidepull and high-step on a polished knob out right. Getting established just below the arête is key before moving up on dished-out feet and small crimps. A sketchy little problem.

2. Middle Route 5.10 ★★★

A few feet to the right of *Black Buttress.* From the ground, step up onto the slab keeping just a few feet right of the arête. If it feels easy then you're on the *Slab* problem.

3. Slab 5.7 ★★★

Climb just to the left of the light-colored rock (This spot was marred by vandals with graffiti. The light color was after it was removed.) High-step up on small edges and smears with good holds to the top.

HEEL HOOK BOULDER

Located to the right of Black Buttress.

4. Heel Hook 5.10 ★★★

The texture on this problem is pretty rough. Look for a lip and wide shelf at chest level, just above a slab. Heel hook, hold on, and gun for the top!

MANTEL BOULDER

Down the trail about 100 yards past the Run and Jump Boulder. Look to your left about 25 feet off the trail for a large, gray boulder with several scoops. This boulder has five problems. A good one for practicing thin footwork and manteling.

1. 5.11 Mantel 5.11 ★★★

The first problem on the far left. Step off the slab onto thin foot holds working your way up to a small dish with thin crystals for your feet.

2. 5.10 Mantel 5.10 ★★★★

Just to the right of 5.11 *Mantel* is a dish on which to mantel. Step up on smears and edges. Work up, palm down, drive feet.

3. Big Mantel 5.7

To the right of 5.10 *Mantel*. Easy practice mantel.

4. 5.6 Mantel 5.6

Easy practice mantle to the right of *Big Mantel*.

5. Edge Traverse 5.8 ★★★

Start on Mantel Boulder's far right side. Step up on a foothold then move left following the thin edge that weaves its way across the boulders lower half. Going the opposite direction is harder.

WATCH ME WALL BOULDERS

From the parking area hike 300 yards down the trail (east). There are two boulders located in front of Watch Me Wall. (See overview map).

Kali's Kids Boulder is a low-angle dark-colored granite boulder with a nice flat base, sitting just in front of a cedar tree.

1. Kali's Kids Boulder 5.Easy ★★★★

A fun, easy boulder problem for kids to learn friction. Located 20 yards to the right of the Grunt Chamber and left of Watch Me Wall.

Logan Lunge Boulder is a dark brown rock that sits 20 feet to the right of Kali's Kid's Boulder. There are two problems on this bullet-hard, polished boulder.

2. Left Edge 5.10 ★★

Starting on the left side, move up the arête on good holds, heel hook across the top trending right.

3. Logan's Lunge 5.10 ★★★

Dyno for the large hueco about 10 feet up or use small holds to reach for the bottom edge of the hueco (harder if you're shorter). Continue on good holds over the lip.

Kali Jo Boren getting the Quartz skills early (6 years old) on the Kid's Boulder, spotted by Logan Boren. | Photo by Tony Mayse

STRAY CATS AREA A.K.A .CEDAR VALLEY

This area is located on the east side of Quartz Mountain. Follow the trail east past the south-facing walls of Quartz Mountain. After passing the last bit of rock on your left there is a faint trail leading left (north). Follow this trail north passing the gray walls with black water streaks on your left. After several hundred yards walking north, you will be able to see the Stray Cats Wall located west and slightly to the north. There are several boulder problems below Stray Cats Wall, some still waiting first ascents and some that are listed here. The first large boulder closest to the trail is the Hutch Boulder.

This majority of the problems are in this area.

Buddha's Eye and Table Top Rock are just south a few hundred yards from the Hutch Boulder (see overview map on page 200).

BUDDHA'S EYE BOULDER

Located south of the Stray Cats/Cedar Valley bouldering area. Buddha's Eye Boulder is the first problem off the trail before reaching Stray Cats Wall. This 12-foot-diameter bowl with its orange color, facing to the east makes for a perfect place to enjoy some bouldering and a bit of meditation. The name was inspired by Lori Mayse.

Approach: As you walk east on the main trail, continue past Old Baldy towards the trees and a wash. From here a faint trail heads north. Walk approximately 100 yards north, look up (west) toward the rock with trees covering the lower reaches. In the morning sun, Buddha's Eye glows orange and is hard to miss. Scramble up the rocks to gain the cave-like bowl.

1. Buddha's Eye 5.10+ ★★★★

Move up the south side of the eye on huecos and jugs to a sloping hold and exit moves over the lip. Namaste. Committing highball.

TABLE TOP ROCK

Continue walking north past the Buddha's Eye boulder for approximately 200 yards.

Table Top Rock is a large boulder sitting high up on the hill below the water streaked walls on Quartz's east side. It is an easy approach and visible from the trail. Look uphill to your left (west) before reaching Hutch Boulder. Table Top Rock is 20 feet tall and about 35 feet in diameter with bright yellow lichen on the upper part of the rock. Currently there is only one problem on this large rock.

1. Table Top Traverse (PROJECT) 5.12? ★★

Start on the northwest corner on good sidepulls and holds. Keeping your feet low and your hands in the middle band, traverse left with crimps, sidepulls, compression presses, and whatever else keeps you on. Work your way around to the east side and up the southwest corner on jugs to the top. The traverse is 20 feet long with 15 more feet up jugs on the southwest corner.

Molly Hennesy on the Table Top Rock project boulder problem spotted by Preston Pettigrew and Elisha G. | Photo by Tony Mayse

Elisha Gallegos contemplates the downclimb on the highball Hutch Boulder. | Photo by Molly Hennesy

HUTCH BOULDER

Located approximately 100 yards north of Table Top Rock. This is the first huge boulder that sits just off the trail and is hard to miss.. The main climbing side faces east. Currently there are three problems on this boulder.

1. The Arête 5.9 ★★★
Climb up on good holds staying left of *Fire Face* and follow the arête on good holds. Highball.

2. Fire Face 5.10 ★★★
The obvious line in the center of the south face. Flakey rock down low and better rock higher up. Climb thin holds up the wall to the top. Highball

3. Monkey Love 5.9 ★
Starting on the northeast side. Follow good holds up and to the right leading to the top.

Stray Cats Area

Table Top Rock

WARM UP BOULDER

Located uphill from Hutch Boulder, with three problems that face to the east. This is a good warm-up boulder featuring big huecos and jugs.

1. Project 5.12
The farthest-most line closest to the overhanging corner.

2. Warm-Up 1 5.9 ★★
Face climb with huecos leading to the top.

3. Warm Up 2 5.9 ★★
Takes the hueco-pocketed face to the right of #2.

MUNGE LUNGE BOULDER

Located uphill from Warm Up Boulder. The problems on the Munge Lunge Boulder are on the overhanging south side and nicely nestled down low; out of the north wind on cold days, and shaded later in the day in the summer months. This boulder is well known at Quartz. *Munge Lunge* was first climbed in 1981 by Duane Raleigh and is one of the more popular boulder problems at Old Baldy.

1. Warm-Up 5.8 ★
On the non-overhanging west side of the boulder. Plenty of pockets and jugs make for a nice warm-up line.

2. Munge Lunge 5.11 ★★★★
The namesake to this boulder. Start down low on good holds, moving up and right to the top.
FA: Duane Raleigh 1981

3. Quality Control 5.12 ★★
Just to the right of *Munge Lunge*. Harder problem than the others, starting with small holds down low and staying just left of the outer edge to the top.

4. Black Streak 5.9 ★★
Climb the black water streak on the east face. Highball.

Preston Pettiegrew on Black Streak 5.9. Photo by Molly Hennesy

Molly Hennesy topping out on the iconic Munge Lunge. | Photo by Tony Mayse

WHALE BOULDER

Walk north past Stray Cats Wall approximately 400 yards. Whale Boulder is hard to miss. Walk north, dropping down and then up the ravine to a large flat area and Whale Boulder. The problems listed are on the east-facing side.

1. Kiddie Pool 5.6 ★

The first problem on the far left end. Climb up to a good flake/crack taking you to the top. A good warm-up.

2. Project 1

Climb the first flake/crack about 40 feet to the right of *Kiddie Pool*. Highball.

3. Project 2

Climb the flake/crack to the right of *Project 1*. Face climb up to the crack and flake until it fades out about four feet from the top.

4. Property Line 5.9 ★★★★

Climb the obvious fingers to tight hands just right of the *Project* problems. In the early 90s there was a property line wire fence next to this problem.

> "I can't climb just a little. I need to crank like a bastard." ~Klem Loskot

DUST BOULDER

Located in the Stray Cats/Cedar Valley Area and just to the north of Munge Lunge Boulder. This boulder has three problems.

1. Captain Beef Heart 5.8

Climb the thin face on the boulders west face.

2. Dust 5.9

Climb the overhanging corner to the top.

3. Mellow Blotch 5.8

Climb the pockets on the east face.

QUARTZ BACKSIDE AREA

From the Practice Wall, follow the trail left (west). The trail wraps around the far west end of Old Baldy then leads north towards the boulders; these are spread out over a large area.

The large boulder on your right as your turn towards Devil's Slide is the Marksism Boulder. Walk about 30 yards north and Hueco Thanks will be on your left. From here follow the map. All boulders are just off the trail and easily spotted (see overview map on page 200).

MARKSISM BOULDER

This boulder is the first large boulder on your right (east) as you hike the trail into the Backside Area. From *Boulder till You Bust*, Marksism Boulder is uphill (south and east) 50 yards. A smaller boulder below and just to the left is the starting point for this line. It currently has only one problem.

1. Marksism 5.8 ★★

Starting on the boulder below and to the left, traverse right then climb the slab to top out.

HUECO THANKS BOULDER

This is the first boulder on your left as you enter the Backside Area. Brown boulder with a hole on its upper left side.

To descend this boulder, either downclimb *Keep Your Powder Dry*, or step down to the large hole of *Hueco Thanks* and hop off.

1. Hueco Thanks 5.10- ★★★

The first problem on the southeast face. Start with a good right hand and small edge for your foot, pop for a left hand crimp, then rail out right before the hueco and exit moves. Good problem with a couple campus moves.
FA: Stanley Vrba

Hueco Thanks

2. Like a Hurricane 5.12b ★★★★

Center line on the Hueco Thanks Boulder. Start with a good left-hand crimp and delicate feet. Hard move gunning for the horizontal rail. Several options available on this problem, none are easy.
Best line on the Hueco Thanks Boulder.

3. Cowgirl in the Sand 5.10- ★★

Five feet to the right of *Like a Hurricane* (on the north side). Good feet left of the arête lead to a few sharp crimps and hand bumps up the arête to better holds up higher. Good warm-up problem.
FA: Tony Mayse

4. Cinnamon Girl 5.9 ★

Climb the steep slab, starting off the boulder just to right of *Cowgirl in the Sand*.
FA: Joe Romero

Tony Mayse on *Like a Hurricane*.

Joe Romero pulling hard on the powerful Like a Hurricane 5.12b.

5. Look out Momma 5.12 (PROJECT)
Steep face closest to the ravine.

6. Ruby in the Dust 5.12 (PROJECT)
Steep face a few feet right of *Look out Momma*.

7. Keep Your Powder Dry 5.7 ★★
Climb good edges and pockets up the face 10 feet left of the *Hueco Thanks* problem.

FA: *Stanley Vrba*

BOULDER TILL YOU BUST
This boulder is located just to the right of the Hueco Thanks Boulder.

1. Boulder Till You Bust 5.11+ ★★★
A line established by Steve Gillam in 1986. This large boulder sits just north of the Hueco Thanks Boulder in the Backside Area. Climb the face on the north side and connect with a left-angling crack up higher. Established on toprope back in the day. Highball.

Kali Jo Boren on the Backside Boulders with spotter Rotes below.

MUSHROOM BOULDER

Sitting about 20 yards from Boulder Till You Bust is a boulder resembling a mushroom.

1. Mushroom Jump 5.9 ★★

Dyno up to a good hold and mantel over the lip. Downclimb the backside.

GUM SHOE

Located just past Devil's Slide. Look uphill and to your right (north and to the east). This curved boulder sits off by itself on the hillside and has three problems.

1. West Face 5.10 ★★

Climbs the face on the west face of *Gum Shoe*.

2. The Arête 5.10 ★★★

Climb the arête to the right of *West Face* starting down low.

3. Gum Shoe 5.10 ★★★★

Classic boulder problem and the namesake for this rock on the Backside. Start on the arête and move up and right on the two obvious chalked up rails leading to a finishing jug/rail.

Preston Pettigrew on *Gum Shoe*. | Photo by Molly Hennesy

Gum Shoe

NOOKIE BOULDER

Located 50 feet up and to the right of Gum Shoe Boulder. There is currently one problem on this boulder.

1. All About the Nookie 5.9 ★

The problem is on the north side of the boulder. Sit start to a jug out left; continue up and to the right for the top out.

Preston Pettigrew on Gum Shoe. | Photo by Tony Mayse

SHIP'S PROW

The first boulder as you walk up from the trail resembling the prow of a ship.

1. Ship's Prow 5.11 ★★★

The obvious boulder resembling a ship's prow.
Sit start, starting on the right side of the prow, heel hook, traversing out to the left making your way to the prow proper. Move up to the top from here.

THE MAIN CIRCUIT

The Main Circuit has three boulders located north and to the west of the Gum Shoe Boulder. Continue past Gum Shoe Boulder heading north and to the west. Before you drop down into the gully you will reach the Main Circuit.

Preston Pettigrew on Ship's Prow 5.11. | Photo by Tony Mayse

BLACK SCRATCH 2

Just right of Ship's Prow. For several years it has been named Black Scratch and mistaken for the *Black Scratch* problem on the Gill Boulder.

1. Beginner's Arête 5.6 ★
Climb the easy left face up the arête.

2. Black Scratch 2 5.11 ★★★
Small foot holds to a sloper at the top. South-facing problem.

HOLE SHOT

Located to the north of Black Scratch 2.

1. Hole Shot Crack 5.9 ★★
Sit start below an overhanging crack. Locker jams lead to a smoothed out finger-lock pocket towards the top.

2. Hole Shot 5.10 ★★
Sit start on good holds to a sloper out right and edges to the top.

Preston Pettigrew on the slopers of Black Scratch 2. | Photo by Tony Mayse

3. Dave's a Bitch 5.10

Campus to good holds, sidepull, and high step. Apparently Dave's pants earned him a boulder problem name due to his pants being to tight and not allowing him to high step.

Stanley Vrba exploring new bouldering potential

W BOULDER

Located on the far north end of the Backside Area. Look to the north, past all of the smaller boulders in the circuit. W Boulder sits on top of a granite slab and is facing to the west with its unmistakable yellow face and the letter "W" on the lower right side of the west face.

1. W 5.10 ★★★

Just left of the "W," mantel up to a comfortable stance. Continue to the top on smaller holds. Downclimb the eastside slab. Highball.

2. Stanley's Project 5.12 (PROJECT)

Located on the boulder's north side. Traverse right over the big drop and move up to the flake with a crack leading to the top. Highball.

W Boulder

In the early 1980s, while some of the routes were being climbed for the first time in the Wichita Mountains and Old Baldy, the notion of climbing rocks was for me about as remote as visiting Mars. I was attached to a Marine Corps Combat Infantry unit during that time. Then in the late 1980s competitive power-lifting inspired my every thought for the next several years, leading to the desire to compete for the coveted title Mr. Oklahoma for bodybuilding. Climbing wasn't even on the radar until my wife introduced me to her cousin, Gary Smith, a climber who was also friends with Duane Raleigh. Lori's first pair of climbing shoes were some of Duane's hand-me-downs, so the good climbing ju-ju was already starting to build.

After six months of climbing at Quartz Lori and I achieved a milestone of sorts. It marked the time we went to Yosemite Valley for our first climbing trip and was a turning point in my climbing ability. By that time I knew enough about climbing that I could lead S Wall, which is a story itself. I had asked Gary about the route and remembered him saying these exact words, "There are bolts all over the place up there." That was all I needed to hear. Lori held the rope, belaying me. I set off with a static line in tow. Once the "S" was reached I kept going, then true to Gary's words another bolt. Continuing up, I reached the horizontal band when I heard Lori yell up, "You have 10 feet of rope left!" At this point I can see where the end of the route was and stepping down was not an option, so I yelled to Lori "let go of the rope!" She did, and I made it to the belay!

Yosemite Valley was unreal! We stopped off in Tuolumne Meadows on Labor Day weekend 1991. The air was crisp and the trees smelled so good! "We are in the mountains" I said to myself! Wow! Our mission was to climb a 10-pitch slab route on North Dome in Yosemite Valley. This type of climbing was what we knew, so this route was the most obvious choice for a big adventure; 10 pitches of bolt-protected Quartz Mountain type climbing. A few days earlier I met a guy at the base of Lembert Dome who, ironically enough, was a former Marine and knew my old roommate and power-lifting buddy, Mark McCurdy. After meeting Tom I knew this was going to be a killer trip!

Tom and I climbed *Crest Jewell* that trip, and then the next day I remember walking up to that giant Valley monolith, El Capitan, and watching climbers swinging around up there. Clueless as to what they were doing, I bought a book about big walls named *Climbing Big Walls* by Mike Strassman. The cover had a climber in a hammock high up on El Cap, it looked scary as hell! I had to figure out how all this worked. Reading everything I could find, buying aiders and jumars, back home I set off to learn big wall

Gary Smith, Tom Thoma & Tony at Glacier Point Apron 1991.

climbing. My first aid route was *Stray Cats*, a short little crack at Quartz Mtn. that had good gear. The very next weekend my buddy, Bob Scheier, and I went out to Yosemite and climbed the *Regular Route* on Half Dome's northwest face. Some other climbers were doing the *Direct Northwest Face* just to the right of us. We met them the day before, it happened to be Yosemite legend and climbing guide Sue McDevitt and her husband Dan.

Spending three days to climb this big wall was scary but we did it! Two days later we were up in Tuolumne Meadows. Getting out of the car at the Fairview Dome parking area, a couple older guys showed up, one of them had a mustache and wore glasses; he asked us what we were going to climb. Before I could answer Bob popped off, "What do you think?" Come to find out it was Steve Roper. Yes, the *Fifty Classic Climbs* author Steve Roper. He was with his partner John Harlin, III whose father died on the Eiger after a rope that he was jugging broke. This infamous incident happened while he was a member of an American climbing team, racing to beat the Europeans, in 1966, for the first ascent of the *Direct North Face* route of the Eiger. In climbing you just never know who you're going to meet.

While at Quartz Mountain, one weekend in 1993, a van rolled up with California license plates. A couple climbers, Todd Ward and Mike Johnson, were in the parking area and said an older guy named Bob from California was visiting Old Baldy for the first time. I had just read about Bob Kamps so I asked "Is it Bob Kamps?" They said they thought that's what he said. I ran down and started up a conversation in hopes I could climb with Bob! Bob was a legend. Just check out some history about him and you'll notice that he was a driving force, the same caliber as Royal Robbins et al. In the 1960s, Bob followed his buddy who led the *Regular Route* on Fairview Dome on aid (it had not been led free). Though Bob freed it, he did not get credit since he was following that day, and Steve Roper got the credit for free climbing it. Mattered not, because Bob set out to free some of the best climbs of the day in Tuolumne Meadows. Routes like *Lucky Streaks, Mr. Kamps, Inverted Staircase* and *Chingadera* in Tahquitz, a hard 5.11 put up on lead with a crux bolt clip that was hand-drilled. Bob also made the first ascent of the Diamond, in Colorado, with Dave Rearick in 1960. On the day I met Bob at Quartz, he onsighted all the classics: *S Wall, Last of the Good Guys, Cruzin' for a Bruzin', Amazon Woman, South Pacific ,*and *Stray Cats.* Bob was

Lori Mayse in El Cap Meadow. | Photo by Andy Chasteen

a climber's climber and watching him cruise up those routes like a youngster—at 63 years young—left an everlasting memory for me.

I climbed with him on other occasions including Joshua Tree, where we ran into Allen Steck, and Eric Beck (2nd ascentionist of *The Nose* of El Cap). Joe Fitschen was also there. That gang was calling themselves the "Wilted Wall Flowers!" You could tell Bob was held in high regard, it was so apparent that I couldn't resist having a little fun with him, as he was fun to tease. I told him, "See Bob, you hang out with me and I'll make you famous! " Bob then looked at me with a serious but smiling grin and held out his hand to shake mine!

That same year I climbed El Capitan with Tom Thoma. We got stormed off when our bivy ledge had six inches of snow and ice from the night before. Tom had read that you could get under a tarp, fastening the top like a cone making a shelter to keep the rain off. We both got soaked! Next day while we were rappelling off the Captain, Tom in his white Converse and cotton sweat pants and Goretex jacket, Merry Braun and her husband Werner along with all of YOSAR (Yosemite Search and Rescue) waited for a rescue opportunity (YOSAR only gets paid while on the job). We made it down in one piece and as we walked by El Cap Meadow, I overheard Merry telling another YOSAR member that "some guy was rappelling in his socks!" Tom and his white Converse...

I was so hooked about being up there on the Captain that I went back six weeks later and climbed *The Nose* with Chris Giancinto, a climber Lori had met at the Devil's Bathtubs area on the previous trip. Chris was a California guy who loved to surf and climb. He had El Capitan tattooed on one shoulder and a surfer on the other, his two loves. We climbed *The Nose* on that trip, then I threw caution to the wind and took multiples leaves of absence from work so I could stay in Yosemite. It was almost to the point where my home was on the verge of going back to the bank, when Bob Kamps lectured me, "Don't quit your day job!" I took his words to heart and forged a path that has allowed me to continue taking trips and still have base camp at home. Bob knew of the "FORCE" that calls out to young climbers, but, he also knew of its downside in the years to come. Climbing all the time doesn't set you up for later years.

Bob shaped my climbing from that very first meeting at Quartz where it seemed that the Kamps footwork "magic dust" was sprinkled on my shoes. My footwork improved just by watching his elegant movement and effortless touch while climbing challenging routes. He set the course for my life with his words and as well as his actions.

The adventures continue with each outing here in Oklahoma, across this country, and around the world. Climbing is just as exciting to me today as the early days. Lori is still encouraging me and humoring me when I ramble on about the days climbing. She is like Bonnie Kamps was to Bob, the balance in my life. After all, it's all about balance and of course, all about the feet. ~TM

"Climbing here saved my life from the confines of the materialistic illusion that we're taught as children in school...

The way I see it, there are two worlds: There's the world where nothing is sacred except money, and the other world where everything is sacred."

~Ron Kauk (Yosemite Climber)

Documentary
Film

guideforaday.com

Photo By Andrew Burr

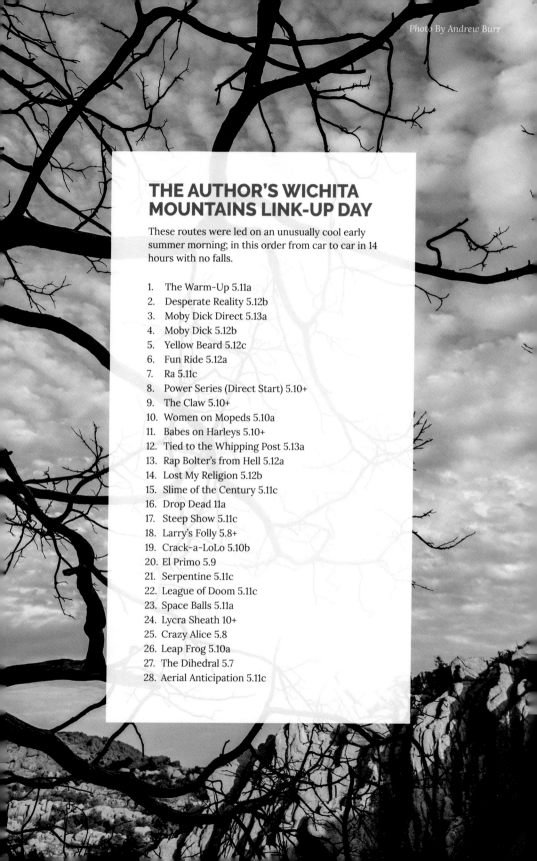

THE AUTHOR'S WICHITA MOUNTAINS LINK-UP DAY

These routes were led on an unusually cool early summer morning; in this order from car to car in 14 hours with no falls.

1.   The Warm-Up 5.11a
2.   Desperate Reality 5.12b
3.   Moby Dick Direct 5.13a
4.   Moby Dick 5.12b
5.   Yellow Beard 5.12c
6.   Fun Ride 5.12a
7.   Ra 5.11c
8.   Power Series (Direct Start) 5.10+
9.   The Claw 5.10+
10. Women on Mopeds 5.10a
11. Babes on Harleys 5.10+
12. Tied to the Whipping Post 5.13a
13. Rap Bolter's from Hell 5.12a
14. Lost My Religion 5.12b
15. Slime of the Century 5.11c
16. Drop Dead 11a
17. Steep Show 5.11c
18. Larry's Folly 5.8+
19. Crack-a-LoLo 5.10b
20. El Primo 5.9
21. Serpentine 5.11c
22. League of Doom 5.11c
23. Space Balls 5.11a
24. Lycra Sheath 10+
25. Crazy Alice 5.8
26. Leap Frog 5.10a
27. The Dihedral 5.7
28. Aerial Anticipation 5.11c

Terry Andrews showing how it's done on Munge Lunge | Photo by Vonda Covington

5.10

5.11

Oklahoma's hard woman Elisha Gallegos sending at Lost Dome! | Photo by Andrew Burr

JON FRANK CAMP FIRE CONVERSATION STARTERS:

1. How did you get into climbing?

2. What was your first climb?

3. What was your first lead?

4. How did the person who got you into climbing get into climbing?

5. What do you think are the top 5 climbs in Oklahoma?

6. What was your scariest climbing moment?

7. What is your favorite climb?

RECOMMENDED READING:

- *My Life at the Limit* ~ Reinhold Messner
- *White Spider* ~ Heinrich Harrier
- *Eiger Dreams* ~ Jon Krakauer
- *Extreme Alpinism* ~ Marc Twight
- *Kiss or Kill* ~ Marc Twight
- *Beyond the Mountain* ~ Steve House
- *A Night on the Ground a Day in the Open* ~ Doug Robinson
- *The Rock Warrior's Way* ~ Arno Ilgner
- *Gorilla Monsoon* ~ John Long
- *The Quotable Climber* ~ Jonathan Waterman
- *Mountaineering: Freedom of the Hills* ~ Multiple authors
- *Fifty Classic Climbs* ~ Steve Roper, Alan Steck
- *One Move Too Many* ~ Volker Schoeffl, Thomas Hochholzer
- *The Good, the Great, and the Awesome* ~ Peter Croft
- *Climbing & Gymnastics* ~ John Gill
- *Climbing Free* ~ Lynn Hill
- *Alone on the Wall* ~ Alex Honnold
- *High Infatuation* ~ Steph Davis
- *Drawn: The Art of Ascent* ~ Jeremy Collins
- *Espresso Lessons* ~ Arno Ilgner
- *Camp IV Recollections of a Yosemite Rock Climber* ~ Steve Roper